MORE KILLER PUZZLES

MURDLE

100 FIENDISHLY FOUL MURDER MYSTERY LOGIC PUZZLES

....

G. T. KARBER

SOUVENIR
PRESS

To my mom

First published in Great Britain in 2023 by
Souvenir Press,
an imprint of Profile Books Ltd
29 Cloth Fair
London
EC1A 7JQ
www.souvenirpress.co.uk

First published in the United States of America as *Murdle: Volume 2* by
St. Martin's Griffin, an imprint of St. Martin's Publishing Group

Copyright © by Gregory Thomas Karber, Jr

Designed by Omar Chapa

1 3 5 7 9 10 8 6 4 2

Printed and bound in Great Britain by Clays Ltd, Elcograf S.p.A.

The moral right of the author has been asserted.

A CIP catalogue record for this book is available from the British Library.

ISBN 978 1 80081 805 7

FSC
www.fsc.org
MIX
Paper | Supporting
responsible forestry
FSC® C018072

CONTENTS

HOW TO SOLVE

Welcome to *Murdle,* the official publication of the case files of the world's greatest mystery-solving mind, Deductive Logico.

Unlike other memoirs of the crime-fighting life, these murdles are not mere tales, but puzzles for you to solve. And all you need to crack these cases is a sharp pencil and an even sharper mind.

To prove it, let's review Deductive Logico's very first case, which he cracked as a junior at Deduction College. The student body president had been murdered, and Logico was certain one of three people had done it:

MAYOR HONEY

He knows where the bodies are buried, and he makes sure they always vote for him.

6'0" • LEFT-HANDED • HAZEL EYES • LIGHT BROWN HAIR

DEAN GLAUCOUS

The dean of some such-and-such department at Deduction College. What does he do? Well, he handles the money, for one . . .

5'6" • RIGHT-HANDED • LIGHT BROWN EYES • LIGHT BROWN HAIR

CHANCELLOR TUSCANY

As the head of Deduction College, she has deduced exactly how much rich parents are willing to pay to get their children a degree in logic.

5'5" • LEFT-HANDED • GREEN EYES • BLOND HAIR

Young Logico also knew that each of them was in one of these places and had one of these weapons.

THE STADIUM
OUTDOORS

The field features the absolute highest quality fake grass money can buy.

THE BOOKSTORE
INDOORS

The biggest money-maker on campus. A sign offers a 2-for-$500 deal on textbooks.

OLD MAIN
INDOORS

The first building on campus and the least maintained. Paint is peeling off the wall!

A SHARP PENCIL
LIGHT-WEIGHT

Back then, they used actual lead. One stab and you'd die from lead poisoning.

A HEAVY BACKPACK
HEAVY-WEIGHT

Finally, a practical use for all those logic textbooks (hitting people with them).

A GRADUATION CORD
LIGHT-WEIGHT

It would be a high academic honor to be strangled by one of these.

Now, Logico knew that he could not make assumptions just from reading these descriptions! Sometimes mayors wore heavy backpacks, and sometimes teachers went to the stadium. No, the way to figure out who had what where was by studying the clues and evidence.

These were the facts he knew to be absolutely, perfectly true:

- Whoever was in the stadium was right-handed.

- The suspect with the sharp pencil resented the person at Old Main.

- The suspect with a graduation cord had beautiful hazel eyes.

- Dean Glaucous seemed to carry a lot of logic textbooks around.

- **The body was found next to peeling paint.**

And finally, he pulled out his detective's notebook and meticulously drew a grid, labeling each column and row with a picture representing each of the suspects, weapons, and locations.

The locations were listed twice—once on top, and once on the side—so that every square represented a unique potential pairing.

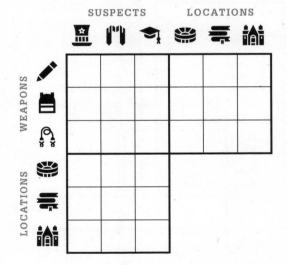

This tool—the deduction grid—was a powerful technology taught at Deduction College. It could help clarify your thoughts and identify the possible conclusions you could make.

But never before had it been used to solve a murder! In Deduction College, they apply logic only to the realm of the purely abstract. If all *X*s are *Y*s and all *Y*s are *Z*s—that kind of thing. What Logico was doing here was new, exciting, and dangerous!

Once he drew his deduction grid, he had arrived at his favorite part: the deducing! He went down the list of clues, and put each of them into his grid.

The first clue is: **Whoever was in the stadium was right-handed.**

According to Logico's notes on the suspects, only Dean Glaucous was right-handed. Therefore, Dean Glaucous was at the stadium.

Logico marked that down on his grid, as seen below. But that was

not all Logico learned from that clue.

If Dean Glaucous was at the stadium, then he wasn't at the bookstore or Old Main, and since only one suspect was at each location, neither Chancellor Tuscany nor Mayor Honey was at the stadium.

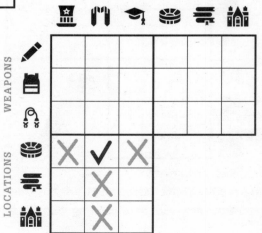

Logico represented this on his grid with *X*s. This illustrates a principle: When you identify somebody's location or their weapon, you can cross out every other possibility in that row and column.

Logico moved on to

the next clue: **The suspect with the sharp pencil resented the person at Old Main.**

It seems like this clue is telling us about personal relationships. But Logico was only concerned with facts. And the only fact this clue told him was that the suspect with the sharp pencil and the suspect at Old Main were two separate people. Therefore, *the sharp pencil was not at Old Main.*

And so, Logico marked that down in his deduction grid, too.

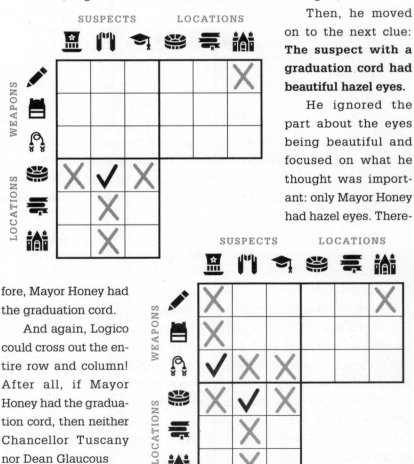

Then, he moved on to the next clue: **The suspect with a graduation cord had beautiful hazel eyes.**

He ignored the part about the eyes being beautiful and focused on what he thought was important: only Mayor Honey had hazel eyes. There-

fore, Mayor Honey had the graduation cord.

And again, Logico could cross out the entire row and column! After all, if Mayor Honey had the graduation cord, then neither Chancellor Tuscany nor Dean Glaucous had it. And since each suspect had only one weapon, Mayor Honey couldn't have the heavy backpack or the sharp pencil.

Logico moved on to the next clue: **Dean Glaucous seemed to carry a lot of logic textbooks around.**

Now, what does that mean? Logic textbooks aren't one

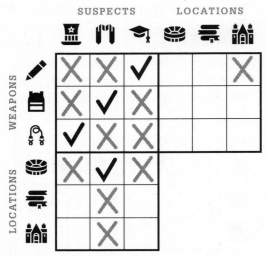

of the weapons! But, if you read the descriptions of each weapon, you'll notice that the heavy backpack's says, "Finally, a practical use for all those logic textbooks (hitting people with them)." If Dean Glaucous was carrying a lot of logic textbooks around, he was using the backpack to do it!

You don't have to make leaps of logic in these puzzles: everything you need to know clearly appears in the descriptions. Is it possible that Dean Glaucous was carrying logic books around without a heavy backpack? Not to Deductive Logico!

Logico marked down that Dean Glaucous had the heavy backpack, and he crossed off the other possibilities in that row and column. Once he did that, Logico smiled. If Mayor Honey had the graduation cord and Dean Glaucous had the heavy backpack, Chancellor Tuscany must have had the sharp pencil. He marked this down as well.

This next step is the key to solving all the murder mysteries that appear in this book: Chancellor Tuscany had the sharp pencil. The sharp pencil is not at Old Main. Therefore, *Chancellor Tuscany could not be at Old Main.*

Therefore, Chancellor Tuscany was at the bookstore, since it was

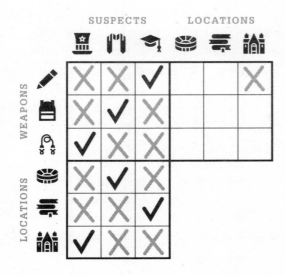

the only remaining location. And since she had the sharp pencil, the sharp pencil must have been at the bookstore, too.

Logico marked this on his deduction grid and crossed off the other boxes in each row and column. And from there, he deduced that Mayor Honey was at Old Main, so he marked that down, too.

Since Mayor Honey was at Old Main with the graduation cord, the graduation cord must have been at Old Main. And since Dean Glaucous had the heavy backpack and was at the stadium, the heavy backpack was at the stadium, too.

So satisfying! Logico thought, as he looked at his completed grid. Now, he was ready for the final clue: **The body was found next to peeling paint.**

This last clue is special. It doesn't tell you who has what weapon where—it tells you about the murder itself!

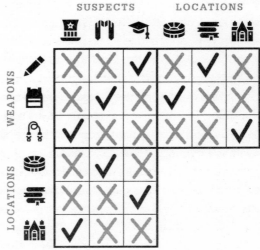

By consulting his notes, Logico knew that this clue meant the murder had been committed in Old Main, because the description of Old Main mentions peeling paint. Therefore, since Mayor Honey was the suspect in Old Main, Mayor Honey must have committed the crime.

Confident in his deductions, Logico marched down to the chancellor's office where he confidently declared: **"It was Mayor Honey with the graduation cord at Old Main!"**

Chancellor Tuscany was impressed with his hard work, and she gave him an A-plus. Mayor Honey, however, was able to win reelection in a landslide, thanks to his populist tirades against the tyranny of logic. But that did not matter, because to Logico, it wasn't the consequences of his deductions that mattered: it was the deductive work itself.

And that is how young Logico became Deductive Logico, and how he first applied the theories of his college education to the problems of the real world. When he graduated, he moved to the city, and he began to offer his services as the only deductive detective in the business.

This book contains one hundred mysteries that Deductive Logico was able to solve using these techniques and others. There are ciphers to decode, witness statements to examine, and many other secrets to unlock. As you progress, and the mysteries become more challenging, you will find your reasoning skills being put to the test.

If you get stuck, do not despair! You can flip to the back of the book for a hint. And when you're ready to make your accusation, flip even farther back to the answers to see if you're right. With every mystery solved, a bigger story begins to emerge.

If you need more help, or want to solve more mysteries with others, then join the Detective Club at Murdle.com. Otherwise, you're on your own!

Good luck, gumshoe!

DEGREE OF DIFFICULTY

Q — ELEMENTARY

QQ — OCCULT MEDIUM

QQQ — HARD BOILED

QQQQ — IMPOSSIBLE

A MAP OF THE VIOLET
ISLAND GARDEN MAZE

ELEMENTARY

After a long night, Deductive Logico came home to an encrypted note nailed to his door. When he couldn't solve it, he asked the esoteric Inspector Irratino for help. When Irratino declared the letter was an occult incantation, Logico took it to the Detective Club. They broke it into words, and they cracked each word one at a time.

Finally, Logico was able to read the entire decoded message:

Dear Logico,
This is a single invitation to our Old Drakonian Holiday Party at my family mega-mansion in the Violet Isles.

Here, we are safe from the "night-eater" and the Red Government, but we have problems of our own, and we need your help. Please hurry!

Yours,
V

Irratino was disappointed that there was no mention of a plus-one. "I'd really love to help them discover their dark secret."

"What dark secret?" Logico said. "There's no mention of a dark secret."

"Oh, there's obviously a dark secret. There's *always* a dark secret."

Can you solve the following twenty-five elementary mysteries? If you get stuck, you can always flip to the back for a hint. And if you think they're too easy, then take the Detective Club Challenge: Discover the dark secret of the Violet Isles before Logico!

1. THE DETECTIVE CLUB KILLER

Before Logico left for the holiday party, he visited the Detective Club headquarters to tell his friends the good news. Unfortunately, they had bad news: the president (now the former president) had been killed. Whodunit?

SUSPECTS

MISS SAFFRON

Miss Saffron is technically an aristocrat, but more accurately, she's just plain rich.

5'2" • LEFT-HANDED • HAZEL EYES • BLOND HAIR

GENERAL COFFEE

Now that Detective Club HQ has added a coffee bar, he's there every day.

6'0" • RIGHT-HANDED • BROWN EYES • BALD

GRANDMASTER ROSE

Chess is a kind of mystery, so Grandmaster Rose fits right in at the DCHQ. (His opponent opened with 1. g4: the Grob.)

5'7" • LEFT-HANDED • BROWN EYES • BROWN HAIR

LOCATIONS

THE DETECTIVE KIT STORAGE ROOM
INDOORS

There is a pile of fedora pins next to a printing press for membership cards. Join today!

THE ROOFTOP LOOKOUT
OUTDOORS

Where you can keep an eye on the entrance and the pigeons.

THE CONSPIRACY BOARD ROOM
INDOORS

The walls are corkboards covered with newspaper articles connected with red string.

WEAPONS

THE FIRST
***MURDLE* BOOK**
MEDIUM-WEIGHT

A copy of the first book: a great gift and an even greater weapon.

A MAGNIFYING GLASS
MEDIUM-WEIGHT

You could use this to find a clue or to start a small fire. Or both!

A RED HERRING
MEDIUM-WEIGHT

If you hold it by the tail, you can get some real momentum behind it.

CLUES & EVIDENCE

- General Coffee was using the printing press to print his manifesto: *On Beans and Bombs*.

- Grandmaster Rose was afraid of heights, so he had never been to the roof.

- The first *Murdle* book was not in the conspiracy board room.

- Miss Saffron had a magnifying glass.

- **Something was fishy about the murder: it was committed with a fish.**

WHO?

WHAT?

WHERE?

2. THE ZEPPELIVING AND THE DEAD 🔍

Whoever said that the air was the fastest way to travel has never taken a zeppelin to Drakonia. Fortunately, Deductive Logico was able to fill the time by solving the murder of the pilot.

SUSPECTS

CAPTAIN SLATE

A real-life astronaut. The first woman to travel around the dark side of the moon, and also the first to be suspected of murdering her copilot.

5'5" • LEFT-HANDED • BROWN EYES • BROWN HAIR

PRESIDENT WHITE

The duly elected president of the Royal Resistance, a party of aristocrats who want to retake power. She wears a signet ring.

5'10" • RIGHT-HANDED • GRAY EYES • WHITE HAIR

DR. CRIMSON

She believes that everyone—no matter their race or creed—deserves the right to medical care, as long as they can afford it.

5'9" • LEFT-HANDED • GREEN EYES • RED HAIR

LOCATIONS

THE PASSENGER CABIN
INDOORS

No commercial plane has this much legroom, or a parachute for every passenger.

THE CARGO HOLD
INDOORS

Every single piece of luggage is designer, and each is worth more than its contents.

THE COCKPIT
INDOORS

Thankfully for the passengers, there is a robotic copilot built by TekCo Futures.

WEAPONS

A STUN GUN
LIGHT-WEIGHT

Advertised as "less-than-lethal," but anything's lethal if you use it right.

A FIRE EXTINGUISHER
HEAVY-WEIGHT

Kill someone by hitting them over the head with this, or by starting a fire and doing nothing with it.

A CUP OF SCALDING COFFEE
MEDIUM-WEIGHT

The hottest coffee you'll ever taste—and the last!

CLUES & EVIDENCE

- Dr. Crimson was trying to sell something to the person who brought a fire extinguisher.

- Captain Slate was not in the cargo hold.

- Brown eyes were reflected in the cup of scalding coffee.

- The robot copilot's proximity sensors detected a nearby fire extinguisher.

- **A weapon that was (apparently not) less-than-lethal was used to kill the pilot.**

SUSPECTS   LOCATIONS

WEAPONS / LOCATIONS

WHO?

WHAT?

WHERE?

3. TOUCH DOWN TO MURDER 🔍

When the zeppelin landed at the People's City airport, Logico was surprised to find it much cleaner, nicer, and more beautiful than the one in his city. He looked for his chauffeur but found a dead body: a security guard had been murdered.

SUSPECTS

CAPTAIN SLATE

A real-life astronaut. The first woman to travel around the dark side of the moon, and also the first to be suspected of murdering her copilot.

5'5" • LEFT-HANDED • BROWN EYES • BROWN HAIR

CHAUFFEUR BRONZE

Lady Violet's chauffeur. He's an aristocrat himself, which shows you how important Lady Violet is.

5'10" • RIGHT-HANDED • BROWN EYES • BLOND HAIR

BOSS CHARCOAL

A mob boss from the good ol' days when being a mob boss from the good ol' days meant something.

5'11" • RIGHT-HANDED • BROWN EYES • BLACK HAIR

LOCATIONS

THE RUNWAY
OUTDOORS

So named because it's a great place for political prisoners to run away.

THE BAGGAGE CLAIM
INDOORS

Good luck getting your luggage: the bags that weren't lost were stolen.

THE CURRENCY EXCHANGE
INDOORS

The exchange rate here is a rip-off. They're trading Drakonian dollars for US dollars one to one.

WEAPONS

AN EXPOSED WIRE
LIGHT-WEIGHT

One of the last things you want to be exposed to. It's shocking!

A WATER BOTTLE
MEDIUM-WEIGHT

Ironic, because you'll die without it, too.

AN '80S CELL PHONE
HEAVY-WEIGHT

Heavier than some '80s cars. At this point, it's ancient technology.

CLUES & EVIDENCE

- Boss Charcoal always carried a variety of currencies, so he would never visit the exchange.

- Captain Slate was suspiciously thirsty: she kept drinking out of her water bottle.

- Due to their refined sensibilities, the aristocrat would never be around exposed wires.

- Ancient technology was found sitting on the runway.

- **The body of the security guard was found in the baggage claim.**

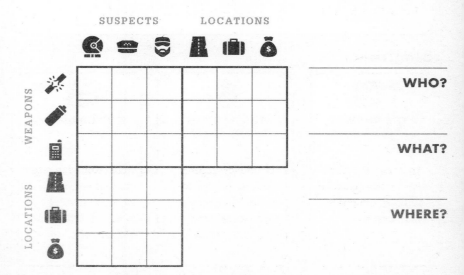

WHO?

WHAT?

WHERE?

4. A LOCKED-ROOM MYSTERY 🔍

The moment Deductive Logico stepped outside the airport, he was arrested by the Free Drakonian police and taken to a holding cell, where he was commanded by an angry soldier to solve the murder of the last prisoner they arrested.

SUSPECTS

OFFICER COPPER

Now that Officer Copper works for the Drakonian government, she is no longer corrupt. (The penalty for corruption is death.)

5'5" • RIGHT-HANDED • BLUE EYES • BLOND HAIR

COMRADE CHAMPAGNE

Now that Comrade Champagne has moved to Drakonia, he has to work like everyone else.

5'11" • LEFT-HANDED • HAZEL EYES • BLOND HAIR

COSMONAUT BLUSKI

An ex-Soviet spaceman whose blood flows red. Sure, that's normal, but for him it's patriotic.

6'2" • LEFT-HANDED • BROWN EYES • BLACK HAIR

LOCATIONS

THE INTERROGATION ROOM
INDOORS

Two uncomfortable chairs and a table are reflected in the wall-sized mirror.

THE "EMERGENCY EXIT"
OUTDOORS

A euphemism for the 25th-floor window. If the guards don't like you, they throw you out of it.

THE OBSERVATION ROOM
INDOORS

On the other side of the two-way mirror, you can watch the interrogation from a plush sofa.

WEAPONS

THE BIG RED BOOK
MEDIUM-WEIGHT

Written by Major Red, it argues for a world without rulers (other than him, of course).

A HEAVY BOOT
HEAVY-WEIGHT

You could swing its steel toes at someone. (Or, better yet, kick them with it!)

A CHEAP PEN
LIGHT-WEIGHT

Getting killed by an expensive pen is bad enough . . .

CLUES & EVIDENCE

- A scrap of paper bearing a famous saying of Major Red ("In a street fight, ten people always beat one.") was discovered under a plush sofa.

- You know what they say: the tallest suspect has the cheapest pen.

- Comrade Champagne had never been near the 25th-floor window.

- Either a cheap pen was found by the "Emergency Exit," or Officer Copper carried the Big Red Book.

- **The prisoner had been killed with a heavy boot. (Probably by being kicked by it.)**

WHO?

WHAT?

WHERE?

5. DEATH ON THE LOW SEAS 🔍

Once he was released from jail, Deductive Logico took a ferry across the Red Bay with a few of Lady Violet's other guests. All of them watched with foreboding as the silhouette of Violet Manor appeared in the fog. All but one, that is. One was dead.

SUSPECTS

ADMIRAL NAVY

The firstborn son of an Admiral Navy who himself was the son of an Admiral Navy.

5'9" • RIGHT-HANDED • BLUE EYES • BROWN HAIR

THE DUCHESS OF VERMILLION

A tall, old woman with tall, old secrets. If she is the murderer, then it certainly wouldn't be the first time.

5'9" • LEFT-HANDED • GRAY EYES • WHITE HAIR

UNCLE MIDNIGHT

When his dad died, he bought a desert mansion with a pool and retired. He was seventeen.

5'8" • LEFT-HANDED • BLUE EYES • BROWN HAIR

LOCATIONS

OVERBOARD
OUTDOORS

Here you might get murdered by the sharks, too.

THE CAPTAIN'S QUARTERS
INDOORS

Here, the captain told Logico the legend that Lord Violet had killed the person who killed his favorite butler.

THE DECK
OUTDOORS

Look out over the ocean, but not too far, or someone might push you.

WEAPONS

**A LIFE
PRESERVER**
MEDIUM-WEIGHT

Getting killed by
this would defi-
nitely be ironic.

**A DIAMOND
NECKLACE**
LIGHT-WEIGHT

Maybe the most
expensive weapon
in the whole book.
It's missing one
diamond!

A FISH BONE
LIGHT-WEIGHT

Historically, what
people have choked
on the most.

CLUES & EVIDENCE

- They combed the deck, and they're certain the missing diamond wasn't there.

- An ironic weapon was discovered beside a shark.

- The suspect on the deck retired at seventeen.

- The Duchess of Vermillion was attracted to the person who brought a life preserver.

- **The dead guest was found where Logico had been told a legend.**

WHO?

WHAT?

WHERE?

6. THE TINY ISLAND MURDER MYSTERY 🔍

Suddenly, the ferry ran aground on a tiny island—halfway to the main Violet Isle—and Deductive Logico took charge: "This has happened to me before," he said, "and the most important thing is to make sure nobody is murdered." It was too late: the captain was already dead.

SUSPECTS

CASTAWAY SABLE

Unkempt and unmoored, Sable has lived on this island for longer than she can remember (six days).

5'5" • LEFT-HANDED • HAZEL EYES • BLACK HAIR

UNCLE MIDNIGHT

When his dad died, he bought a desert mansion with a pool and retired. He was seventeen.

5'8" • LEFT-HANDED • BLUE EYES • BROWN HAIR

ADMIRAL NAVY

The firstborn son of an Admiral Navy who himself was the son of an Admiral Navy.

5'9" • RIGHT-HANDED • BLUE EYES • BROWN HAIR

LOCATIONS

THE LONE PALM TREE
OUTDOORS

A small bunch of coconuts hangs from it. Iconic, really.

THE SHIP-WRECKED FERRY
INDOORS

This ship running aground has almost doubled the size of the island.

A SINGLE HEADSTONE
OUTDOORS

It has a message engraved on it: "RIP Beloved Butler Beryl. Buried in a private ceremony."

WEAPONS

SPOILED SOUP MEDIUM-WEIGHT	**AN ATTACK CRAB** MEDIUM-WEIGHT	**A HUMAN SKULL** MEDIUM-WEIGHT
One bite of this soup and you'll croak. (Ironically, it's frog soup.)	You might not be afraid of this until you hear its claws are dipped in poison!	"Alas, poor Yorick, I knew him. And now I'm swinging his skull at people."

CLUES & EVIDENCE

- An attack crab was not found anywhere in the shipwrecked ferry.

- Admiral Navy held in his hands a human skull to which he quoted Shakespeare.

- Uncle Midnight was attracted to the person with spoiled soup.

- Castaway Sable was relaxing beneath a coconut, as she had been for six days.

- **The murder took place next to an engraved message.**

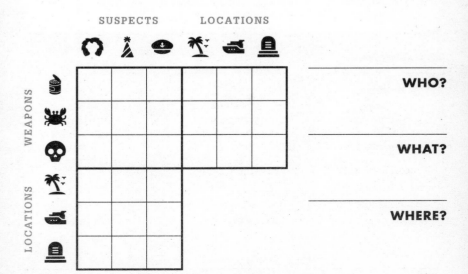

WHO?

WHAT?

WHERE?

7. TICK-TOCK—HE DIED ON THE DOCK! 🔍

When they finally arrived on the Violet Isles, Lady Violet had planned to meet them at the docks in a grand ceremony. Unfortunately, the occasion was ruined when one of her dockworkers was killed.

SUSPECTS

ADMIRAL NAVY

The firstborn son of an Admiral Navy who himself was the son of an Admiral Navy.

5'9" • RIGHT-HANDED • BLUE EYES • BROWN HAIR

LADY VIOLET

The heiress of the Violet Isles, the largest extrajudicial territory in the world.

5'0" • RIGHT-HANDED • BLUE EYES • BLOND HAIR

CASTAWAY SABLE

Stepping onto the dock, she is given a drink, and a glimmer of her life back.

5'5" • LEFT-HANDED • HAZEL EYES • BLACK HAIR

LOCATIONS

THE TACKLE SHACK
INDOORS

A shack filled with all the equipment you need to go fishing.

THE WOODEN DOCK
OUTDOORS

The wood is incredibly expensive mahogany.

THE STONE STAIRS
OUTDOORS

A set of narrow stairs winding up the cliffs—the only way to or from the docks.

WEAPONS

A BROKEN SWORD
HEAVY-WEIGHT

Half of a sword. Un-
fortunately for any
potential victims,
it's the deadly half.

A TOXIC BLOWFISH
MEDIUM-WEIGHT

Prepared carefully,
it's safe to eat. Pre-
pared even more
carefully, it can kill.

A VIAL OF POISON
LIGHT-WEIGHT

Your typical vial
of poison. Don't
underestimate the
classics.

CLUES & EVIDENCE

- Admiral Navy never even set foot on the stone stairs.

- Someone found Lord Violet's famous sword just sitting in the tackle shack.

- Castaway Sable fell in love with the person who brought a toxic blowfish.

- A scrambled tip was given to Deductive Logico: "TEH OSHETRST PTSCSEU LUHDDDE NI HTE ETKCAL CAKSH."

- **The body was found on mahogany.**

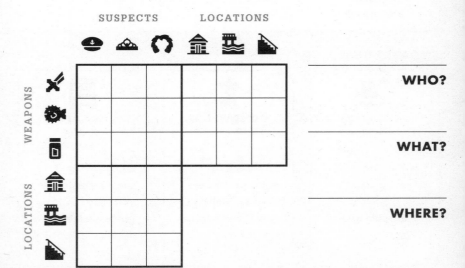

8. A DEADLY TOUR 🔍

Despite the deadly voyage, Lady Violet was determined to continue her party as usual, so she gave Logico a tour of the grounds. During the tour, he was able to solve another murder: the death of the original tour guide.

SUSPECTS

BARON MAROON

An incredibly haughty man who famously holds a grudge. Nobody wants to offend the baron. At least, nobody who's still alive . . .

6'2" • RIGHT-HANDED • HAZEL EYES • RED HAIR

LADY VIOLET

She is actually a rather charming tour guide, and her knowledge of the island's history is vast.

5'0" • RIGHT-HANDED • BLUE EYES • BLOND HAIR

SIGNOR EMERALD

An Italian jeweler of great renown, Signor Emerald has traveled the world in search of rare, precious stones, which are always falling out of his pockets.

5'8" • LEFT-HANDED • BROWN EYES • BLACK HAIR

LOCATIONS

THE CLIFFS
OUTDOORS

Huge cliffs surround the main island. The docks are the only way to leave.

THE STATUE OF LORD VIOLET
OUTDOORS

An enormous statue of Lord Violet, Lady Violet's father: there's a mask over his face.

THE GUEST HOUSE
INDOORS

If Logico hadn't seen the main mansion, this would be the biggest house he'd ever seen.

WEAPONS

A BAG OF ACORNS
MEDIUM-WEIGHT

Tasty enough to eat, easy enough to bury, heavy enough to kill.

A DECK OF MAROT CARDS
LIGHT-WEIGHT

You can use these murder-themed tarot cards to read your future.

A BOTTLE OF WINE
MEDIUM-WEIGHT

Watch out for stains, because the red doesn't come out.

CLUES & EVIDENCE

- The tallest suspect had known the person who brought a deck of marot cards for years.

- The bag of acorns was found outside, and something had gotten into it . . .

- A marot card—the Scimitar of Death—was found on the cliffs. That's a bad sign.

- Brown eyes were reflected in the bottle of wine.

- **A masked stone face had gazed down upon the murder of the guide.**

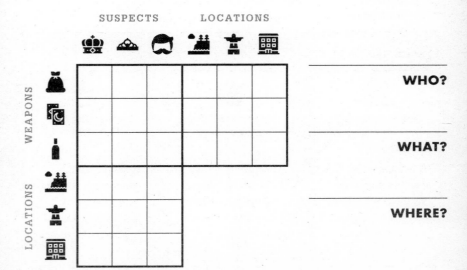

WHO?

WHAT?

WHERE?

9. THE END OF THE TOUR (AND A LIFE) 🔍

Lady Violet continued the tour—substituting the recently arrived President White for Baron Maroon—and (of course) someone else was killed. This time, it was the radio operator: now, nobody could radio the mainland!

SUSPECTS

LADY VIOLET

Lady Violet seems very relaxed about all of the murders, but so far, they've only affected the staff.

5'0" • RIGHT-HANDED • BLUE EYES • BLOND HAIR

PRESIDENT WHITE

It is interesting that the president of the Royal Resistance made it to the island after Logico, despite all the delays that Logico faced . . .

5'10" • RIGHT-HANDED • GRAY EYES • WHITE HAIR

SIGNOR EMERALD

Unbelievably, jewels are still falling out of Signor Emerald's pockets.

5'8" • LEFT-HANDED • BROWN EYES • BLACK HAIR

LOCATIONS

THE GARDEN MAZE
OUTDOORS

A beautiful maze of thorny roses. The fastest way across the island—if you know the path!

THE GREENHOUSE
OUTDOORS

Only strange plants grow here. Plants that feed on blood.

THE MAIN HOUSE
OUTDOORS

This house has more than two hundred rooms (including sixteen libraries and twenty-seven bathrooms).

WEAPONS

A SHOVEL
MEDIUM-WEIGHT

A multipurpose tool: kill someone and bury them with the same shovel!

A BOOK OF WAR POETRY
MEDIUM-WEIGHT

Poems about the war between the Royals and the Reds, full of glory, betrayal, and loss.

A FLAG
LIGHT-WEIGHT

A flag of the Royal Resistance, featuring the motto "God Fights For Us—St. Lupine."

CLUES & EVIDENCE

- The tallest suspect carried a shovel—but what were they doing with it?

- Signor Emerald hated reading: he did not bring a book of war poetry.

- A symbol of the Royal Resistance was not found in the greenhouse.

- The book of war poetry was found in an apiary. (See Exhibit A.)

- **The body of the radio operator was found in a library.**

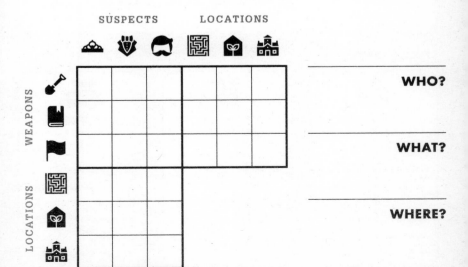

WHO?

WHAT?

WHERE?

10. GRAND ENTRANCE, GRAND EXIT 🔍

Lady Violet stood in the grand entrance and declared that her holiday party had officially begun: "First, you will move into your bedrooms—" But she was wrong, because first, another of her staff was murdered—this time, it was one of the guards.

SUSPECTS

AGENT APPLEGREEN

From literary assistant to Hollywood agent, Applegreen will stop at nothing to get what she wants: everything.

5'3" • LEFT-HANDED • BLUE EYES • BLOND HAIR

VISCOUNT EMINENCE

The oldest man you have ever seen. It is said that he outlived all of his sons and was born before his father.

5'2" • LEFT-HANDED • GRAY EYES • BROWN HAIR

SILVERTON THE LEGEND

An acclaimed actor of the Golden Age, now in his golden years.

6'4" • RIGHT-HANDED • BLUE EYES • SILVER HAIR

LOCATIONS

THE GIANT DOORWAY
INDOORS

The motto "God Fights For Us—St. Lupine" is engraved above the door, too.

THE DRIVEWAY
OUTDOORS

Lined with giant hedge animals, and completely unnecessary since it's on an island.

THE ENORMOUS STAIRS
INDOORS

Covered in gold and lit by torches, it represents all the wealth of the world.

WEAPONS

A PIECE OF WOOD
HEAVY-WEIGHT

Taken from a lifeboat. So, it's probably already killed those poor people.

A SATIN CHOKER
LIGHT-WEIGHT

Pretty obvious how this would be used as a weapon, right?

A BAG OF CASH
HEAVY-WEIGHT

Great for bribery, graft, or just general corruption.

CLUES & EVIDENCE

- A brown hair was found on a golden step.

- A satin choker was not on the enormous stairs.

- Silverton the Legend loved pretending to pet a hedge rabbit.

- A bag of cash was not in the giant doorway.

- The shortest suspect would never stoop so low as to carry their own cash.

- **A bloodstain was found on the piece of wood. (And the piece of wood was found in the head of the guard.)**

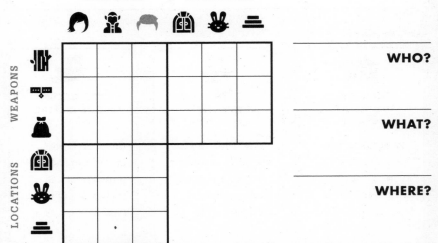

WHO?

WHAT?

WHERE?

11. THE GUEST BEDROOM BURGLAR BEATING 🔍

Logico was led up to his bedroom suite, which was still being cleaned, when suddenly he heard a scream. A burglar had broken in! And then, someone had murdered the burglar. But who?

SUSPECTS

MAID MARBLE

She resents everything and everyone, and she expresses that resentment by being really bad at her job.

5'7" • LEFT-HANDED • BLUE EYES • BLOND HAIR

MANSERVANT BROWNSTONE

Manservant Brownstone's brother is devoted to God, but he is devoted to the Violets.

6'2" • RIGHT-HANDED • BROWN EYES • BROWN HAIR

CHAUFFEUR BRONZE

Lady Violet's chauffeur. He's an aristocrat himself, which shows you how important Lady Violet is.

5'10" • RIGHT-HANDED • BROWN EYES • BLOND HAIR

LOCATIONS

THE GUEST BEDROOM
INDOORS

The bed is a size you haven't even heard of (Imperial Sun King).

THE BALCONY
OUTDOORS

In Logico's apartment, the balcony is a fire escape. This one has a fountain on it.

THE GUEST BATHROOM
INDOORS

Logico's private bathroom in the guest house is larger than his whole apartment.

WEAPONS

A BIOGRAPHY OF LORD VIOLET
MEDIUM-WEIGHT

The story of how Lord Violet joined the Royal Resistance when his Beloved Butler Beryl was killed.

A POISONED TINCTURE
LIGHT-WEIGHT

According to the label, one drop of this will cure all your ails. Two will kill you.

A MARBLE BUST
HEAVY-WEIGHT

A bust of Lord Violet: his face is covered with a mask.

CLUES & EVIDENCE

- A poisoned tincture was in the guest bedroom.

- Manservant Brownstone had a poisoned tincture.

- Chauffeur Bronze had never been in the guest bedroom.

- A bust of an aristocrat was discovered in the guest bathroom.

- Maid Marble had not been out on the balcony.

- **A bloodstained biography of Lord Violet was found beside the burglar.**

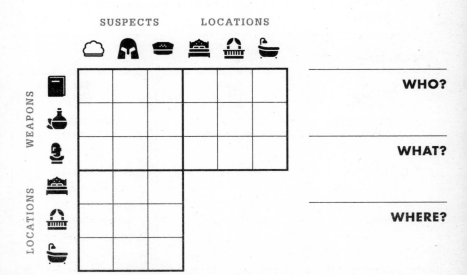

WHO?

WHAT?

WHERE?

12. THE MURDER OF THE BUTLER 🔍

Deductive Logico took some time to read the bloodstained biography of Lord Violet. When the Drakonian Civil War broke out, at first he was an oddity—a noble who supported the Reds. Everything changed when his Beloved Butler Beryl was murdered.

SUSPECTS

LORD VIOLET

Burnt in a fire that killed his parents, he wore a mask from the time he was a boy.

5'9" • RIGHT-HANDED • BROWN EYES • BROWN HAIR

LADY VIOLET

The heiress of the Violet Isles, the largest extrajudicial territory in the world.

5'0" • RIGHT-HANDED • BLUE EYES • BLOND HAIR

THE BLOODY ASSASSIN

A hired killer for the Red Revolution: he shows no mercy.

5'5" • LEFT-HANDED • BLUE EYES • BLOND HAIR

LOCATIONS

THE TWIN BED
INDOORS

Actually, it takes two of these beds together to make one twin.

THE TINY WINDOW
INDOORS

It's about six inches wide, but from 4:15 to 4:22 P.M. it lets in some light.

THE SINGLE CHAIR
INDOORS

It's supposed to have four legs but it only has three (which is why they let the butler have it).

WEAPONS

A STANDARD SWORD
HEAVY-WEIGHT

A typical sword with no particular distinguishing feature.

A HEAVY PURSE
HEAVY-WEIGHT

Finally, all that junk in there will be put to use (providing inertia).

LEATHER GLOVES
LIGHT-WEIGHT

Beware someone who wears leather gloves. They've already killed a cow: Who's next?!

CLUES & EVIDENCE

- The shortest suspect sat in the single chair with a regal pose.

- A brown hair was found in the tiny window.

- The Bloody Assassin was a Red, so he did not carry a heavy purse.

- A standard sword was certainly not in the single chair.

- Lady Violet did not carry a heavy purse.

- **The body of Beloved Butler Beryl was found on his tiny bed.**

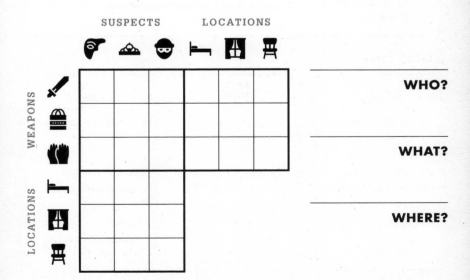

WHO?

WHAT?

WHERE?

13. CHAOS ON THE CLIFFSIDE 🔍

Suddenly, Logico heard an explosion! He ran outside and saw Independence Day fireworks exploding over the cliffs, and all the other guests were applauding. He hurried to join the crowd, but by the time he had found a seat, the fireworks guy had been killed.

SUSPECTS

PATRIARCH PORPOISE

The Holy Drakonian patriarch, the one true leader of all St. Lupinian Orthodox believers, and he won't let you forget it.

5'4" • RIGHT-HANDED • BLACK EYES • BLACK HAIR

THE DUCHESS OF VERMILLION

A tall, old woman with tall, old secrets. If she is the murderer, then it certainly wouldn't be the first time.

5'9" • LEFT-HANDED • GRAY EYES • WHITE HAIR

SEARCHING SABLE

She's searching for the pieces of her identity to put herself back together.

5'5" • LEFT-HANDED • HAZEL EYES • BLACK HAIR

LOCATIONS

THE STATUE OF LORD VIOLET
OUTDOORS

The mask on the statue has a haunting quality to it, as if there's nothing behind it.

THE CLIFFSIDE
OUTDOORS

Clearly, you get a better (and more dangerous) view with your feet dangling over the edge.

THE SEATING AREA
OUTDOORS

Plastic folding chairs have been set up for the guests to relax in while they enjoy the show.

WEAPONS

THE BOOK OF ST. LUPINE
MEDIUM-WEIGHT

A religious text, revered by the Holy Drakonian Church, about their great hero, St. Lupine.

A CARROT
HEAVY-WEIGHT

The most dangerous of vegetables: it's the only one that's sharp.

COMMERCIAL-GRADE FIREWORK
MEDIUM-WEIGHT

Used to celebrate Drakonian independence. Just point it at your enemy and light the fuse.

CLUES & EVIDENCE

- A page of scripture was found fluttering off of the cliffside.

- Someone with black eyes read a verse from the Book of St. Lupine. The verse read, "The purpose of life is to die, so good news . . ."

- A dangerous vegetable was discovered under a plastic folding chair.

- The second tallest suspect was not in the seating area.

- **A burnt fuse was found beside the victim.**

SUSPECTS · LOCATIONS

WEAPONS · LOCATIONS

WHO?

WHAT?

WHERE?

14. THE THANKSGIVING DINNER MURDER 🔍

In the Holy Republic of Drakonia, Thanksgiving was a sacred holiday which commemorated the crushing of a peasant uprising. Perhaps it was in honor of this great day that someone had killed the cook.

SUSPECTS

EXECUTIVE PRODUCER STEEL

The richest, smartest, and meanest producer in Hollywood. She's never seen a check she couldn't cash.

5'6" • RIGHT-HANDED • GRAY EYES • WHITE HAIR

FATHER MANGO

Father Mango has taken a vow of poverty, but he drives a BMW. He's taken a vow of obedience, but he has a staff of twenty-five. He's taken a vow of chastity, too, which is why he's on vacation.

5'10" • LEFT-HANDED • BROWN EYES • BALD

LADY VIOLET

The heiress of the Violet Isles, the largest extrajudicial territory in the world.

5'0" • RIGHT-HANDED • BLUE EYES • BLOND HAIR

LOCATIONS

THE DINING ROOM
OUTDOORS

Topped with a beautiful centerpiece commemorating the slaughter of the peasants.

THE KITCHEN
OUTDOORS

Where the chefs prepare the customary Thanksgiving foods: anything brown.

THE PANTRY
OUTDOORS

Where the brown foods are stored. (Honestly, a lot of them used to be white.)

WEAPONS

A GRAVY BOAT
MEDIUM-WEIGHT

A beautiful ceramic heirloom filled with hot, poisoned gravy.

A FORK
LIGHT-WEIGHT

Actually a lot more gruesome than a knife, if you think about it.

A TURKEY LEG
MEDIUM-WEIGHT

A turkey's had its leg ripped off, and you're worried about another murder?

CLUES & EVIDENCE

- The second tallest suspect thought the person who brought a gravy boat had an interesting vibe.

- Either Father Mango was in the kitchen, or Executive Producer Steel was beside a chef.

- A fork was discovered next to a grisly centerpiece.

- Father Mango was seen snooping around some stored brown food.

- **A turkey leg was used to commit the murder.**

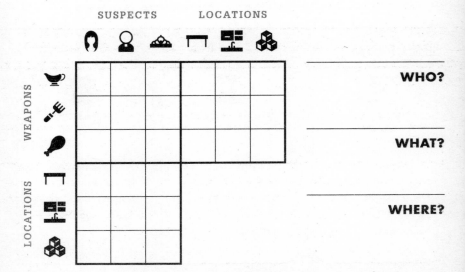

WHO?

WHAT?

WHERE?

15. CHRISTMAS IN THE GARDEN MAZE 🔍

Christmas in Drakonia was a celebration to support the restoration of the monarchy. The aristocrats gathered around, exchanged presents, and talked about how great things used to be back then, before the guy playing Santa was murdered.

SUSPECTS

MAID MARBLE

She resents everything and everyone, and she expresses that resentment by being really bad at her job.

5'7" • LEFT-HANDED • BLUE EYES • BLOND HAIR

CHRISTMAS-LOVER SABLE

Sable has decided to make Christmas her entire identity: her sweater has LED lights on it.

5'5" • LEFT-HANDED • HAZEL EYES • BLACK HAIR

BISHOP AZURE

A bishop in the Church, Azure has been known to pray for both her friends and her enemies. Of course, she asks for different things . . .

5'4" • RIGHT-HANDED • BROWN EYES • BROWN HAIR

LOCATIONS

THE FOUNTAIN
OUTDOORS

The water in the fountain is frozen over (well, it's an acrylic ice substitute).

THE LOOKOUT TOWER
INDOORS

The tower is covered in snow (imported from Switzerland).

THE SECRET GARDEN
OUTDOORS

A secret garden inside a larger garden? This is too meta.

WEAPONS

A LUMP OF COAL
HEAVY-WEIGHT

If you're on somebody's naughty list and they come at you with one of these, watch out!

A GIFT-WRAPPED BOMB
MEDIUM-WEIGHT

It's in a beautiful package and it's triggered to explode if it's unwrapped.

A CANDY CANE
LIGHT-WEIGHT

Someone has licked the end of it until it was sharpened into a deadly point.

CLUES & EVIDENCE

- The second tallest suspect was jealous when they saw someone else bring a gift-wrapped bomb: what a good present!

- A lump of coal was not found on the path between the fountain and the main house. (See Exhibit A.)

- Bishop Azure must have been on the naughty list, because she had a lump of coal.

- Maid Marble stopped to rest at a spot on the path between the fountain and the greenhouse. (See Exhibit A.)

- **The body of the fake Santa was found atop fake ice.**

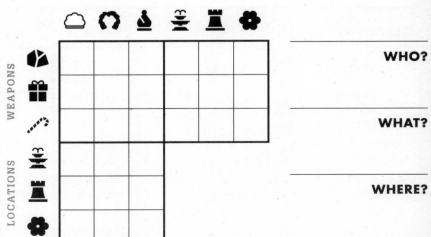

WHO?

WHAT?

WHERE?

16. YULE PAY FOR THIS 🔍

Later in the evening, everyone went into the mega-mansion to celebrate Yule. Nobody knew exactly what Yule was, so they basically just celebrated the cold. But then, the heater broke down, and the heater-repair technician was murdered.

SUSPECTS

CHAIRMAN CHALK

He figured out the publishing business years ago and never looked back. He called ebooks a "fad" and still owns a rotary phone. He is worth a billion dollars.

5'9" • RIGHT-HANDED • BLUE EYES • WHITE HAIR

PHILOLOGIST FLINT

You can learn a lot about a word from its etymology, like where it came from, and what it used to mean.

5'2" • LEFT-HANDED • GREEN EYES • BLOND HAIR

SECRETARY CELADON

The secretary of defense, and someone who is personally responsible for a number of war crimes, some of which are now named after her.

5'6" • LEFT-HANDED • GREEN EYES • BROWN HAIR

LOCATIONS

THE STAIRWELL
INDOORS

The only way to get onto or off of the roof (other than jumping).

THE BAR
OUTDOORS

Here they have all the best Yule drinks, and some of the worst, too.

THE DANCE FLOOR
OUTDOORS

They've set up a huge dance floor to celebrate Yule properly (they think).

WEAPONS

A LOG
HEAVY-WEIGHT

A big, heavy oak log. Somebody killed the tree so that the tree could kill somebody.

A REGULAR SNOWBALL
MEDIUM-WEIGHT

Okay, so, that's what it looks like, but actually, there's a grenade inside of it.

A FIRE POKER
MEDIUM-WEIGHT

You can use this to start a fire . . . or end a life.

CLUES & EVIDENCE

- Either Philologist Flint or a war criminal was on the dance floor.

- The second tallest suspect had previously employed the person who brought a fire poker.

- A billionaire brought a log.

- The second tallest suspect was seen next to an awful drink.

- **The body was found in the only path to or from the roof.**

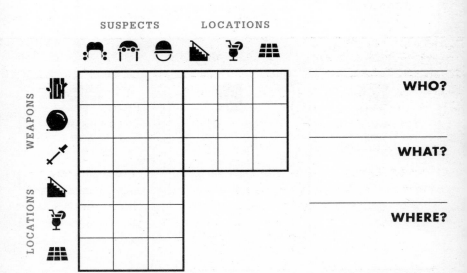

SUSPECTS   LOCATIONS

WEAPONS

LOCATIONS

WHO?

WHAT?

WHERE?

17. NEW YEAR, NEW MURDER 🔍

To celebrate the New Year, everyone gathered in the library, which was filled with DJ music and lighting that was so dim it made it hard to read, and even harder to discover the dead body of the DJ.

SUSPECTS

A-LIST ABALONE

The most talented and in-demand actress of all time this month.

5'6" • RIGHT-HANDED • HAZEL EYES • RED HAIR

LADY VIOLET

The heiress of the Violet Isles, the largest extrajudicial territory in the world.

5'0" • RIGHT-HANDED • BLUE EYES • BLOND HAIR

JUDGE PINE

Master of the courtroom and possessed of a firm belief in justice, as decided by her and her alone.

5'6" • RIGHT-HANDED • BROWN EYES • BLACK HAIR

LOCATIONS

THE MAP ROOM
INDOORS

Filled with maps of Drakonia, highlighting its strategic chokepoints.

THE STACKS
INDOORS

Hundreds and hundreds of books on Drakonian history and economic theory.

THE SECRET PASSAGEWAY
INDOORS

To open this door, pull out a book nobody would intentionally read: *The Accountant's Guide to Having Fun.*

WEAPONS

A CHAMPAGNE FLUTE
LIGHT-WEIGHT

Break it and stab someone with it, or just fill it with poisoned champagne.

A REALLY HIGH HEEL
MEDIUM-WEIGHT

Stilettos should have to be registered as deadly (and uncomfortable) weapons.

GHOST PEPPER FLAKES
LIGHT-WEIGHT

A deadly spice. Throw these in someone's face and they'll become a ghost.

CLUES & EVIDENCE

- Judge Pine had not been anywhere near any books on history.

- No stilettos were found in the map room.

- A deadly spice was certainly not in the map room.

- The heiress of Violet Isles had a champagne flute.

- A-List Abalone was seen with a really high heel.

- **The DJ's body was hard to find because it was hidden in the secret passage.**

SUSPECTS   LOCATIONS

WEAPONS

LOCATIONS

WHO?

WHAT?

WHERE?

18. THE SECRET PASSAGE

Once Logico had discovered there was a secret passage, he had to investigate it. And once he did that, he discovered a dead body. And once he did *that*, he had to investigate that, too.

SUSPECTS

PATRIARCH PORPOISE

The Holy Drakonian patriarch, the one true leader of all St. Lupinian Orthodox believers, and he won't let you forget it.

5'4" • RIGHT-HANDED • BLACK EYES • BLACK HAIR

CHEF AUBERGINE

It is said that she once killed her husband, cooked him, and then served him at her restaurant. It's not true, but even the fact that it's said about her tells you something.

5'2" • RIGHT-HANDED • BLUE EYES • BLOND HAIR

VICE PRESIDENT MAUVE

A vice president of TekCo Futures. She has been tasked with developing the latest TekCo product: TekTopia. It's like a metaverse in real life.

5'8" • RIGHT-HANDED • BROWN EYES • BLACK HAIR

LOCATIONS

A BIG LOCKED DOOR
INDOORS

A locked iron door at the end of the tunnel: What the heck is behind it?

AN EMPTY ROOM
INDOORS

A brick room with a single drain in the floor. Honestly, the creepiest thing Logico's seen.

THE MAIN PASSAGEWAY
INDOORS

Brick-walled and lit by bare incandescent bulbs. Not comforting!

WEAPONS

A HEAVY CANDLE
HEAVY-WEIGHT

It's heavy, yet it really lightens up the room.

A CROWBAR
MEDIUM-WEIGHT

Honestly, they're used more often for crime than anything else.

A HEAVY CODEBOOK
HEAVY-WEIGHT

Filled with key-words and ciphers, you can use it to crack codes or skulls.

CLUES & EVIDENCE

- Patriarch Porpoise had not been near a big locked door.

- Chef Aubergine was afraid of the person who brought a heavy codebook.

- A drop of wax was found beneath a bare lightbulb.

- In the harsh light of a bare incandescent bulb, Vice President Mauve looked evil.

- **The body was found beside a creepy drain, which made it even creepier.**

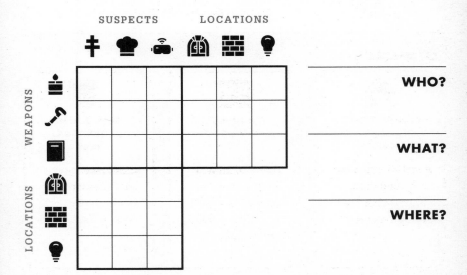

19. THE PRIVATE HOSPITAL PUBLIC MURDER 🔍

When Logico pushed open the heavy iron doors he found . . . "A private hospital," Dr. Crimson explained. They were illegal in Free Drakonia, so Lady Violet had built one beneath the Violet Manor. But that wasn't the only crime, she said: they had just found the body of the last patient—murdered!

SUSPECTS

SECRETARY CELADON

The secretary of defense, and someone who is personally responsible for a number of war crimes, some of which are now named after her.

5'6" • LEFT-HANDED • GREEN EYES • BROWN HAIR

DR. CRIMSON

She believes that everyone—no matter their race or creed—deserves the right to medical care, as long as they can afford it.

5'9" • LEFT-HANDED • GREEN EYES • RED HAIR

MISS SAFFRON

Miss Saffron is technically an aristocrat, but more accurately, she's just plain rich.

5'2" • LEFT-HANDED • HAZEL EYES • BLOND HAIR

LOCATIONS

A GIANT MEDI-CAL MACHINE
INDOORS

It does something with your ions or your cells or something.

AN OPERATING TABLE
INDOORS

Honestly, the leather straps are a little freaky, but I guess you'd need them.

A MEDICINE CABINET
INDOORS

It has all the greats in it: arsenic, cyanide, and some helpful ones, too.

WEAPONS

A BRAIN IN A JAR
HEAVY-WEIGHT

Philosophers argue you might be a brain in a jar. A great rebuttal is to hit them over the head with one.

A CHEAP PEN
LIGHT-WEIGHT

Getting killed by an expensive pen is bad enough . . .

A CRANIAL SAW
MEDIUM-WEIGHT

Just a regular bone saw. It can be used for brain surgery, vivisection, or murder.

CLUES & EVIDENCE

- The suspect who had a brain in a jar also had hazel eyes (in their head, not in a jar).

- Logico could barely read his own scrambled handwriting: EYARSRCTE ENDCOLA ASW NEES TNEX OT EMOS KDNI OF HEANICM.

- The tallest suspect brought a cheap pen.

- The suspect who's just plain rich never got near an operating table.

- **The last patient had their cranium sawed . . . to death!**

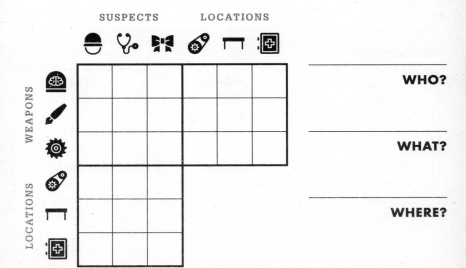

20. GATHERING THE SUSPECTS

Finally, Deductive Logico gathered the suspects in the sitting room to reveal that there *was* a dark secret, and he had figured it out. However, before he could reveal what it was, he was killed! But—aha!—it was only a decoy Logico who had been murdered!

SUSPECTS

LADY VIOLET

The heiress of the Violet Isles, the largest extra-judicial territory in the world.

5'0" • RIGHT-HANDED • BLUE EYES • BLOND HAIR

CHEF AUBERGINE

It is said that she once killed her husband, cooked him, and then served him at her restaurant. It's not true, but even the fact that it's said about her tells you something.

5'2" • RIGHT-HANDED • BLUE EYES • BLOND HAIR

MAID MARBLE

She resents everything and everyone, and she expresses that resentment by being really bad at her job.

5'7" • LEFT-HANDED • BLUE EYES • BLOND HAIR

LOCATIONS

THE FIREPLACE
INDOORS

For gazing at the flaming logs, thoughtfully, while the supersleuth explains the mystery.

THE BALCONY
OUTDOORS

For gazing over the grounds, really pensively, while the gumshoe cracks the case.

THE LEATHER COUCH
INDOORS

For sprawling out on, really casually, while the detective describes the murder.

WEAPONS

AN EMPTY CAGE
HEAVY-WEIGHT

It smells like a tiny rodent, like a ferret or a mongoose.

A CANDELABRA
HEAVY-WEIGHT

You could smash somebody in the head with this, or just light some candles.

A PAINTING OF LORD VIOLET
HEAVY-WEIGHT

Lord Violet's striking blue eyes seem to follow you wherever you go.

CLUES & EVIDENCE

- Lady Violet was either gazing at the fire or sprawling out.
- Chef Aubergine was staring thoughtfully.
- Maid Marble was lit spookily with her candelabra.
- A painting of Lord Violet was not on the leather couch.
- **The decoy Logico smelled like a tiny rodent.**

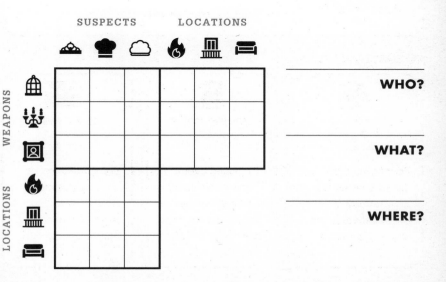

WHO?

WHAT?

WHERE?

21. THE MURDER OF LORD VIOLET 🔍

"There *is* a dark secret on this island!" Logico declared. "And if we are to uncover it, we must ask ourselves: Who killed Lord Violet? For it happened in the Drakonian Civil War, after he had joined with the Royal Resistance to fight the Reds."

SUSPECTS

GOVERNOR LEAD

He would become the most feared and least loved of the Free Drakonian governors.

6'2" • RIGHT-HANDED • BROWN EYES • BLACK HAIR

THE IRON TSAR

The meanest, cruelest, and most powerful strongman in history. He always wears a helmet.

5'6" • LEFT-HANDED • GRAY EYES • UNKNOWN

MAJOR RED

The revolutionary leader who freed Drakonia from the grasp of the Tsar and then immediately grasped it himself.

6'2" • LEFT-HANDED • BROWN EYES • BROWN HAIR

LOCATIONS

THE GRAND BALCONY
OUTDOORS

Where the Iron Tsar would make his annual appearance to watch the military parade.

THE GREAT HALL
INDOORS

Not only are the floors and the walls made of marble, but the forks, spoons, and knives are, too.

THE THRONE ROOM
INDOORS

The great throne of the Iron Tsar stands in the middle. (It's made, perhaps ironically, of gold.)

WEAPONS

A BAZOOKA
HEAVY-WEIGHT

Probably the worst possible weapon for your enemy to point at you.

THE BIG RED BOOK
MEDIUM-WEIGHT

Written by Major Red, some say it single-handedly won the revolution. Others say the weapons played a part.

IVORY NIGHT-EATER FANGS
MEDIUM-WEIGHT

Ancient Drakonian warriors would wear these to terrify their enemies.

CLUES & EVIDENCE

- The Iron Tsar had previously appointed the person who brought the Big Red Book to a government post, and yet they betrayed him.

- Pieces of the story were scrambled over time: VORYI FNGAS WREE OTN NI HET RDGAN BYAOLCN.

- Governor Lead attempted to take his place on a golden throne.

- The revolutionary leader carried a heavy-weight weapon.

- **Lord Violet was struck down in the great hall!**

	SUSPECTS			LOCATIONS		
WEAPONS						
LOCATIONS						

WHO?

WHAT?

WHERE?

22. THE REDS ARRIVE

The Red Army was storming the island! Lady Violet shouted for people to follow her to the secret passage in the garden maze, but as she led the guests there, one of them was killed! Which of the Reds did it?

SUSPECTS

SERGEANT GUNMETAL

A serious, hard-edged soldier who doesn't take "no" for an answer.

6'0" • RIGHT-HANDED • BROWN EYES • BLACK HAIR

COMRADE CHAMPAGNE

A communist and a rich one. Comrade Champagne likes nothing more than to travel the world, sharing the message of communism with his fellow vacationers.

5'11" • LEFT-HANDED • HAZEL EYES • BLOND HAIR

COSMONAUT BLUSKI

An ex-Soviet spaceman whose blood flows red. Sure, that's normal, but for him it's patriotic.

6'2" • LEFT-HANDED • BROWN EYES • BLACK HAIR

LOCATIONS

THE GARDEN MAZE
OUTDOORS

A beautiful maze, not made of hedges, but of beautiful (and thorny) roses.

THE CLIFFS
OUTDOORS

Jagged rocks, crushing waves, and sharks are below. A beautiful moonlit sky is above.

THE MAIN HOUSE
INDOORS

This house has more than two hundred rooms, all of which are larger than Logico's apartment.

WEAPONS

AN EXPLODING CIGAR
LIGHT-WEIGHT

A classic of practical joking and American "diplomacy."

A HAMMER AND SICKLE
HEAVY-WEIGHT

When one weapon won't do, you can use these two!

A BAYONET
MEDIUM-WEIGHT

The official weapon of the Red Army, mostly because it doesn't require paying for bullets.

CLUES & EVIDENCE

- Whoever had the bayonet was left-handed.

- Sergeant Gunmetal had not passed the lookout tower when he went from the fountain in the center of the maze to the place where he was during the murder. (See Exhibit A.)

- An exploding cigar was discovered next to a beautiful rose.

- Deductive Logico intercepted a coded message sent by the Reds: RAGIC GNIDOLPXE NA HTIW NEES SAW ENGAPMAHC EDARMOC.

- **The guest fell on jagged rocks. And then they were eaten by sharks.**

SUSPECTS   LOCATIONS

WHO?

WHAT?

WHERE?

23. THE FLIGHT UNDERGROUND 🔍

Logico expected another surprise at the end of this underground tunnel, but he did not expect that surprise to be an enormous crystal cove, and an underground lake, and a submarine! He did expect a murder, though: the submarine captain was dead.

SUSPECTS

MISS SAFFRON

Miss Saffron is technically an aristocrat, but more accurately, she's just plain rich.

5'2" • LEFT-HANDED • HAZEL EYES • BLOND HAIR

CHEF AUBERGINE

It is said that she once killed her husband, cooked him, and then served him at her restaurant. It's not true, but even the fact that it's said about her tells you something.

5'2" • RIGHT-HANDED • BLUE EYES • BLOND HAIR

MANSERVANT BROWNSTONE

Manservant Brownstone's brother is devoted to God, but he is devoted to the Violets.

6'2" • RIGHT-HANDED • BROWN EYES • BROWN HAIR

LOCATIONS

THE CRYSTAL FIELDS
INDOORS

Thousands of violet sapphires jut out from every rock surface.

A GIANT HOLE
INDOORS

A huge pit in the ground. If you shine a light in it, you see nothing.

THE UNDER-GROUND LAKE
INDOORS

There is a lake underground with a submarine at the dock.

WEAPONS

A PUFFY TAIL COMB
LIGHT-WEIGHT

Perfectly suited for combing a fluffy tail. Squirrel hairs stick out of it.

A HOLY DRAKO-NIAN AWARD
MEDIUM-WEIGHT

"To Lord Violet. For honor and bravery in the fight against the Reds."—The Iron Tsar

A GEODE
MEDIUM-WEIGHT

It probably has beautiful crystals inside but you won't know unless you hit someone with it.

CLUES & EVIDENCE

- Miss Saffron was not in a giant hole, and a puffy tail comb was not in the underground lake.

- Manservant Brownstone carried a rock that might contain crystals inside.

- Logico made some scrambled notes in the dark: A DOEEG SAW NTO UDNFO NI ETH DRGDUNNOREU KEAL.

- The suspect with a restaurant was childhood friends with the person who brought a puffy tail comb.

- **The submarine captain had a violet sapphire clutched in his hand.**

SUSPECTS · LOCATIONS

WHO?

WHAT?

WHERE?

24. UNDER THE SEA, OVER THE LINE 🔍

The remaining three guests plus Lady Violet and Deductive Logico boarded the submarine, only to discover that a fourth guest was on board, and also that the fourth guest had been murdered.

SUSPECTS

SILVERTON THE LEGEND

An acclaimed actor of the Golden Age, now in his golden years.

6'4" • RIGHT-HANDED • BLUE EYES • SILVER HAIR

CAPTAIN SLATE

A real-life astronaut. The first woman to travel around the dark side of the moon, and also the first to be suspected of murdering her copilot.

5'5" • LEFT-HANDED • BROWN EYES • BROWN HAIR

THE DUKE OF VERMILLION

He just wanted to enjoy a party. That's all he wanted to do. And yet, even that is out of reach.

5'9" • LEFT-HANDED • GRAY EYES • WHITE HAIR

LOCATIONS

THE QUARTERS
INDOORS

All of the evacuees are complaining that the bunks are too small.

THE CONTROL ROOM
INDOORS

People take turns looking through the periscope.

THE ENGINE ROOM
INDOORS

A massive industrial engine powered by a nuclear reactor.

WEAPONS

A FLYING SQUIRREL
MEDIUM-WEIGHT

A throw-and-go weapon, if you don't mind making an enemy of the squirrel.

A TORPEDO
HEAVY-WEIGHT

This could sink a battleship, but if you hit someone over the head with it, it'll probably just sink them.

A BRIEFCASE FULL OF MONEY
MEDIUM-WEIGHT

Wait a second—all of the faces on the bills have mustaches on them!

CLUES & EVIDENCE

- Either the Duke of Vermillion was in the engine room or Captain Slate brought a torpedo.

- Neither the tallest suspect nor the suspect with brown eyes had been in the quarters.

- The second tallest suspect was in love with the person who brought a briefcase full of money.

- Logico found a report written in a scrambled hand: A OEDPTOR WAS NOT NI TEH GENIEN RMOO.

- **A flying squirrel was used to commit the murder.**

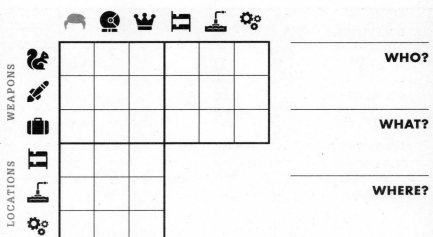

25. THE BIG REVEAL 🔍

When the submarine was surfacing off the coast of France, everyone asked Logico to explain the dark secret of Lord Violet. And so, he did: "The Bloody Assassin did not kill Beloved Butler Beryl. The true story is different from the one you know."

SUSPECTS

BELOVED BUTLER BERYL

The beloved butler of Lord Violet, who is honored everywhere in the mansion.

5'9" • RIGHT-HANDED • BROWN EYES • BROWN HAIR

LORD VIOLET

Remember: he's worn this mask since he was very young.

5'9" • RIGHT-HANDED • BLUE EYES • BLOND HAIR

LADY VIOLET

The heiress of the Violet Isles, the largest extrajudicial territory in the world.

5'0" • RIGHT-HANDED • BLUE EYES • BLOND HAIR

LOCATIONS

THE SINGLE CHAIR
INDOORS

It's supposed to have four legs but it only has three (which is why they let the butler have it).

THE TINY WINDOW
INDOORS

It's about six inches wide, but from 4:15 to 4:22 P.M. it lets in some light.

THE TWIN BED
INDOORS

Actually, it takes two of these beds together to make one twin.

WEAPONS

**LEATHER
GLOVES**
LIGHT-WEIGHT

Beware someone
who wears leather
gloves. They've al-
ready killed a cow:
Who's next?!

**A HEAVY
PURSE**
HEAVY-WEIGHT

Finally, all that junk
in there will be put
to use (to provide
inertia).

**A BROKEN
SWORD**
MEDIUM-WEIGHT

The famous broken
sword of legend:
only the truth is a
little different from
the tale.

CLUES & EVIDENCE

- The Detective Club sent Logico a message written in their secret
  code: OLIW ERLOVG XZIIRVW Z SVZEB KFIHV. (See the first *Murdle*
  book or the hints.)

- Leather gloves were certainly not in the single chair.

- Logico discovered a strange message in the marginalia of the biography of Lord Violet: NA SSERIEH SAW GNIDNATS NI EHT YNIT
  WODNIW.

- The person on the twin bed was a Violet.

- **The murderer used a broken sword to dispatch his foe.**

WHO? _____

WHAT? _____

WHERE? _____

EXHIBIT B

LETTER VALUES

1	2	3	4	5	6	7	8	9
A	B	C	D	E	F	G	H	I
J	K	L	M	N	O	P	Q	R
S	T	U	V	W	X	Y	Z	

NUMEROLOGICAL ASSOCIATIONS

0. Origins, opportunities

1. Unity, leadership

2. Duality, the Dialectic

3. Creativity, magick

4. Matter, minerals, work

5. Adventure, nature

6. Death, sincerity, home

7. Luck, spirituality, life

8. Money, motivation

9. Pain, revolution

HOW TO CALCULATE A SIGNIFICANT FIGURE

1. Add the values of each letter of a last name.
   (e.g. for Red, R = 9, E = 5, D = 4, so 9 + 5 + 4 = 18)

2. If they sum to more than 9, add their digits together.
   (e.g. since 18 > 9, 1 + 8 = 9)

3. Repeat Step 2 until the value is 9 or less. When they sum to a single digit, that is your significant figure.
   (e.g. Red's is 9, associated with pain & revolution)

INSPECTOR IRRATINO'S GUIDE TO NUMEROLOGY

OCCULT MEDIUM

Once Deductive Logico and Inspector Irratino were reunited, Irratino convinced him to stop worrying about politics, and to enjoy a short respite from the troubles of the world.

"Let's travel around the world solving mysteries!" Irratino said. "I have recently been introduced to some interesting numerological ideas, which I would like to put into practice." These ideas are collected in Irratino's numerological primer (Exhibit B, seen on the left).

Logico did not believe in numerology and Irratino did not believe in mathematics, but the two of them worked together well and solved all the mysteries before them.

In these twenty-five mysteries, you must examine the statements of the suspects in addition to the clues and evidence.

The murderer will always lie, and the other suspects will always tell the truth.

You might be able to spot the killer right away. Or you might have to think through each suspect in turn, examining if it is logically possible for them to be the only liar, while the others are telling the truth. The one and only liar will always be the murderer.

For an even more difficult task, take the Detective Club Challenge: Solve the Seven Riddles of Pythagoras, which will appear throughout this section, and use them to unlock the secrets of his tomb.

26. INSTITUTIONALIZED MURDER

Investigator Irratino was excited to tell his fellow esoterics at the Investigation Institute about Logico's wild experience on the Violet Isles. Unfortunately, all they wanted to talk about was how one of their top occultists had been murdered.

SUSPECTS

DR. SEASHELL, DDS

He's an amateur physicist with a new theory of the universe, and also, a working dentist.

5'7" • RIGHT-HANDED • GREEN EYES • GRAY HAIR • PISCES

HERBALIST ONYX

In her greenhouse, she's grown every kind of plant required in the culinary, magick, and poisoning arts.

5'0" • RIGHT-HANDED • BROWN EYES • BLACK HAIR • VIRGO

NUMEROLOGIST NIGHT

Not only do they know the value of x, they know the meaning of x.

5'9" • LEFT-HANDED • BLUE EYES • BROWN HAIR • PISCES

LOCATIONS

THE GREAT TOWER
INDOORS

A towering tower specifically built to drop things for experimental purposes.

THE OBSERVATORY
INDOORS

For studying the stars, or having a romantic evening.

AN IMPOSSIBLE HEDGE MAZE
OUTDOORS

No ordinary hedge maze. This one was designed by the late M.C. Escher.

WEAPONS

A POISONED TINCTURE
LIGHT-WEIGHT

According to the label, one drop of this will cure all your ails. Two will kill you.

A PRAYER CANDLE
MEDIUM-WEIGHT

If you were praying that somebody died, your wish came true.

A CRYSTAL BALL
HEAVY-WEIGHT

If you look into it, it will tell you your future, so long as your future is a crystal ball.

CLUES & EVIDENCE

- A Virgo had a weapon that could supposedly tell the future.

- Dr. Seashell, DDS, did not bring a poisoned tincture.

STATEMENTS
(Remember: The murderer is lying. The others are telling the truth.)

Dr. Seashell, DDS: A prayer candle was not in the observatory.

Herbalist Onyx: If I tell you, can I get back to my work? A poisoned tincture was in the observatory.

Numerologist Night: I was not in an impossible hedge maze.

WHO?

WHAT?

WHERE?

27. YOUR DAYS ARE NUMBERED 🔍🔍

At the Investigation Institute, the one department you could count on was the numerology department. Unfortunately, their new director had been killed, right as he was on the verge of discovering a new number. Who had killed him?

SUSPECTS

ASTROLOGER AZURE

A stargazer, full of wonder and questions about the exact time and place of your birth.

5'6" • RIGHT-HANDED • HAZEL EYES • BROWN HAIR • CANCER

SUPREME MASTER COBALT

He has a long, white beard, and he wears long, white robes.

5'9" • RIGHT-HANDED • BLUE EYES • SILVER HAIR • AQUARIUS

NUMEROLOGIST NIGHT

Not only do they know the value of *x*, they know the meaning of *x*.

5'9" • LEFT-HANDED • BLUE EYES • BROWN HAIR • PISCES

LOCATIONS

THE CALCULA-TOR ROOM
INDOORS

They're multiplying 367 by 673 and seeing if it equals the same as it did yesterday.

THE APPLE ORCHARD
INDOORS

Used to empirically test those questions about how many apples you have.

123

THE COUNTING ROOM
INDOORS

Here, they have people counting, seeing if they can find the highest number.

WEAPONS

A CUTE ANGEL
LIGHT-WEIGHT

A little doll who is supposedly the patron saint of math.

A PRIME STEAK
MEDIUM-WEIGHT

The finest cut of (genetically modified soy) steak.

A HYPERCUBE
HEAVY-WEIGHT

Technically impossible, which makes for a great impossible crime.

CLUES & EVIDENCE

- Supreme Master Cobalt had not been in the counting room.

- A little doll was discovered in the apple orchard.

STATEMENTS
(Remember: The murderer is lying. The others are telling the truth.)

Astrologer Azure: Look at the stars! They say I brought a prime steak.

Supreme Master Cobalt: Based on my visions, Astrologer Azure was in the calculator room.

Numerologist Night: Based on the numbers, I brought a hypercube.

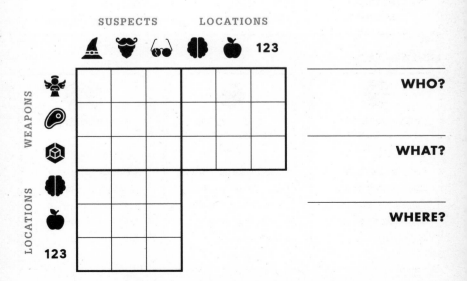

WHO?

WHAT?

WHERE?

28. BANKING ON MURDER

The Investigation Institute offered $1 million to anyone who could provide proof of the occult. Irratino had given it out so many times, his bank's manager demanded to speak to him. But when Logico and Irratino arrived, the manager was dead.

SUSPECTS

CHAIRMAN CHALK

He figured out the publishing business years ago and never looked back. He called ebooks a "fad" and still owns a rotary phone. He is worth a billion dollars.

5'9" • RIGHT-HANDED • BLUE EYES • WHITE HAIR • SAGITTARIUS

FATHER MANGO

Father Mango has taken a vow of poverty, but he drives a BMW. He's taken a vow of obedience, but he has a staff of twenty-five. He's taken a vow of chastity, too, which is why he's on vacation.

5'10" • LEFT-HANDED • BROWN EYES • BALD • TAURUS

SIGNOR EMERALD

An Italian jeweler of great renown, Signor Emerald has traveled the world in search of rare, precious stones, which are always falling out of his pockets.

5'8" • LEFT-HANDED • BROWN EYES • BLACK HAIR • SAGITTARIUS

LOCATIONS

THE BACK ROOM
INDOORS

Unquestionably, the printing press back here is the source of the funny mustache money.

THE CLOCK ROOM
INDOORS

Cogs and gears and brass that operate the outdoor clock. Explore at your own risk!

THE VAULT
INDOORS

Inside a safety deposit box on ancient papyrus is the 1st Riddle: *The only odd number between half 10 and twice 4.*

WEAPONS

LEATHER GLOVES
LIGHT-WEIGHT

Beware someone who wears leather gloves. They've already killed a cow: Who's next?!

A LAPTOP
MEDIUM-WEIGHT

The machine you work on. It's connected to every distraction ever made.

A BAG OF GOLD
HEAVY-WEIGHT

Heavy and expensive! Gold coins keep falling out.

CLUES & EVIDENCE

- A scrambled message was handed to Logico from the bank teller: A SRAUUT AWS IN EHT BKCA OMOR.

- A cowhide weapon was not by the safety deposit boxes.

STATEMENTS
(Remember: The murderer is lying. The others are telling the truth.)

Chairman Chalk: Hmm . . . a bag of gold was in the clock room.
Father Mango: A laptop was in the back room.
Signor Emerald: Chairman Chalk brought a laptop.

SUSPECTS   LOCATIONS

WHO?

WHAT?

WHERE?

29. THE HOTEL BY THE CONVENTION CENTER

Inspector Irratino agreed to accompany Logico to a mathematics convention. First, they checked into a hotel, and Irratino was already so bored that he was relieved when the concierge was murdered.

SUSPECTS

SIGNOR EMERALD

An Italian jeweler of great renown, Signor Emerald has traveled the world in search of rare, precious stones, which are always falling out of his pockets.

5'8" • LEFT-HANDED • BROWN EYES • BLACK HAIR • SAGITTARIUS

SOCIOLOGIST UMBER

As a representative from the hard sciences, Sociologist Umber is always asking people to question their priors and if they've read Weber.

5'4" • LEFT-HANDED • BLUE EYES • BLOND HAIR • LEO

MATHEMATICIAN MARBLE

Finally, she had quit her job as a maid and left to pursue her true passion: mathematics.

5'7" • LEFT-HANDED • BLUE EYES • BLOND HAIR • CANCER

LOCATIONS

ROOM 101
INDOORS

The nicest room in the hotel.

ROOM 202
INDOORS

The most expensive room in the hotel.

ROOM 303
INDOORS

The one they call the "Presidential Suite."

WEAPONS

A POISONED MUFFIN
LIGHT-WEIGHT

Not only poisoned, but rock hard. So you could use it two ways.

A π-DIMENSIONAL HYPERCUBE
HEAVY-WEIGHT

Impossible to imagine, so the crime will be impossible to solve.

A LAUNDRY BAG FILLED WITH KNIVES
HEAVY-WEIGHT

Sometimes you gotta clean your knives.

CLUES & EVIDENCE

- A rare, precious stone was found in a room with a number that was exactly half the number of one of the two other rooms.

- Sociologist Umber had once been ripped off by the person who brought a technically impossible weapon.

STATEMENTS
(Remember: The murderer is lying. The others are telling the truth.)

Signor Emerald: Listen: I brought a laundry bag filled with knives.
Sociologist Umber: A poisoned muffin was in Room 202.
Mathematician Marble: My room number was three times another.

SUSPECTS   LOCATIONS

WEAPONS

LOCATIONS

WHO?

WHAT?

WHERE?

30. A² + B² = MURDER!

Deductive Logico and Inspector Irratino headed over to the mathematics convention. Logico was delighted to learn about the new mathematical developments, but Irratino was disappointed that there didn't seem to be much on the esoteric significance of them. Their differences were resolved when a presenter was murdered.

SUSPECTS

BROTHER BROWNSTONE

A monk who has dedicated his life to the Church, specifically to making money for it.

5'4" • LEFT-HANDED • BROWN EYES • BROWN HAIR • CAPRICORN

THE AMAZING AUREOLIN

A touring magician who has perfected the whole sawing-the-husband-in-two routine. Then, she made the body disappear.

5'6" • LEFT-HANDED • GREEN EYES • BLOND HAIR • ARIES

PRINCIPAL APPLEGREEN

A strict principal about everything except getting away with murder. His hands are always covered in chalk.

5'11" • RIGHT-HANDED • BLUE EYES • BALD • LIBRA

LOCATIONS

THE CHECK-IN STAND
INDOORS

Solve the 2nd Riddle to check in: *1 3 5 7. Three are the side lengths of a triangle. Which one isn't?*

THE BATHROOM
INDOORS

There is never a line: the mathematicians figured out a way to optimize bathrooms.

THE GREAT HALL
INDOORS

They're unveiling a new theorem that proves the tomb of Pythagoras is still lost.

WEAPONS

A 3D PRINTER
HEAVY-WEIGHT

You could 3D print a knife, or just drop it on someone.

A PROTRACTOR
LIGHT-WEIGHT

With this you can protract the time it takes for a guy to recover from being stabbed by it.

A COMPASS
HEAVY-WEIGHT

The kind for drawing circles, not navigating. If you're lost and this is all you have, you're dead.

CLUES & EVIDENCE

- Principal Applegreen had expelled the suspect who had a compass.

- A brown-eyed man was trying to solve the Riddle of Pythagoras.

STATEMENTS
(Remember: The murderer is lying. The others are telling the truth.)

Brother Brownstone: The Amazing Aureolin was in the bathroom.
The Amazing Aureolin: Magician's honor: a 3D printer was in the great hall.
Principal Applegreen: The Amazing Aureolin brought a protractor.

SUSPECTS · LOCATIONS

WEAPONS

LOCATIONS

WHO?

WHAT?

WHERE?

31. SKI LODGE A COMPLAINT: THERE'S BEEN A MURDER

Inspector Irratino took Deductive Logico to a ski lodge that a friend of his owned. But when they got there, the friend had been killed. (This cut down on their skiing.)

SUSPECTS

GRANDMASTER ROSE

A chess grandmaster who is always plotting his next move. Like how to bump off his next opponent! (He replied: 1 . . . e5.)

5'7" • LEFT-HANDED • BROWN EYES • BROWN HAIR • SCORPIO

DEACON VERDIGRIS

A deacon in the Church. She handles the parishioners' donations and, sometimes, their secrets.

5'3" • LEFT-HANDED • BLUE EYES • GRAY HAIR • LEO

EDITOR IVORY

The greatest romance editor of all time. She invented the enemies-to-lovers genre, and she was the first person to put a naked man on the cover of a book.

5'6" • LEFT-HANDED • BROWN EYES • GRAY HAIR • SCORPIO

LOCATIONS

THE SLOPES
OUTDOORS

Some of the finest slopes in the world. Long runs and moguls are fun for skiers and snowboarders alike.

A HIDDEN CAVE
OUTDOORS

A cave on the back side of the mountain, filled with stalactites and stalagmites and who knows what else.

THE WOODS
INDOORS

A deep, dark pine forest that encircles the ski resort. People have been known to go into it and never come out . . .

WEAPONS

A STRANGLIN' SCARF
LIGHT-WEIGHT

My, what a nice scarf Grandma knitted with a malicious gleam in her eyes.

POISONED HOT CHOCOLATE
LIGHT-WEIGHT

It's the last warm drink you'll ever have.

A SKI POLE
LIGHT-WEIGHT

The hardest part of using this to kill is skiing away with just one pole.

CLUES & EVIDENCE

- Poisoned hot chocolate was not anywhere near a mogul.

- A double-black-diamond skier handed Logico a scrambled message: ON PROCISO WSA IN HTE DWSOO.

STATEMENTS
(Remember: The murderer is lying. The others are telling the truth.)

Grandmaster Rose: Editor Ivory was not in a hidden cave.

Deacon Verdigris: As a godly woman, I say that Grandmaster Rose brought poisoned hot chocolate.

Editor Ivory: Grandmaster Rose did not bring a ski pole.

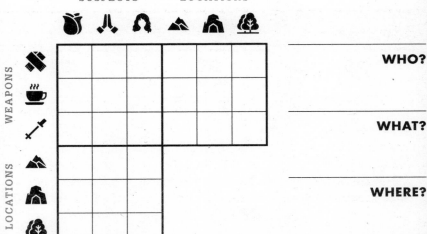

32. COUNTRY CLUBBED TO DEATH

Deductive Logico wondered why he and Inspector Irratino encountered this many murders. For example, when they joined a country club, one of its members was murdered almost immediately. Logico knew country club politics were cutthroat, but this seemed like overkill . . .

SUSPECTS

MX. TANGERINE

Proving that non-binary people can be murderers, too, Mx. Tangerine is an artist, poet, and potential suspect.

5'5" • LEFT-HANDED • HAZEL EYES • BLOND HAIR • PISCES

JUDGE PINE

Master of the courtroom and possessed of a firm belief in justice, as decided by her and her alone.

5'6" • RIGHT-HANDED • BROWN EYES • BLACK HAIR • TAURUS

VICE PRESIDENT MAUVE

A vice president of TekCo Futures. She has been tasked with developing the latest TekCo product: TekTopia. It's like a metaverse in real life.

5'8" • RIGHT-HANDED • BROWN EYES • BLACK HAIR • TAURUS

LOCATIONS

THE DINING HALL
INDOORS

The finest and whitest tablecloths covered by the most expensive silverware.

THE CADDY SHACK
INDOORS

Filled with rusty old tools, it's the perfect place for a caddy to hide their ▮▮▮▮ . . . or a body.

THE EIGHTEENTH HOLE
OUTDOORS

After a long exhausting round of golf, the last thing you want is to be murdered.

WEAPONS

A POISONED COCKTAIL
LIGHT-WEIGHT

Technically, it contains two poisons: alcohol and whatever the other one is.

A FIRST-PLACE TROPHY
HEAVY-WEIGHT

It features a statue of a golfer holding a smaller trophy (also of a golfer).

A SACK FULL OF GOLF BALLS
MEDIUM-WEIGHT

You could hit someone with this, or you could throw them behind you to trip your pursuers.

CLUES & EVIDENCE

- Whoever was in the caddy shack was left-handed.

- On a receipt, someone had scrawled a scrambled message for Logico: IERHETN AURTSU DAH HET FITSR CEPAL POHRTY.

STATEMENTS
(Remember: The murderer is lying. The others are telling the truth.)

Mx. Tangerine: A poisoned cocktail was not in the dining hall.

Judge Pine: All I know is Vice President Mauve was in the dining hall.

Vice President Mauve: A sack full of golf balls was not on the eighteenth hole.

SUSPECTS   LOCATIONS

WEAPONS

LOCATIONS

WHO?

WHAT?

WHERE?

33. GAMBLING AND MURDER ARE BOTH ILLEGAL

Logico received an invitation to an underground gambling ring. He invited Irratino, who swore he had devised a system for winning at poker. Irratino lost a lot of money, but another gambler lost their life.

SUSPECTS

BOSS CHARCOAL

A mob boss from the good ol' days when being a mob boss from the good ol' days meant something.

5'11" • RIGHT-HANDED • BROWN EYES • BLACK HAIR • TAURUS

SILVERTON THE LEGEND

An acclaimed actor of the Golden Age, now in his golden years.

6'4" • RIGHT-HANDED • BLUE EYES • SILVER HAIR • LEO

BABYFACE BLUE

This is absolutely one fully grown man, and not two kids in a trench coat. They can do adult things like see R-rated movies, buy beer, and stay out way past bedtime.

7'8" • RIGHT-HANDED • BLUE EYES • BLOND HAIR • GEMINI

LOCATIONS

THE FRONT DOOR
OUTDOORS

To get in, answer the 3rd Riddle: *Five halves is half of it.*

THE POKER TABLE
INDOORS

Hold up: do five aces beat a royal flush?

THE CASHIER
INDOORS

All the Benjamin Franklins have mustaches on them . . .

WEAPONS

A BAG OF GOLD
HEAVY-WEIGHT

Heavy and expensive! Gold coins keep falling out.

A SHOE KNIFE
MEDIUM-WEIGHT

Stomp your foot and a knife comes out of the leather.

A SLEEVE PIPE
MEDIUM-WEIGHT

A regular pipe hidden in a regular sleeve.

CLUES & EVIDENCE

- A Gemini was at the poker table.

- A secret message, written in a numerological code, was passed to Logico beneath the table: 52 62 71 62 32 41 21 11 71 11 23 61 92 62 52 23 41 62 62 92. (See Exhibit B.)

STATEMENTS
(Remember: The murderer is lying. The others are telling the truth.)

Boss Charcoal: Look here: Silverton the Legend was at the cashier.

Silverton the Legend: Let me tell you how it is: Boss Charcoal brought a sleeve pipe.

Babyface Blue: We, I mean I, know this: a shoe knife was at the cashier.

SUSPECTS   LOCATIONS

WEAPONS

LOCATIONS

WHO?

WHAT?

WHERE?

34. STATISTICALLY SPEAKING, YOU'RE PROBABLY DEAD

Deductive Logico was concerned the number of murders he was solving was improbable, so he visited his alma mater, the Deduction College, and discovered the stats professor had been killed. What are the odds?

SUSPECTS

MATHEMATICIAN MARBLE

Finally, she had quit her job as a maid and left to pursue her true passion: mathematics.

5'7" • LEFT-HANDED • BLUE EYES • BLOND HAIR • CANCER

THE DUCHESS OF VERMILLION

A tall, old woman with tall, old secrets. If she is the murderer, then it certainly wouldn't be the first time.

5'9" • LEFT-HANDED • GRAY EYES • WHITE HAIR • PISCES

SOCIOLOGIST UMBER

As a representative from the hard sciences, Sociologist Umber is always asking people to question their priors and if they've read Weber.

5'4" • LEFT-HANDED • BLUE EYES • BLOND HAIR • LEO

LOCATIONS

THE COMPUTER ROOM
INDOORS

In here, a computer is calculating the number of things it could possibly calculate.

COIN-FLIPPING ROOM
INDOORS

This is the room where they flip coins to make sure the odds really are even.

THE TYPE-WRITER ROOM
OUTDOORS

They have 26 monkeys on 26 typewriters, and they'll have a draft of *Hamlet* in 40 billion years.

WEAPONS

A FIRE EXTINGUISHER
HEAVY-WEIGHT

You can hit someone over the head with it or just start a fire and do nothing with it.

A SHARP PENCIL
LIGHT-WEIGHT

Filled with actual lead. One stab and you'd die from lead poisoning.

A CALCULATOR
MIDDLE-WEIGHT

This has more computing power than it took to put a man on the moon. Also, you can spell dirty words upside down.

CLUES & EVIDENCE

- A monkey found a white hair.

- Sociologist Umber hated the person who brought a fire extinguisher.

STATEMENTS
(Remember: The murderer is lying. The others are telling the truth.)

Mathematician Marble: Well, sir, a calculator was in the coin-flipping room.
The Duchess of Vermillion: Marble was in the computer room.
Sociologist Umber: Marble brought a sharp pencil.

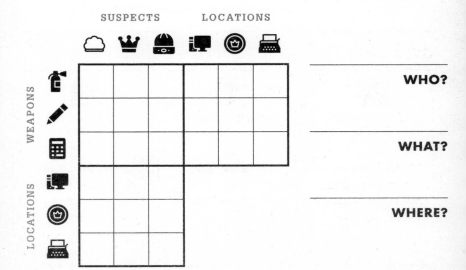

WHO?

WHAT?

WHERE?

35. A SURPRISE FOR A PSYCHIC

Inspector Irratino told Deductive Logico that he had agreed to give the Psychic Research Lab one more shot to prove themselves legitimate. But the fact that another so-called psychic had been killed really undermined their case.

SUSPECTS

ASTROLOGER AZURE

A stargazer, full of wonder and questions about the exact time and place of your birth.

5'6" • RIGHT-HANDED • HAZEL EYES • BROWN HAIR • CANCER

VICE PRESIDENT MAUVE

A vice president of TekCo Futures. She has been tasked with developing the latest TekCo product: TekTopia. It's like a metaverse in real life.

5'8" • RIGHT-HANDED • BROWN EYES • BLACK HAIR • TAURUS

DEAN GLAUCOUS

The dean of some such-and-such department at a massively funded research university. What does he do? Well, he handles the money, for one . . .

5'6" • RIGHT-HANDED • BROWN EYES • BROWN HAIR • VIRGO

LOCATIONS

THE GROUNDS
OUTDOORS

Filled with holes as a result of dowsing experiments.

THE KITCHEN
INDOORS

All the silverware has been removed from the drawers for experiments.

THE ISOLATION CHAMBER
INDOORS

A water tank in a dark room. You can regress in time, or just get really bored.

WEAPONS

A DOWSING ROD
MEDIUM-WEIGHT

You can find water, oil, and suckers with these.

A QUASI-PER-PETUAL MOTION MACHINE
HEAVY-WEIGHT

It doesn't run forever. More like two or three minutes.

A CRYSTAL BALL
HEAVY-WEIGHT

If you look into it, it will tell you your future, so long as your future is a crystal ball.

CLUES & EVIDENCE

- Dean Glaucous was hoping to get money from the person who brought a machine that runs for two or three minutes.

- A scrambled message was written on the wall of the Psychic Research Lab: A TSAUUR AWS NI EHT IHKNTCE.

STATEMENTS
(Remember: The murderer is lying. The others are telling the truth.)

Astrologer Azure: I was not in the isolation chamber.
Vice President Mauve: A crystal ball was not on the grounds.
Dean Glaucous: A quasi-perpetual motion machine was on the grounds.

SUSPECTS   LOCATIONS

WEAPONS

LOCATIONS

WHO?

WHAT?

WHERE?

36. A MIDNIGHT MOVIE SEQUEL

Two representatives from the Drakonian Royal Resistance were lobbying Midnight Movies to make an epic film against the Red Revolution, but negotiations had stalled when their chosen director was murdered. Once again, Logico was called to Hollywood to crack the case.

SUSPECTS

PATRIARCH PORPOISE

The Holy Drakonian patriarch, the one true leader of all St. Lupinian Orthodox believers, and he won't let you forget it.

5'4" • RIGHT-HANDED • BLACK EYES • BLACK HAIR • CANCER

EARL GREY

He comes from a long line of Earl Greys. Yes, those Earl Greys. No, he doesn't sign autographs. But he does always have some bags with him.

5'9" • RIGHT-HANDED • BROWN EYES • WHITE HAIR • CAPRICORN

PRESIDENT MIDNIGHT

His son once tried to steal the studio from him. Now he still has the studio, but he doesn't have a son.

6'2" • RIGHT-HANDED • BLACK EYES • BLACK HAIR • CAPRICORN

LOCATIONS

THE STATUE OF MIDNIGHT I
OUTDOORS

A statue to the founder of Midnight Movies, the great Midnight I.

SOUNDSTAGE A
INDOORS

Now they're filming a new murder mystery because *Murdle: The Movie* was such a hit.

THE SECURITY BUILDING
INDOORS

A more sophisticated security system than most military bases.

WEAPONS

A BOOM MIC
MEDIUM-WEIGHT

Unlike other microphones, this one can kill from a distance.

A STAGE LIGHT
HEAVY-WEIGHT

Shine it in their eyes and they can't see for a moment. Hit them on the head and they can't see forever.

A PENCIL
LIGHT-WEIGHT

For tracking continuity or stabbing somebody.

CLUES & EVIDENCE

- President Midnight clutched a weapon that could kill from a distance.

- Logico noticed a flashing scrambled message projected at the beginning of a screening: A CEARNC ASW YB HET TSTUAE FO IGHTMDIN I.

STATEMENTS
(Remember: The murderer is lying. The others are telling the truth.)

Patriarch Porpoise: As St. Lupine might say, Earl Grey was in the security building.

Earl Grey: If you must, President Midnight was in Soundstage A.

President Midnight: Earl Grey brought a pencil, you see?

	✝	🧐	🎩	⛩	A	📹
🎤						
🔦						
✏						
⛩						
A						
📹						

SUSPECTS   LOCATIONS

WEAPONS

LOCATIONS

WHO?

WHAT?

WHERE?

To truly test his mathematical acumen, Logico visited an organic grocery store where the prices contained numbers he had never seen before. Irratino was convinced they were in some kind of alternate dimension, but Logico was convinced it was a murder scene: the butcher had been butchered.

SUSPECTS

HIGH ALCHE-MIST RAVEN

There's an old joke that all alchemists are high alchemists. Raven hates it.

5'8" • RIGHT-HANDED • BROWN EYES • BROWN HAIR • PISCES

CHEF AUBERGINE

It is said that she once killed her husband, cooked him, and then served him at her restaurant. It's not true, but even the fact that it's said about her tells you something.

5'2" • RIGHT-HANDED • BLUE EYES • BLOND HAIR • LIBRA

OFFICER COPPER

The best part of being a policewoman criminal is that you can cut out the middleman and fail to investigate your own crimes.

5'5" • RIGHT-HANDED • BLUE EYES • BLOND HAIR • ARIES

LOCATIONS

THE PRODUCE SECTION
INDOORS

All the produce is farm-to-table, fair-trade, and far-too-expensive.

THE BAKERY
INDOORS

Fresh-baked rye bread by a freshly baked wry head.

THE DELI COUNTER
INDOORS

All the best vegan meats, from seitan sausage to soy beef.

WEAPONS

A CORKSCREW
LIGHT-WEIGHT

Once Logico started looking, he saw weapons everywhere.

A FORK
LIGHT-WEIGHT

A lot more gruesome than a knife, if you think about it.

A SPOON
LIGHT-WEIGHT

If a fork is more gruesome than a knife, think how bad killing someone with a spoon would be.

CLUES & EVIDENCE

- A spoon was not found near fair-trade food.

- Chef Aubergine was seen staring at the price tag on a warm rye.

STATEMENTS
(Remember: The murderer is lying. The others are telling the truth.)

High Alchemist Raven: Alchemically speaking, a corkscrew was at the deli counter.

Chef Aubergine: Officer Copper was at the deli counter.

Officer Copper: High Alchemist Raven did not bring a corkscrew.

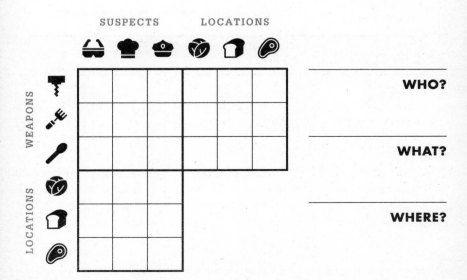

WHO?

WHAT?

WHERE?

38. DREAM A DREAM OF MURDER 🔍🔍

Exhausted from all the murders, Deductive Logico fell asleep on Irratino's couch and—even in his dream—he had to crack a case. Everyone knows that if you don't solve a dream murder before you wake up, the dream killer gets away.

SUSPECTS

INSPECTOR IRRATINO

Logico had a lot of dreams about Irratino, mostly involving ███████.

6'2" • LEFT-HANDED • GREEN EYES • BROWN HAIR • AQUARIUS

DIRECTOR DUSTY

Director Dusty seems to be directing the dream. But also, he's in the dream? It's confusing.

5'10" • LEFT-HANDED • HAZEL EYES • BALD • PISCES

BOOKIE-WINNER GAINSBORO

Ever since Logico showed him up by winning that Bookie, Logico's been having stress dreams where the author murders him.

6'0" • LEFT-HANDED • HAZEL EYES • BROWN HAIR • GEMINI

LOCATIONS

A LOCAL COFFEE SHOP
INDOORS

Everyone is acting totally normal, but the coffee shop is also on fire.

HIS CHILDHOOD HOME
INDOORS

And yet, it also seems to be a scene from a movie he liked.

THE CLOUDS
INDOORS

They are floating above an island that is also Logico's apartment.

WEAPONS

A PIANO
HEAVY-WEIGHT

It represents the heavy burden of solving so many murders.

GHOST PEPPER FLAKES
LIGHT-WEIGHT

Incredibly hot spice. They represent the fiery passion Logico has for ██████.

THE BIG RED BOOK
MEDIUM-WEIGHT

Written by Major Red, but in Logico's dream, it contains an exam he hadn't studied for.

CLUES & EVIDENCE

- The suspect in Logico's childhood home had a significant figure of 8. (See Exhibit B.)

- The weapon that represented Logico's fiery passion was not found in the clouds.

STATEMENTS
(Remember: The murderer is lying. The others are telling the truth.)

Inspector Irratino: I promise I did not bring a piano.
Director Dusty: I'm very busy, but a piano was in the clouds.
Bookie-Winner Gainsboro: I swear I was not in a local coffee shop.

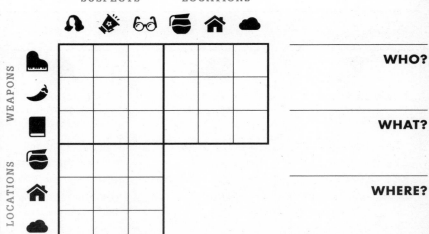

WHO?

WHAT?

WHERE?

39. THUNDER FOLLOWS LIGHTNING; LOGICO FOLLOWS LEADS

Deductive Logico and Inspector Irratino probably should have found a safe place inside to take shelter. Unfortunately, murder called: someone had taken this valuable opportunity to kill a meteorologist.

SUSPECTS

CAPTAIN SLATE

A real-life astronaut. The first woman to travel around the dark side of the moon, and also the first to be suspected of murdering her copilot.

5'5" • LEFT-HANDED • BROWN EYES • BROWN HAIR • AQUARIUS

COSMONAUT BLUSKI

An ex-Soviet spaceman whose blood flows red. Sure, that's normal, but for him it's patriotic.

6'2" • LEFT-HANDED • BROWN EYES • BLACK HAIR • ARIES

SIR RULEAN

A sophisticated gentleman who just happens to have been knighted, if you believe the Official Knighting Documents he is always waving around.

5'8" • RIGHT-HANDED • BLUE EYES • RED HAIR • LEO

LOCATIONS

A TORNADO
OUTDOORS

Wind that is spinning so quickly it can kill you, or transport you to a magical world.

A STORM-CHASING VAN
OUTDOORS

Speeding down the freeway in the opposite direction of everyone else.

A STORM SHELTER
INDOORS

They've got table tennis, vending machines, and TVs that show you how badly everyone is doing.

WEAPONS

A SATELLITE DISH
HEAVY-WEIGHT

This complicated piece of machinery can be used to track storms or hit people on the head.

A LIGHTNING ROD
MEDIUM-WEIGHT

Ask someone to hold on to this and wait: what happens next will shock them!

A MOTORCYCLE HELMET
HEAVY-WEIGHT

Sometimes the best weapons are life-saving devices.

CLUES & EVIDENCE

- A stack of Official Knighting Documents flew out the window of the storm-chasing van.

- Captain Slate hated the person who brought a satellite dish.

STATEMENTS
(Remember: The murderer is lying. The others are telling the truth.)

Captain Slate: Cosmonaut Bluski was in a storm shelter.
Cosmonaut Bluski: Comrade, a helmet was in the tornado.
Sir Rulean: I brought a lightning rod.

SUSPECTS   LOCATIONS

WEAPONS

LOCATIONS

WHO?

WHAT?

WHERE?

40. TEKCO FUTURES: WHERE THE PAST GOES TO DIE

Deductive Logico and Inspector Irratino were invited to the corporate headquarters of TekCo Futures in order to meet with the CEO. I know what you're thinking: the CEO was dead when they got there. But he wasn't dead. He was just busy and couldn't make it. But the secretary who was supposed to pass that along? She was dead.

SUSPECTS

COMRADE CHAMPAGNE

A communist and a rich one. Comrade Champagne likes nothing more than to travel the world, sharing the message of communism with his fellow vacationers.

5'11" • LEFT-HANDED • HAZEL EYES • BLOND HAIR • CAPRICORN

VICE PRESIDENT MAUVE

A vice president of TekCo Futures. She has been tasked with developing the latest TekCo product: TekTopia. It's like a metaverse in real life.

5'8" • RIGHT-HANDED • BROWN EYES • BLACK HAIR • TAURUS

PRESIDENT WHITE

The duly elected president of the Royal Resistance, a party of aristocrats who want to retake power. She wears a signet ring.

5'10" • RIGHT-HANDED • GRAY EYES • WHITE HAIR • LEO

LOCATIONS

THE NATURE ROOM
INDOORS

Everything here is made of plastic, but it's a perfect model of what the real nature room will look like.

THE HOLOSTAGE
INDOORS

Famous actor Silverton the Legend was paid a million dollars to pretend to be a hologram.

THE CONFERENCE ROOM
INDOORS

Nobody ever uses this room because the CEO makes all the decisions.

WEAPONS

A BRIEF-CASE FULL OF MONEY
HEAVY-WEIGHT

Honestly, this counterfeiting operation is going to debase the currency.

THE GOLDEN CUBE
HEAVY-WEIGHT

A one-meter cube of solid gold is worth one billion dollars, despite having no utility. Until now . . .

A LAPTOP
MEDIUM-WEIGHT

At TekCo Futures, a laptop was old-school, like rotary phones or VHS.

CLUES & EVIDENCE

- Comrade Champagne hated the person who brought a briefcase full of money.

- TekCo computers transmitted an encrypted message using the Next Letter Code: VGNDUDQ VZR NM SGD GNKNRSZFD GZC FQZX DXDR.

STATEMENTS
(Remember: The murderer is lying. The others are telling the truth.)

Comrade Champagne: Vice President Mauve brought the golden cube.
Vice President Mauve: As a VP, I'm certain a laptop was in the nature room.
President White: Vice President Mauve was in the conference room.

SUSPECTS   LOCATIONS

WEAPONS

LOCATIONS

WHO?

WHAT?

WHERE?

41. DEATH TO CARNIVORES! 🔍🔍

Inspector Irratino took Logico to an animal rescue run by one of his friends. His friend was fine, but a carnivorous guest at the animal rescue wasn't. In fact, he was dead. And only Logico could solve the case.

SUSPECTS

BABYFACE BLUE

This is absolutely one fully grown man, and not two kids in a trench coat. They can do adult things like see R-rated movies, buy beer, and stay out way past bedtime.

7'8" • RIGHT-HANDED • BLUE EYES • BLOND HAIR • GEMINI

CRYPTOZOOLO-GIST CLOUD

They know every sighting of Bigfoot, Yeti, Sasquatch, and what the difference is.

5'7" • RIGHT-HANDED • GRAY EYES • WHITE HAIR • SCORPIO

MX. TANGERINE

Proving that non-binary people can be murderers, too, Mx. Tangerine is an artist, poet, and potential suspect.

5'5" • LEFT-HANDED • HAZEL EYES • BLOND HAIR • PISCES

LOCATIONS

THE SQUIRREL PRESERVE
OUTDOORS

Millions of squirrels are frolicking. Walnut shells are everywhere.

THE LLAMA BED
INDOORS

Please do not wake the llamas. They are sleeping.

THE PIG PEN
INDOORS

You'd think this would be dirty, but it's the cleanest part of the rescue.

WEAPONS

A HEAD OF CABBAGE
MEDIUM-WEIGHT

It's frozen solid and rock hard. Afterward, you can eat the evidence.

A CARROT
LIGHT-WEIGHT

The most dangerous vegetable: perfect for stabbing.

A BROCCOLI
LIGHT-WEIGHT

This is green and good for you, like money. It's also the perfect size for choking.

CLUES & EVIDENCE

- One of the more intelligent pigs had written Logico a message. Unfortunately, it kept scrambling its letters: A NIMIEG DHA ETH LOCOCIBR.

- A frozen vegetable was found next to a dozing animal.

STATEMENTS
(Remember: The murderer is lying. The others are telling the truth.)

Babyface Blue: We, I mean, I know this: Mx. Tangerine was in the pig pen.

Cryptozoologist Cloud: First, I thought I saw a Bigfoot. Then, I realized it was only Mx. Tangerine with a head of cabbage.

Mx. Tangerine: Cryptozoologist Cloud did not bring a carrot.

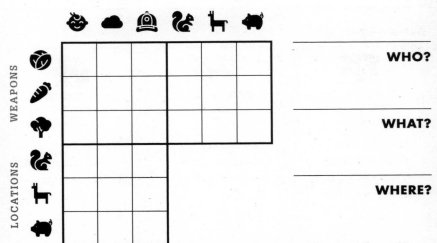

WHO?

WHAT?

WHERE?

42. CRYPT OR CURRENCY? 🔍🔍

Inspector Irratino took Logico to the Bahamas, where he was excited to enjoy a relaxing beach vacation. But Irratino said first he needed to check on his investments in a cryptocurrency company. Things weren't looking good when they discovered the CEO was *D-E-D*.

SUSPECTS

MATHEMATICIAN MARBLE

She has discovered you can use mathematics to discover the secrets of the universe—or to make a ton of money!

5'7" • LEFT-HANDED • BLUE EYES • BLOND HAIR • CANCER

EXECUTIVE PRODUCER STEEL

The richest, smartest, and meanest producer in Hollywood. She's never seen a check she couldn't cash.

5'6" • RIGHT-HANDED • GRAY EYES • WHITE HAIR • ARIES

SIR RULEAN

A sophisticated gentleman who just happens to have been knighted, if you believe the Official Knighting Documents he is always waving around.

5'8" • RIGHT-HANDED • BLUE EYES • RED HAIR • LEO

LOCATIONS

THE PENTHOUSE
INDOORS

Each TV uses a fifth of the energy of the server room, but there are six TVs.

THE SERVER ROOM
INDOORS

This room consumes enough energy to solve world hunger.

THE COMPUTER ROOM
INDOORS

Each computer costs enough to feed a small country; they're used to play solitaire.

WEAPONS

A HOODIE
MEDIUM-WEIGHT

Wrap up this leisure-wear and use it to strangle someone.

A BUNCH OF MAGIC MUSHROOMS
LIGHT-WEIGHT

What's magic about these fungi is that they make people disappear.

AN ATTACK CRAB
MEDIUM-WEIGHT

You might not be afraid of this until you hear its claws are dipped in poison!

CLUES & EVIDENCE

- Sir Rulean was childhood friends with the person who brought a bunch of magic mushrooms.

- The suspect in the computer room had a significant figure of 7. (See Exhibit B.)

STATEMENTS
(Remember: The murderer is lying. The others are telling the truth.)

Mathematician Marble: Well, sir, I brought a hoodie.
Executive Producer Steel: Mathematician Marble was in the server room.
Sir Rulean: A hoodie was not in the penthouse.

SUSPECTS   LOCATIONS

WEAPONS

LOCATIONS

WHO?

WHAT?

WHERE?

43. MURDER ON THE BOARD 🔍🔍

Finally, Logico convinced Irratino to come with him to a chess tournament. He tried to make it interesting to Irratino by explaining the esoteric significance of the pieces and moves, but Irratino wasn't truly invested until one of the referees was murdered.

SUSPECTS

GENERAL COFFEE

An espresso connoisseur, he always drinks his morning brew before sending his men across the battlefield to die. Is it for honor? Glory? Riches? Or is it for the love of the bean?

6'0" • RIGHT-HANDED • BROWN EYES • BALD • SAGITTARIUS

BOSS CHARCOAL

A mob boss from the good ol' days when being a mob boss from the good ol' days meant something.

5'11" • RIGHT-HANDED • BROWN EYES • BLACK HAIR • TAURUS

GRANDMASTER ROSE

A chess grandmaster who is always plotting his next move. Like how to bump off his opponent! (2. f4, attacking the pawn.)

5'7" • LEFT-HANDED • BROWN EYES • BROWN HAIR • SCORPIO

LOCATIONS

THE TOP BOARD
INDOORS

The world's two greatest players play an eighteen-hour game that ends in a draw. Riveting!

THE COFFEE SHOP ACROSS THE STREET
OUTDOORS

Where the real chess is played. (And the real coffee is drunk, too.)

THE ANALYSIS ROOM
INDOORS

The 4th Riddle:
One more than the number of chess pieces you must draw to guarantee two of one color.

WEAPONS

AN EXPLODING BISHOP
LIGHT-WEIGHT

There are 16 white and 16 black pieces, but only one explodes!

A CHESS BOOK
MEDIUM-WEIGHT

Who would buy a book that's filled with puzzles and inscrutable diagrams?

AN ANTIQUE CHESS CLOCK
HEAVY-WEIGHT

Tick-tock, tick-tock. Technically, time is killing us all slowly.

CLUES & EVIDENCE

- An exploding chess piece was found outdoors.
- Boss Charcoal had once put a hit out on the person who brought a chess book.

STATEMENTS
(Remember: The murderer is lying. The others are telling the truth.)

General Coffee: Boss Charcoal brought an exploding bishop.
Boss Charcoal: General Coffee was not in the analysis room.
Grandmaster Rose: General Coffee was playing on the top board.

	SUSPECTS			LOCATIONS		
WEAPONS						
♟						
📖						
🕐						
LOCATIONS						
▦						
☕						
🚪						

WHO? _____

WHAT? _____

WHERE? _____

44. AMBASSADOR'S MANSION MYSTERY 🔍🔍

The Convocation of Countries still did not recognize Free Drakonia, so their only acknowledged ambassador was the representative from the deposed Holy Drakonian government. Except he probably wouldn't be recognized anymore, on account of being dead. Logico investigated his mansion to discover who had killed him.

SUSPECTS

PATRIARCH PORPOISE

The Holy Drakonian patriarch, the one true leader of all St. Lupinian Orthodox believers, and he won't let you forget it.

5'4" • RIGHT-HANDED • BLACK EYES • BLACK HAIR • CANCER

COSMONAUT BLUSKI

An ex-Soviet spaceman whose blood flows red. Sure, that's normal, but for him it's patriotic.

6'2" • LEFT-HANDED • BROWN EYES • BLACK HAIR • ARIES

PRESIDENT WHITE

The duly elected president of the Royal Resistance, a party of aristocrats who want to retake power. She dreams of yesterday.

5'10" • RIGHT-HANDED • GRAY EYES • WHITE HAIR • LEO

LOCATIONS

THE FRONT ENTRANCE
OUTDOORS

Where the dignitaries are greeted.

THE BACK ENTRANCE
OUTDOORS

Where the bribes are delivered.

THE SIDE ENTRANCE
OUTDOORS

Where the ambassador's bros enter when they drop by.

WEAPONS

AN ANTIQUE FLINTLOCK
MEDIUM-WEIGHT

The gun that fired the silver bullet that started the Drakonian Civil War.

AN '80S CELL PHONE
HEAVY-WEIGHT

Heavier than some '80s cars. At this point, it's ancient technology.

A CHESS BOARD
HEAVY-WEIGHT

Made of marble and heavier than God.

CLUES & EVIDENCE

- A scrambled fax from the Detective Club was received with a clue: EHT SCEPTUS HWIT EHT S08 LCLE OEHPN DAH ITHWE IAHR.

- A marble weapon was not found by the back entrance.

STATEMENTS
(Remember: The murderer is lying. The others are telling the truth.)

Patriarch Porpoise: Cosmonaut Bluski was not in the front entrance.
Cosmonaut Bluski: An antique flintlock was in the front entrance.
President White: Patriarch Porpoise brought an antique flintlock.

	SUSPECTS			LOCATIONS		

WHO?

_____

WHAT?

_____

WHERE?

45. YOUR DAYS ARE NUMBERED! 🔍🔍

An old math professor of Deductive Logico's called him up and told him to hurry to his mansion. When they got there, all Logico could think was, how could a mathematician afford a mansion this big? And also, who had murdered him?

SUSPECTS

NUMEROLOGIST NIGHT

Not only do they know the value of x, they know the meaning of x.

5'9" • LEFT-HANDED • BLUE EYES • BROWN HAIR • PISCES

VICE PRESIDENT MAUVE

A vice president of TekCo Futures. She has been tasked with developing the latest TekCo product: TekTopia. It's like a metaverse in real life.

5'8" • RIGHT-HANDED • BROWN EYES • BLACK HAIR • TAURUS

DAME OBSIDIAN

A mystery writer whose books have sold more copies than the Bible and Shakespeare combined.

5'4" • LEFT-HANDED • GREEN EYES • BLACK HAIR • LEO

LOCATIONS

THE BACK PORCH
OUTDOORS

The professor's porch looks out over the lake. How could he afford this?

THE STUDY
INDOORS

A note on the desk contains the 5th Riddle: *If it takes 2 students 4 days to solve 8 problems, how many can 3 solve in 2 days?*

THE LIBRARY
INDOORS

All of the books are just filled with long lists of numbers.

WEAPONS

A TITANIUM SPHERE
HEAVY-WEIGHT

It is exactly three inches in diameter. It's beautiful.

A LETTER OPENER
LIGHT-WEIGHT

An envelope next to it says, *Thanks for your work. Love, the CIA.* That explains the mansion!

A PRIME STEAK
MEDIUM-WEIGHT

The finest cut of (genetically modified soy) steak. Also, it's been poisoned.

CLUES & EVIDENCE

- Someone with a significant figure associated with leadership had the letter opener. (See Exhibit B.)

- The tallest suspect had a crush on the person who brought a three-inch weapon.

STATEMENTS
(Remember: The murderer is lying. The others are telling the truth.)

Numerologist Night: Based on the numbers, a prime steak was in the study.
Vice President Mauve: I was not in the study.
Dame Obsidian: A prime steak was not in the library.

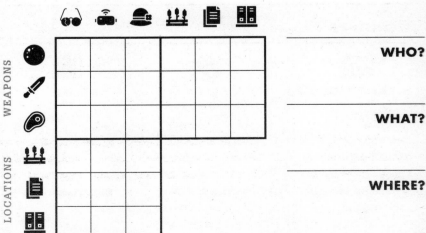

WHO?

WHAT?

WHERE?

46. THE CLOCKTOWER KILLING 🔍🔍

The mathematician's map led all around the world, and Logico followed it until he arrived at a massive ruined city. In the middle of it was a clocktower, and in the middle of that was a dead body and three suspicious interlopers . . .

SUSPECTS

THE DUCHESS OF VERMILLION

A tall, old woman with tall, old secrets. If she is the murderer, then it certainly wouldn't be the first time.

5'9" • LEFT-HANDED • GRAY EYES • WHITE HAIR • PISCES

BARON MAROON

An incredibly haughty man who famously holds a grudge. Nobody wants to offend the baron. At least, nobody who's still alive . . .

6'2" • RIGHT-HANDED • HAZEL EYES • RED HAIR • SCORPIO

MX. TANGERINE

Proving that non-binary people can be murderers, too, Mx. Tangerine is an artist, poet, and potential suspect.

5'5" • LEFT-HANDED • HAZEL EYES • BLOND HAIR • PISCES

LOCATIONS

THE GROUNDS
OUTDOORS

In a bush Logico found the 6th Riddle: *How many degrees will the hour hand move in 18 minutes?*

THE CLOCKWORKS
INDOORS

A room filled with rusted cogs and gears that now tell time in centuries.

THE STAIRWELL
INDOORS

Rotting wooden steps all the way up: every third, fifth, and seventh one is broken.

WEAPONS

AN ATTACK GOOSE	**A GIANT METAL ZERO**	**A RUSTED HOUR HAND**
MEDIUM-WEIGHT	HEAVY-WEIGHT	HEAVY-WEIGHT
The most fearsome weapon in the book. Beware the attack goose!	Now there are two one o'clocks on the clock face.	This thing is big enough to use as a sword and rusty enough to give your victim tetanus.

CLUES & EVIDENCE

- Someone with hazel eyes, as well as a significant figure associated with creativity and magick, brought a giant metal zero. (See Exhibit B.)

- A rusted hour hand was not in the stairwell.

STATEMENTS
(Remember: The murderer is lying. The others are telling the truth.)

The Duchess of Vermillion: If you ask me, I brought an attack goose.
Baron Maroon: I was not on the grounds.
Mx. Tangerine: An attack goose was on the grounds.

SUSPECTS   LOCATIONS

WEAPONS

LOCATIONS

WHO?

WHAT?

WHERE?

47. THE TOMB OF PYTHAGORAS AND ANOTHER GUY

The map led to the legendary lost tomb of Pythagoras, but when Logico and Irratino arrived, they found it was also the tomb of another person who had just been murdered. For a lost tomb, there certainly were a lot of people hanging around.

SUSPECTS

COSMONAUT BLUSKI

An ex-Soviet spaceman whose blood flows red. Sure, that's normal, but for him it's patriotic.

6'2" • LEFT-HANDED • BROWN EYES • BLACK HAIR • ARIES

SOCIOLOGIST UMBER

As a representative from the hard sciences, Sociologist Umber is always asking people to question their priors and if they've read Weber.

5'4" • LEFT-HANDED • BLUE EYES • BLOND HAIR • LEO

SISTER LAPIS

A nun who travels the world, doing God's work on His dime. Her habit is cashmere, and her habit is spending.

5'2" • RIGHT-HANDED • BROWN EYES • BROWN HAIR • CANCER

LOCATIONS

THE NUMERO-LOGICAL HALL
INDOORS

Legend has it that these walls contain numbers people have only dreamed about.

THE CRYPT ITSELF
INDOORS

The body of Pythagoras is supposedly inside this giant stone box.

THE CRUMBLING ENTRANCE
OUTDOORS

The stone columns have collapsed around the entrance.

WEAPONS

A MATHEMATICS TEXTBOOK
HEAVY-WEIGHT

The equations are so hard they're head-splitting (and so is the textbook).

ANCIENT PAPYRUS
LIGHT-WEIGHT

This ancient papyrus contains a horrifying secret that kills whoever reads it.

THE ARM OF A STATUE
HEAVY-WEIGHT

A great stone arm. Like, really great. Amazing, even.

CLUES & EVIDENCE

- A mathematics textbook was not found in the crumbling entrance.

- Someone shorter than six feet who has brown eyes was in the crypt itself.

STATEMENTS
(Remember: The murderer is lying. The others are telling the truth.)

Cosmonaut Bluski: I did not bring ancient papyrus.
Sociologist Umber: I did not bring the arm of a statue.
Sister Lapis: In His name, Sociologist Umber brought ancient papyrus.

SUSPECTS   LOCATIONS

WEAPONS

LOCATIONS

WHO?

WHAT?

WHERE?

48. THE SECRET CHAMBER SECRET 🔍🔍

Pythagoras's grave opened mechanically, revealing a dark stone tunnel. Logico and Irratino crept down the tunnel until it opened up into a large, bizarre chamber. It seemed like some kind of puzzle. But taking away from the elegance of the puzzle was a recently deceased corpse, as well as the three suspects still inside.

SUSPECTS

ARISTOCRAT SABLE

She has been searching the whole world for herself, and it brought her here.

5'5" • LEFT-HANDED • HAZEL EYES • BLACK HAIR • LIBRA

DR. SEASHELL, DDS

He's an amateur physicist with a new theory of the universe, and also, a working dentist.

5'7" • RIGHT-HANDED • GREEN EYES • GRAY HAIR • PISCES

ARCHEOLOGIST ECRU

A great archeologist/grave robber who is famed worldwide for her archeology/grave robbing.

5'8" • LEFT-HANDED • HAZEL EYES • GRAY HAIR • SAGITTARIUS

LOCATIONS

123
A WALL OF NUMBERS
INDOORS

It contains the 7th Riddle: MATTER, MAGICK, DUALITY, *and a blank line.*

A STONE STATUE
INDOORS

It seems to be a statue of Pythagoras, but it's missing an arm.

A GIANT STONE DIAL
INDOORS

Enter the 7 Answers of Pythagoras and pull a lever. If you're right, a prize! If you're wrong . . .

WEAPONS

A MATHEMATICS TEXTBOOK
HEAVY-WEIGHT

The equations are so hard they're head-splitting (and so is the textbook).

A BLOCK OF STONE
HEAVY-WEIGHT

A crumbled piece of the chamber, now turned into a weapon.

A CHALICE
MEDIUM-WEIGHT

You can use it to celebrate a religious ritual, like the murder of a heretic.

CLUES & EVIDENCE

- Archeologist Ecru hated the person with a set of hard equations.
- Logico saw a scrambled message scrawled on the stone wall: A IC-CHALE AWS YB A NETSO TSTEAU.

STATEMENTS
(Remember: The murderer is lying. The others are telling the truth.)

Aristocrat Sable: Tut-tut! I was by a wall of numbers.
Dr. Seashell, DDS: According to my metaphysic, I brought a chalice.
Archeologist Ecru: Hmm . . . a block of stone was by a giant stone dial.

WHO?

WHAT?

WHERE?

49. THE DIPLOMATIC CONVOY DECEPTION

Because of the dangerous nature of their mission, Logico rode to the Convocation in a private security convoy. Someone tried to murder him, but fortunately for Logico, they killed his driver instead. (It was, however, unfortunate for the driver.)

SUSPECTS

RADICAL CRIMSON

Just as smart as her sister, Dr. Crimson, but she wants to perform surgery on society.

5'7" • LEFT-HANDED • GREEN EYES • RED HAIR • LIBRA

OFFICER COPPER

The best part of being a policewoman criminal is that you can cut out the middleman and fail to investigate your own crimes.

5'2" • LEFT-HANDED • BROWN EYES • BROWN HAIR • LEO

TINY TAUPE

He's actually really huge, which is why people call him Tiny.

6'3" • LEFT-HANDED • BLUE EYES • BLOND HAIR • TAURUS

LOCATIONS

THE ROAD
OUTDOORS

The road that the convoy is traveling on toward the Convocation of Countries.

THE DECOY CAR
INDOORS

This car is meant to seem like Logico's car, so that it might get blown up instead of him.

THE TRANSPORT CAR
INDOORS

This is the car that Deductive Logico is actually riding in.

WEAPONS

A KNIFE PEN LIGHT-WEIGHT	**A RED HERRING** MEDIUM-WEIGHT	**A BULLET-PROOF VEST** MEDIUM-WEIGHT
It's a pen. It's a knife. It's a knife pen. Carried by all secret agent diplomats.	If you hold it by the tail, you can get some real momentum behind it.	It would be very ironic to be beaten to death by one of these.

CLUES & EVIDENCE

- Logico received an important scrambled note on a piece of paper: A OLE SWA NI HET TRARNPSOT RCA.

- A bulletproof vest was not found in the decoy car.

STATEMENTS
(Remember: The murderer is lying. The others are telling the truth.)

Radical Crimson: As a real revolutionary, I was in the road.
Officer Copper: Some advice from a cop: a knife pen was on the road.
Tiny Taupe: As a big dude, I brought a red herring.

SUSPECTS   LOCATIONS

WEAPONS

LOCATIONS

WHO?

WHAT?

WHERE?

50. KILLER AT THE CONVOCATION

In the towering edifice where representatives from every country meet to discuss issues of global significance, Logico was booked to make a speech. However, just before he was about to go on, the head of the Convocation was murdered.

SUSPECTS

PRÉSIDENT AMARANTH

The literal French *président*, Amaranth loves spending time with his constituents, especially a certain 1 percent of them.

5'10" • RIGHT-HANDED • GRAY EYES • RED HAIR • GEMINI

PRESIDENT WHITE

The duly elected president of the Royal Resistance, a party of aristocrats who want to retake power. She dreams of yesterday.

5'10" • RIGHT-HANDED • GRAY EYES • WHITE HAIR • LEO

MAJOR RED

The revolutionary leader who freed Drakonia from the grasp of the Tsar and then immediately grasped it himself.

6'2" • LEFT-HANDED • BROWN EYES • BROWN HAIR • ARIES

LOCATIONS

THE GALLERIES
INDOORS

Where the non-ambassadors watch, and occasionally spit on their representatives.

THE FLOOR
INDOORS

Where the ambassadors sit, debate, and occasionally challenge each other to duels.

THE ROSTRUM
INDOORS

Where the head of the Convocation (and others) give their speeches.

WEAPONS

A GAVEL
MEDIUM-WEIGHT

Let's be frank: there's a reason they give the judge a big hammer. (Intimidation.)

AN EXCLUSIVE PIN
LIGHT-WEIGHT

If this is pinned to someone's lapel, they're a member of a secret society.

A REAM OF PAPER
MEDIUM-WEIGHT

You could use these blank pages to give someone a thousand paper cuts or one paper bash.

CLUES & EVIDENCE

- Logico received a scrambled message from one of the delegates: A ELGAV WAS TNO DFUON NO TEH FOORL.

- Whoever was in the galleries had a significant figure associated with revolution. (See Exhibit B.)

STATEMENTS
(Remember: The murderer is lying. The others are telling the truth.)

Président Amaranth: As ze *président*, I brought an exclusive pin.

President White: By decree of the Old Drakonians, a ream of paper was in the rostrum.

Major Red: By the revolution, an exclusive pin was in the galleries.

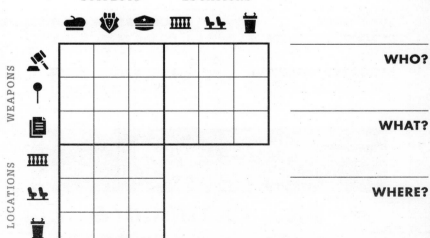

WHO?

WHAT?

WHERE?

EXHIBIT C

BISHOP AZURE
CCTGTTTGTAGCATTAA

COSMONAUT BLUSKI
ATAAAGCTGCGCATGAT

MANSERVANT BROWNSTONE
ACATCCGGCACAGTTGA

SECRETARY CELADON
TTTCGAACATGACGAGC

COMRADE CHAMPAGNE
CATTTGGGCATGTTCCT

GENERAL COFFEE
GTCTCCAGGTCTAGATT

OFFICER COPPER
TCAAAGTGGTTTTTCA

DR. CRIMSON
TACTTCAGATGAGGGTC

VISCOUNT EMINENCE
CGCTCTGAGAAAGCGCC

EARL GREY
GCTGCCGCTGACCTATT

SERGEANT GUNMETAL
TACTGAAGGCCATGAGT

SISTER LAPIS
CCCGTCGAGCCGCTGGC

BARON MAROON
ACATAAAATTCGTTGCA

UNCLE MIDNIGHT
TGGACCGATTGAGTATA

PATRIARCH PORPOISE
GGAAGAGATAATGTGCC

COACH RASPBERRY
TTATGTTTACAAGTACC

HIGH ALCHEMIST RAVEN
TCGCTGCTATGGTAAAG

MAJOR RED
GGCGCTTTCTCAGAGCG

SIR RULEAN
CAGCTGCTCACTTCTTT

ARISTOCRAT SABLE
TTATCTAGGGGTATTGG

DUCHESS OF VERMILLION
CGAACTAAACAGTGCGC

PRESIDENT WHITE
GCTGGCGTACGACCGAG

MYSTERIOUS BLOOD SAMPLE
GCGAGACTCTTTCGCGG

DR. CRIMSON'S
DNA REGISTRY

HARD BOILED

Inspector Irratino was alone!

Logico had vanished at the Convocation of Countries before he could reveal what he had figured out in the Tomb of Pythagoras, and now, Irratino had no one to confide in.

There was only one thing he needed to do: find Deductive Logico. He had to save him from whatever fate had befallen him, and he had to do it using his greatest weakness: logic.

And so, he studied Deductive Logico's textbooks from Deduction College, and he taught himself the latest in forensic science, including the art of DNA matching. He collected samples of DNA, through means both honest and less so, and he had Dr. Crimson test them all in her lab, which produced a table of DNA nucleotide sequence samples (Exhibit C, seen to the left).

By using this scientific knowledge, along with his gut instincts, Inspector Irratino believed he could discover what had happened to Deductive Logico and solve any other mysteries that appeared along the way, no matter how difficult.

In addition to solving the who, what, and where of these hard-boiled murders, each of these mysteries features an extra aspect: everything from what car the suspects drove, to their blood type, to their favorite Dame Obsidian novel.

The Detective Club Challenge for this section is deceptively simple: Discover what happened to Deductive Logico before it's too late!

51. AN EXPERIMENT IN MURDER! 🔍🔍🔍

Inspector Irratino first went to the people who would know where Logico was if nobody else did: his friends at the Psychic Research Laboratory. He interrupted a test of their psychic abilities, but that experiment had already ended when the chief experimenter was murdered.

SUSPECTS

THE CRYSTAL GODDESS

Her followers regard her as a divine being, which is why they give her money.

5'9" • LEFT-HANDED • BLUE EYES • WHITE HAIR • LEO

DR. SEASHELL, DDS

He's an amateur physicist with a new theory of the universe, and also, a working dentist.

5'7" • RIGHT-HANDED • GREEN EYES • GRAY HAIR • PISCES

HERBALIST ONYX

In her greenhouse, she's grown every kind of plant required in the culinary, magick, and poisoning arts.

5'0" • RIGHT-HANDED • BROWN EYES • BLACK HAIR • VIRGO

SUPREME MASTER COBALT

He has a long, white beard, and he wears long, white robes.

5'9" • RIGHT-HANDED • BLUE EYES • SILVER HAIR • AQUARIUS

LOCATIONS

THE ROOF
OUTDOORS

Here they have done successful experiments with astral projection and failed ones with psychic levitation.

THE GROUNDS
OUTDOORS

Filled with holes as a result of dowsing experiments.

THE ISOLATION CHAMBER
INDOORS

A water tank in a dark room. You can regress in time or just get really bored.

THE ACTUAL LABORATORY
INDOORS

Here they've run all manner of tests except those that detect cheating.

WEAPONS

A CHANNELED TEXT
HEAVY-WEIGHT • MADE OF PAPER

This book is longer than Gainsboro's masterpiece and was supposedly written by ghosts.

A DOWSING ROD
MEDIUM-WEIGHT • MADE OF WOOD

You can find water, oil, and suckers with these.

A PSEUDO-SCIENTIFIC APPARATUS
HEAVY-WEIGHT • MADE OF METAL

It measures quantonic currents to evaluate your inner blaxons.

A HYPNOTIC POCKET WATCH
LIGHT-WEIGHT • MADE OF METAL

If you look deeply into this watch, you can tell the time.

PSYCHIC EXPERIMENTS

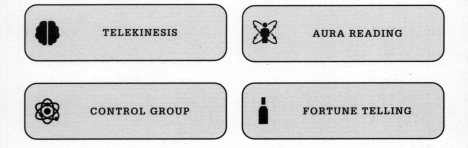

🧠	TELEKINESIS	🦋	AURA READING
⚛	CONTROL GROUP	🍾	FORTUNE TELLING

CLUES & EVIDENCE

- Supreme Master Cobalt was seen tinkering in the actual laboratory.

- A white hair was found on a device that measures quantonic currents.

- Herbalist Onyx was carrying a ghost-written book.

- The person with a dowsing rod was not in the control group.

- Irratino used a technique called spirit writing to produce a scrambled message: EHT EROPSN OWH DOTL ESORTUFN SAW IN HET IOT-NLOSIA HBAREMC.

- The person with the blaxon-evaluator was being tested for telekinesis.

- The suspect with a hypnotic pocket watch had blue eyes.

- The person with a theory of the universe was standing in a hole.

- **The chief experimenter's body was found on the roof.**

SUSPECTS EXPERIMENTS LOCATIONS

WEAPONS

LOCATIONS

EXPERIMENTS

WHO?

WHAT?

WHERE?

AND?

52. DRIVEN TO KILL 🔍🔍🔍

Inspector Irratino decided he needed to investigate this mystery like Logico would: not by talking to psychics but by running down leads. So he traveled to Logico's hometown to see if they knew anything about his disappearance. But when he arrived, he had to solve the murder of the mayor.

SUSPECTS

SUPERFAN SMOKY

He knows the shooting locations of every Midnight mystery, but not how to make friends.

5'10" • LEFT-HANDED • BLACK EYES • BROWN HAIR • VIRGO

SISTER LAPIS

A nun who travels the world, doing God's work on His dime. Her habit is cashmere, and her habit is spending.

5'2" • RIGHT-HANDED • BROWN EYES • BROWN HAIR • CANCER

BOSS CHARCOAL

A mob boss from the good ol' days when being a mob boss from the good ol' days meant something.

5'11" • RIGHT-HANDED • BROWN EYES • BLACK HAIR • TAURUS

MX. TANGERINE

Proving that non-binary people can be murderers, too, Mx. Tangerine is an artist, poet, and potential suspect.

5'5" • LEFT-HANDED • HAZEL EYES • BLOND HAIR • PISCES

LOCATIONS

A CHAIN RESTAURANT
INDOORS

This opened up after the family diner couldn't afford their lease. They have a fried onion.

A USED CAR LOT
INDOORS

The salesman tells you the cars will not explode, and also that they're bought as is.

THE RUN-DOWN MALL
INDOORS

The fountain is dry and only two stores are open: a payday loan company and one that buys gold.

A SECONDHAND SHOP
INDOORS

Honestly, most of the stuff in here looks thirdhand, even the moths.

WEAPONS

AN AXE
MEDIUM-WEIGHT • MADE OF WOOD & METAL

This axe could chop a tree down. Or a person down!

AN ORDINARY BRICK
MEDIUM-WEIGHT • MADE OF BRICK

Just a regular, ordinary brick. With a chip in it.

AN ANTIQUE CLOCK
HEAVY-WEIGHT • MADE OF WOOD & METAL

Tick-tock, tick-tock. Technically, time is killing us all slowly.

A BOTTLE OF WINE
MEDIUM-WEIGHT • MADE OF GLASS & ALCOHOL

Watch out for stains, because the red doesn't come out.

CARS THEY DROVE

 GAS-GUZZLING SUV

 MOTORCYCLE + SIDECAR

 TWELVE-PASSENGER VAN

 MIDLIFE-CRISIS CONVERTIBLE

CLUES & EVIDENCE

- A blond hair was found in a fried onion: yuck!

- Boss Charcoal loved cruising around in his gas guzzler.

- The HD cameras at the run-down mall caught someone with brown eyes.

- In the glass of a crystal ball, Irratino could make out a scrambled clue: HTE RENSPO HTWI NA AXE EORVD A OIVLEENBRTC.

- Superfan Smoky had a weapon made of glass.

- An antique clock was covered in moths.

- The person with an ordinary brick drove a vehicle with a sidecar.

- Ever since "the Incident," the chain restaurant did not allow people to bring bricks inside.

- **The mayor's body was found in the trunk of a car for sale as is.**

WHO?

WHAT?

WHERE?

AND?

53. THE BLOODY, BLOODY HOSPITAL 🔍🔍🔍

Irratino visited Dr. Crimson's private hospital to see if she could help him identify the mysterious blood stain from Logico's disappearance. She seemed like she really wanted to help, but she was a little distracted by the murder of the hospital director.

SUSPECTS

DR. CRIMSON

She believes that everyone—no matter their race or creed—deserves the right to medical care, as long as they can afford it.

5'9" • LEFT-HANDED • GREEN EYES • RED HAIR • AQUARIUS

COACH RASPBERRY

One of the best coaches this side of the Mississippi, regardless of which side you happen to be on. Some people say he has a gambling problem, but he just says he loves danger.

6'0" • LEFT-HANDED • BLUE EYES • BLOND HAIR • ARIES

BARON MAROON

An incredibly haughty man who famously holds a grudge. Nobody wants to offend the baron. At least, nobody who's still alive . . .

6'2" • RIGHT-HANDED • HAZEL EYES • RED HAIR • SCORPIO

UNCLE MIDNIGHT

When his dad died, he bought a desert mansion with a pool and retired. He was seventeen.

5'8" • LEFT-HANDED • BLUE EYES • BROWN HAIR • SAGITTARIUS

LOCATIONS

THE PARKING LOT
OUTDOORS

An enormous parking lot with uniformed valets parking luxury sedans.

THE BREAK ROOM
INDOORS

The vending machines and coffee pots for the staff are noticeably less nice than the ones for the patients.

THE GIFT SHOP
INDOORS

This hospital is so nice you can buy jewelry at the gift shop. But don't worry, there's still a discount rack as well.

THE ROOF
OUTDOORS

Huge AC units and other industrial equipment cover the roof, providing a number of excellent hiding spots.

WEAPONS

A FIRE EXTINGUISHER
HEAVY-WEIGHT • MADE OF METAL

You can kill someone by hitting them over the head with this, or by starting a fire and doing nothing with it.

A CLIPBOARD
MEDIUM-WEIGHT • MADE OF PAPER & WOOD

A checklist of things to do today. Does one say "murder the director"?

A HEAVY MICROSCOPE
HEAVY-WEIGHT • MADE OF METAL & PLASTIC

The slides are so tiny, but the microscope's so heavy!

A SURGICAL SCALPEL
LIGHT-WEIGHT • MADE OF METAL

Somehow it being smaller makes it more dangerous.

BLOOD TYPES

A TYPE A	**AB** TYPE AB
B TYPE B	**O** TYPE O

CLUES & EVIDENCE

- According to the hospital records, there was a sample of type O blood with the following DNA signature: ACATAAAATTCGTTGCA. (See Exhibit C.)

- The suspect who was carrying a clipboard had green eyes.

- The person who had type A blood was looking to buy jewelry.

- Uncle Midnight had type AB blood.

- The heavy microscope could only be held by a right-handed person.

- Irratino had a horrifying (but visionary) dream where the ghost of the hospital director kept repeating the following scrambled words: A SLECHCTKI SWA NFUOD SBEDEI A DOTSCIUN CARK.

- Whoever was next to a uniformed valet could famously hold a grudge.

- Irratino identified a fire hazard: no fire extinguisher was on the roof.

- Coach Raspberry wasn't allowed to go outside: doctor's orders!

- **The hospital director had been stabbed to death with a surgical scalpel.**

SUSPECTS · BLOOD TYPES · LOCATIONS

WEAPONS · LOCATIONS · BLOOD TYPES

WHO?

WHAT?

WHERE?

AND?

54. INVESTIGATE THE INSTITUTE! 🔍🔍🔍

Inspector Irratino returned to the Investigation Institute and put the entire staff on Logico's disappearance. Well, not the entire staff: one of them had been murdered.

SUSPECTS

HIGH ALCHE-MIST RAVEN

There's an old joke that all alchemists are high alchemists. Raven hates it.

5'8" • RIGHT-HANDED • BROWN EYES • BROWN HAIR • PISCES

SUPREME MASTER COBALT

He has a long white beard, and he wears long white robes.

5'9" • RIGHT-HANDED • BLUE EYES • SILVER HAIR • AQUARIUS

SIR RULEAN

A sophisticated gentleman who just happens to have been knighted, if you believe the Official Knighting Documents he is always waving around.

5'8" • RIGHT-HANDED • BLUE EYES • RED HAIR • LEO

THE AMAZING AUREOLIN

The Amazing Aureolin is a touring magician who has perfected the whole sawing-the-husband-in-two routine. Then, she made the body disappear.

5'6" • LEFT-HANDED • GREEN EYES • BLOND HAIR • ARIES

LOCATIONS

THE BIG GATE
OUTDOORS

This is the biggest gate you've ever heard of (besides Watergate).

THE GRAND CHATEAU
INDOORS

A sprawling, ornate mansion that has a tree growing in the middle of it.

THE OBSERVATORY
INDOORS

For studying the stars, or having a romantic evening.

THE MINIATURE GOLF COURSE
OUTDOORS

Eighteen holes. Windmills, caves, and loop-de-loops. The works!

WEAPONS

A DAME OBSIDIAN NOVEL
LIGHT-WEIGHT • MADE OF PAPER

Hey, this is just the plot of the first *Murdle* book—she plagiarized Logico's casebook!

A BOTTLE OF WINE
MEDIUM-WEIGHT • MADE OF GLASS & ALCOHOL

Watch out for stains, because the red doesn't come out.

A POISONED MUFFIN
LIGHT-WEIGHT • MADE OF FLOUR, SUGAR, & POISON

Not only are the raisins poisoned, but it's rock hard. So you could use it two ways.

A RITUAL DAGGER
MEDIUM-WEIGHT • MADE OF BONE

It's made out of bone. Hopefully not human!

OCCULT INTERESTS

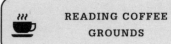 READING COFFEE GROUNDS

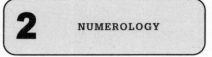 NUMEROLOGY

 ASTROLOGY

THE MAROT

CLUES & EVIDENCE

- The ritual dagger was right-handed only.

- A red stain was discovered on the roots of an indoor tree.

- The person who loved reading coffee grounds was not at a good place for a romantic evening.

- Supreme Master Cobalt was found indoors: he said the sun could kill today.

- Sir Rulean loved astrology; don't all Leos?

- High Alchemist Raven was seen under an enormous gate.

- Whoever studied numerology was an Aries.

- The Institute issued a statement to all its members through a psychic medium, but the letters were scrambled in transit: A ZPAELAIIGRD ONELV SWA ODFNU OORODTSU.

- The tallest suspect never set foot in a sprawling, ornate mansion.

- Forensics determined a weapon made of bone was present at the miniature golf course.

- **A rock-hard raisin was found beside the victim.**

SUSPECTS   INTERESTS   LOCATIONS

WEAPONS

LOCATIONS

INTERESTS

_____ WHO?

_____ WHAT?

_____ WHERE?

_____ AND?

55. THE BODY BURIED BENEATH THE BEANS 🔍🔍🔍

Inspector Irratino went to a coffee shop that Logico had once called "magical," hoping for a magical lead. But all he found was another murder: one of the regulars had tipped their last barista.

SUSPECTS

BOOKIE-WINNER GAINSBORO

Gainsboro has written the Great American Novel, which he will tell you within two minutes of meeting him. It's six thousand pages long, and it's about dirt.

6'0" • LEFT-HANDED • HAZEL EYES • BROWN HAIR • GEMINI

MAYOR HONEY

He knows where the bodies are buried, and he makes sure they always vote for him.

6'0" • LEFT-HANDED • HAZEL EYES • BROWN HAIR • SCORPIO

DAME OBSIDIAN

A mystery writer whose books have sold more copies than the Bible and Shakespeare combined.

5'4" • LEFT-HANDED • GREEN EYES • BLACK HAIR • LEO

GENERAL COFFEE

An espresso connoisseur, he always drinks his morning brew before sending his men across the battlefield to die. Is it for honor? Glory? Riches? Or is it for the love of the bean?

6'0" • RIGHT-HANDED • BROWN EYES • BALD • SAGITTARIUS

LOCATIONS

THE COURTYARD
OUTDOORS

Sun-dappled tables and chairs sit beneath a magnificent oak. A great place for conversation . . . or murder.

THE COUNTER
INDOORS

There is a little bell that alerts the barista you are here so he can start ignoring you.

THE BEAN ROOM
INDOORS

Full of bags and bags of beans. The smell reminds Irratino of Logico's love of coffee.

THE BATHROOM
INDOORS

It's a coffee shop. So obviously, it's going to have a bathroom. This one is always out of paper towels.

WEAPONS

A BUTTER KNIFE
LIGHT-WEIGHT • MADE OF METAL

An embarrassing way to be killed, honestly.

A BOILING POT
HEAVY-WEIGHT • MADE OF METAL & WATER

Hot and heavy! For murderers, that's called a double feature.

A BRICK
HEAVY-WEIGHT • MADE OF CLAY

Just a regular, ordinary brick. Nothing special. Just a brick.

A METAL STRAW
HEAVY-WEIGHT • MADE OF METAL

Better for the planet than a plastic straw, but more deadly! Maybe it'll leave a small hole behind.

COFFEE ORDERS

 REGULAR JOE DRIP

 CHRISTMAS-FLAVORED LATTE

 QUADRUPLE ESPRESSO SHOT

 TEA WITH MILK AND HONEY

CLUES & EVIDENCE

- Dame Obsidian was working on her latest novel indoors.

- A boiling pot was sitting next to a bell.

- At this coffee shop, only Scorpios order Christmas-flavored drinks.

- Inspector Irratino drank his coffee and saw that the grounds at the bottom of it magically spelled a scrambled message: HET EOSPNR HTWI A CRIKB REODDRE ETA.

- Whoever was in the bathroom was right-handed.

- General Coffee ordered a quadruple espresso shot: he was feeling slightly sleepy.

- Mayor Honey had not been at the counter.

- The butter knife reflected the hazel eyes of its wielder.

- Analysts discovered traces of metal from a weapon on the clothing of Bookie-Winner Gainsboro.

- **The body was buried beneath bags of beans.**

SUSPECTS   COFFEE ORDERS   LOCATIONS

WEAPONS

LOCATIONS

COFFEE ORDERS

_____

WHO?

_____

WHAT?

_____

WHERE?

_____

AND?

56. THE MOVIE THEATER MURDER 🔍🔍🔍

Exhausted and disappointed, Inspector Irratino went to see a movie, hoping the film would reveal a clue esoterically. Unfortunately, before the movie even began, the projectionist was murdered.

SUSPECTS

A-LIST ABALONE

The most talented and in-demand actress of all time this month.

5'6" • RIGHT-HANDED • HAZEL EYES • RED HAIR • LIBRA

SILVERTON THE LEGEND

An acclaimed actor of the Golden Age, now in his golden years.

6'4" • RIGHT-HANDED • BLUE EYES • SILVER HAIR • LEO

AGENT APPLEGREEN

From literary assistant to Hollywood agent, Applegreen will stop at nothing to get what she wants: everything.

5'3" • LEFT-HANDED • BLUE EYES • BLOND HAIR • VIRGO

BOOKIE-WINNER GAINSBORO

Gainsboro has written the Great American Novel, which he will tell you within two minutes of meeting him. It's six thousand pages long, and it's about dirt.

6'0" • LEFT-HANDED • HAZEL EYES • BROWN HAIR • GEMINI

LOCATIONS

THE THEATER
INDOORS

For legal reasons, we can't say that it's an IMAX. But also, we can't say that it's not an IMAX.

THE LOBBY
INDOORS

Back in the day, there was a giant chandelier. But it kept falling and crushing people in mysterious ways. Now there are just framed posters.

THE BOX OFFICE
INDOORS

Tickets are expensive, but not as expensive as popcorn, which is not as expensive as beer.

THE CONCESSION STAND
INDOORS

You can buy a soda here if you can afford it: a large is ten times bigger than a small and costs a nickel more.

WEAPONS

POISONED POPCORN
MEDIUM-WEIGHT • MADE OF CORN & OIL

Freshly popped and freshly poisoned, too. Almond flavored!

A STALE CANDY BAR
LIGHT-WEIGHT • MADE OF CHOCOLATE

Hard as a crowbar, it's been here since *Lawrence of Arabia*. Look for rock-hard chocolate crumbs.

A RITUAL DAGGER
MEDIUM-WEIGHT • MADE OF BONE

It's made out of bone. Hopefully not human! It can be identified by a chip of actual bone left behind.

A BAG OF CASH
HEAVY-WEIGHT • MADE OF CLOTH & PAPER

The day's receipts. If a superhero movie was playing, this could kill.

FAVORITE FILMS

 MURDLE: THE MOVIE

 WHO FRAMED BOBERT BUNNY?

 THE MALTESE PENGUIN

 SPOONS OUT

CLUES & EVIDENCE

- Someone complained that a single red hair on the not-not-an-IMAX ruined the movie, and they demanded a refund.

- An oil stain was found on the clothing of Silverton the Legend.

- A light-weight weapon was hidden where people bought their (expensive) tickets.

- Irratino screened the movie backward and found this hidden message: DEDNAH-TFEL SAW YBBOL EHT NI SAW REVEOHW.

- Whoever loved *Who Framed Bobert Bunny?* had a heavy-weight weapon.

- Everybody who loved *Spoons Out* was a Virgo.

- The person with a ritual dagger loved *The Maltese Penguin.*

- Bookie-Winner Gainsboro loved *Who Framed Bobert Bunny?*.

- **The projectionist's body was found sprawled over the concession stand.**

SUSPECTS   FILMS   LOCATIONS

WEAPONS

LOCATIONS

FILMS

WHO?

WHAT?

WHERE?

AND?

57. THE CHECKMATE MURDER 🔍🔍🔍

Inspector Irratino's quest for the missing Logico took him to darker and bloodier places, until he found himself at an illegal underground chessboxing match. Not only was the match illegal, the murder was, too.

SUSPECTS

THE AMAZING AUREOLIN

The Amazing Aureolin is a touring magician who has perfected the whole sawing-the-husband-in-two routine. Then, she made the body disappear.

5'6" • LEFT-HANDED • GREEN EYES • BLOND HAIR • ARIES

ADMIRAL NAVY

The firstborn son of an Admiral Navy who himself was the son of an Admiral Navy.

5'9" • RIGHT-HANDED • BLUE EYES • BROWN HAIR • CANCER

BOSS CHARCOAL

A mob boss from the good ol' days when being a mob boss from the good ol' days meant something.

5'11" • RIGHT-HANDED • BROWN EYES • BLACK HAIR • TAURUS

MX. TANGERINE

Proving that non-binary people can be murderers, too, Mx. Tangerine is an artist, poet, and potential suspect.

5'5" • LEFT-HANDED • HAZEL EYES • BLOND HAIR • PISCES

LOCATIONS

THE ROOFTOP LOUNGE
OUTDOORS

Where the rich hang out and bet on the blood/brainsport.

THE RING
INDOORS

They alternate between rounds of boxing and rounds of chess in here.

THE STANDS
INDOORS

Fans are cheering, "Take the knight!" or "Knock his head off!"

RINGSIDE
INDOORS

Here they've got a table set up with commentators: one knows chess, the other knows boxing.

WEAPONS

BOXING GLOVES
MEDIUM-WEIGHT • MADE OF VINYL

Counterintuitive to use as a weapon, because they'll actually make your punches weaker.

A CHESS BOARD
HEAVY-WEIGHT • MADE OF MARBLE

Made of marble and heavier than God.

A GIANT CHESS KNIGHT
HEAVY-WEIGHT • MADE OF METAL

It was meant for one of those giant floorboards. But it can be used for murder.

A FOLDING CHAIR
HEAVY-WEIGHT • MADE OF METAL

Sometimes chessboxing gets out of hand, and some-body comes in with a folding chair . . .

CHESS OPENINGS

 THE ITALIAN GAME

 THE KING'S GAMBIT

 THE RUY LOPEZ

 THE FRIED LIVER

CLUES & EVIDENCE

- The suspect who was wearing boxing gloves had brown eyes.

- Whoever played the Ruy Lopez was right-handed.

- The person with a folding chair played the Fried Liver.

- The microphone started to fritz out when the following announcement was made: XM AIERNGTEN RNVEE EST OOTF NI EHT RGIN.

- Blue eyes watched the match from the ringside.

- It is a well-known fact in chessboxing circles that those with Aries as their sign only play the King's Gambit.

- Boxing gloves were not found in the ring—bare-knuckle chessboxing, baby!

- A chess board was being studied by someone chanting about a knight.

- **The murder took place not in the ring, but where the rich hang out.**

SUSPECTS OPENINGS LOCATIONS

WEAPONS

LOCATIONS

OPENINGS

WHO?

WHAT?

WHERE?

AND?

58. THE DETECTIVE CLUBHOUSE KILLING 🔍🔍🔍

Irratino had a great idea! Recruit the detectives of the Detective Club to solve the mystery of Logico's disappearance. But when he got there, they were already trying to solve another mystery: the murder of their treasurer.

SUSPECTS

CHEF AUBERGINE

It is said that she once killed her husband, cooked him, and then served him at her restaurant. It's not true, but even the fact that it's said about her tells you something.

5'2" • RIGHT-HANDED • BLUE EYES • BLOND HAIR • LIBRA

COMRADE CHAMPAGNE

A communist and a rich one. Comrade Champagne likes nothing more than to travel the world, sharing the message of communism with his fellow vacationers.

5'11" • LEFT-HANDED • HAZEL EYES • BLOND HAIR • CAPRICORN

JUDGE PINE

Master of the courtroom and possessed of a firm belief in justice, as decided by her and her alone.

5'6" • RIGHT-HANDED • BROWN EYES • BLACK HAIR • TAURUS

BABYFACE BLUE

This is absolutely one fully grown man, and not two kids in a trench coat. They can do adult things like see R-rated movies, buy beer, and stay out way past bedtime.

7'8" • RIGHT-HANDED • BLUE EYES • BLOND HAIR • GEMINI

LOCATIONS

THE MAIN ENTRANCE
OUTDOORS

A sign in the door always says "Closed," and the door is always locked.

THE ENCYCLOPEDIA ROOM
INDOORS

They have dozens of encyclopedia sets and hundreds of Dame Obsidian novels.

THE SECRET ENTRANCE
OUTDOORS

The only actual way to get into the club: it's through ▮▮▮▮▮▮.

THE PARKING GARAGE
OUTDOORS

This is mostly for secret rendezvous with trench-coat-wearing sources.

WEAPONS

A BRIEFCASE FULL OF MONEY
HEAVY-WEIGHT • MADE OF LEATHER & MONEY

Wait a second—all the faces on the bills have mustaches on them!

A FAKE TREASURE MAP
LIGHT-WEIGHT • MADE OF PAPER

This map leads someone straight into a booby-trapped pit.

A GOLDEN BIRD
HEAVY-WEIGHT • MADE OF GOLD

This flamingo statue is worth a fortune.

A BOOBY-TRAPPED FEDORA
MEDIUM-WEIGHT • MADE OF ▮▮▮▮▮

Whatever you do, don't try it on.

FAVORITE MYSTERY MEDIUM

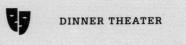 ONLINE GAMES

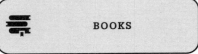 MURDER PARTIES

DINNER THEATER

BOOKS

CLUES & EVIDENCE

- Whoever preferred mystery books always turned the pages with their dominant left hand.

- Traces of a weapon made of gold were found in the main entrance.

- A dangerous hat was found near a secret rendezvous.

- A detective slipped Inspector Irratino a message and told him to read it in a mirror: FEHC ENIGREBUA DID TON GNIRB A EKAF ERUSAERT PAM.

- A Capricorn was in the encyclopedia room studying Capricorn stuff.

- One of the suspects kept a golden bird hidden in their trench coat.

- Whoever preferred murder parties was giving off real Taurus vibes.

- Chef Aubergine loved to solve dinner theater mysteries. A meal and a murder, what's not to love?!

- The person with a booby-trapped fedora did not enjoy dinner theater.

- **The treasurer's body was found in the secret entrance.**

SUSPECTS   MEDIA   LOCATIONS

WEAPONS

LOCATIONS

MEDIA

_____
WHO?

_____
WHAT?

_____
WHERE?

_____
AND?

59. THE PARKING GARAGE FOLLOW-UP 🔍🔍🔍

In the shadowy parking lot outside the Detective Clubhouse, Inspector Irratino met with a secret source who claimed to have information on Logico's disappearance. But when he got there, the secret source had been murdered: But by whom?!

SUSPECTS

MANSERVANT BROWNSTONE

Manservant Brownstone's brother is devoted to God, but he is devoted to the Violets.

6'2" • RIGHT-HANDED • BROWN EYES • BROWN HAIR • CANCER

SISTER LAPIS

A nun who travels the world, doing God's work on His dime. Her habit is cashmere, and her habit is spending.

5'2" • RIGHT-HANDED • BROWN EYES • BROWN HAIR • CANCER

COACH RASPBERRY

One of the best coaches this side of the Mississippi, regardless of which side you happen to be on. Some people say he has a gambling problem, but he just says he loves danger.

6'0" • LEFT-HANDED • BLUE EYES • BLOND HAIR • ARIES

HIGH ALCHEMIST RAVEN

There's an old joke that all alchemists are high alchemists. Raven hates it.

5'8" • RIGHT-HANDED • BROWN EYES • BROWN HAIR • PISCES

LOCATIONS

THE STAIRWELL
INDOORS

A great place to murder, but maybe not a great place to hide a body.

THE ELECTRICAL ROOM
INDOORS

Hidden in a corner of the garage, this room is filled with wires and machines that could easily hide a body.

THE TOP FLOOR
OUTDOORS

You could look out over the whole city and wonder if Logico was in it somewhere.

THE BASEMENT
INDOORS

Irratino had never seen so many cardboard boxes, except for that murder at the cardboard box factory.

WEAPONS

A CROWBAR
MEDIUM-WEIGHT • MADE OF METAL

Honestly, they're used more often for crime than anything else.

A SPARE TIRE
HEAVY-WEIGHT • MADE OF RUBBER & METAL

Where the rubber meets your head!

AN EXPLODING CIGAR
LIGHT-WEIGHT • MADE OF TOBACCO & A BOMB

A classic of practical joking and American "diplomacy."

THE BIG RED BOOK
MEDIUM-WEIGHT • MADE OF PAPER

One of the quotes reads, "In an arm wrestling match, nobody expects you to stab them."

CARS THEY DROVE

 CLASSIC STRETCH LIMO

 TOP-OF-THE-LINE HYBRID

TANDEM BICYCLE

INCONSPICUOUS HEARSE

CLUES & EVIDENCE

- The person with a spare tire drove a hearse.

- A blood sample taken from inside the limo contained the following DNA signature: ACATCC. (See Exhibit C.)

- If you're riding a bicycle, you can only carry a light-weight weapon.

- Whoever was in the stairwell was left-handed.

- The person with the crowbar had a habit of spending.

- Irratino was convinced some scrambled graffiti was the clue he needed: A ESARP EITR SAW NOT IN HTE RLETCACLIE MOOR.

- High Alchemist Raven was seen hanging around beneath a bunch of wires.

- The person who drove a hybrid was in the basement.

- **The last thing the victim saw was a view of the city.**

SUSPECTS   CARS   LOCATIONS

WEAPONS

LOCATIONS

CARS

WHO?

WHAT?

WHERE?

AND?

60. DIVE UNDER THE BAR! 🔍🔍🔍

Inspector Irratino knew, by the principles of esotericism, that everything was connected. And nowhere was that more clear than in the town bar, where you could find people debating the fine points of the latest political developments (like what to do about the Red Revolution) and occasionally murdering each other (probably because of the political debate).

SUSPECTS

UNCLE MIDNIGHT

When his dad died, he bought a desert mansion with a pool and retired. He was seventeen.

5'8" • LEFT-HANDED • BLUE EYES • BROWN HAIR • SAGITTARIUS

TINY TAUPE

He's actually really huge, which is why people call him Tiny.

6'3" • LEFT-HANDED • BLUE EYES • BLOND HAIR • TAURUS

BOOKER-WINNER GAINSBORO

Gainsboro has written the Great American Novel, which he will tell you within two minutes of meeting him. It's six thousand pages long, and it's about dirt.

6'0" • LEFT-HANDED • HAZEL EYES • BROWN HAIR • GEMINI

ARCHEOLOGIST ECRU

A great archeologist/grave robber who is famed worldwide for her archeology/grave robbing.

5'8" • LEFT-HANDED • HAZEL EYES • GRAY HAIR • SAGITTARIUS

LOCATIONS

THE ACTUAL BAR
INDOORS

According to the drink menu, you can get a beer for the price of an arm or a cocktail for the cost of a leg.

THE CORNER BOOTH
INDOORS

It's sticky. It's poorly lit. The upholstery is ripped. And it's the nicest seat here.

THE PATIO
OUTDOORS

Even though you're outside, the air is so thick with smoke you can't breathe.

THE BATHROOM
INDOORS

It's covered in stickers for the worst bands you'll ever hear.

WEAPONS

POISONED TIKI DRINK
MEDIUM-WEIGHT • MADE OF GLASS, SUGAR, & TOXINS

Sure, it's cultural appropriation, and it's poisoned, too, but it's so delicious!

A HARPOON
HEAVY-WEIGHT • MADE OF METAL

A little rusty, which might actually make it a better weapon?

A HEAVY PURSE
HEAVY-WEIGHT • MADE OF VELVET

Finally, all that junk in there will be put to use (to provide inertia).

A CHEAP PEN
LIGHT-WEIGHT • MADE OF PLASTIC

Filled with cheap ink, too. If bars had nice pens they'd spend their whole budget on them.

POLITICAL OPINIONS

 FUND THE ROYAL RESISTANCE

 RECOGNIZE THE RED GOVERNMENT

 INVADE DRAKONIA

 BOMB THE WHOLE COUNTRY

CLUES & EVIDENCE

- The person with a harpoon wanted to invade Drakonia.

- A drop of cheap ink was found beneath the sticker for a band called LEAD GUITAR.

- The suspect who was in the corner booth had hazel eyes.

- A Taurus had the heavy purse.

- Uncle Midnight did not want to fund the Royal Resistance.

- The suspect who wanted to bomb the whole country was found indoors.

- Forensics determined a weapon made at least partially out of toxins was present in the patio.

- Bookie-Winner Gainsboro wanted to recognize the Red Government.

- **The victim's body was found by an expensive menu.**

SUSPECTS   OPINIONS   LOCATIONS

WEAPONS

LOCATIONS

OPINIONS

_____
WHO?

_____
WHAT?

_____
WHERE?

_____
AND?

61. THE CATHEDRAL KILLING 🔍🔍🔍

Inspector Irratino snuck across the secured border into Free Drakonia and visited the People's Cathedral Community Center, formerly the Great Cathedral of St. Lupine, where the tour guide had recently been killed. To untangle this mystery, he was going to have to discern everyone's religious beliefs.

SUSPECTS

OFFICER COPPER

The best part of being a policewoman criminal is that you can cut out the middleman and fail to investigate your own crimes.

5'5" • RIGHT-HANDED • BLUE EYES • BLOND HAIR • ARIES

MISS SAFFRON

Miss Saffron is technically an aristocrat, but more accurately, she's just plain rich.

5'2" • LEFT-HANDED • HAZEL EYES • BLOND HAIR • LIBRA

MX. TANGERINE

Proving that non-binary people can be murderers, too, Mx. Tangerine is an artist, poet, and potential suspect.

5'5" • LEFT-HANDED • HAZEL EYES • BLOND HAIR • PISCES

CHAIRMAN CHALK

He figured out the publishing business years ago and never looked back. He called ebooks a "fad" and still owns a rotary phone. He is worth a billion dollars.

5'9" • RIGHT-HANDED • BLUE EYES • WHITE HAIR • SAGITTARIUS

LOCATIONS

THE PEWS
INDOORS

Each of these wooden pews was made by old wood from the Screaming Forests.

THE BELLTOWER
INDOORS

A giant cracked bell that used to be rung seven times a day before the revolution.

THE GRAND STEPS
OUTDOORS

Sixty-six steps, representing each of the sixty-six noble families of Drakonia.

THE ALTAR
INDOORS

It's made of marble, which was excavated by Drakonian indentured servants.

WEAPONS

A STRING OF PRAYER BEADS
LIGHT-WEIGHT • MADE OF IVORY

Ivory prayer beads covered with tiny engraved symbols.

SACRAMENTAL WINE
MEDIUM-WEIGHT • MADE OF GLASS & WINE

A great way to show your devotion is to drink a lot of this holy red wine.

A HOLY RELIC
MEDIUM-WEIGHT • MADE OF BONE

It's a totem of some long forgotten god with a terrifying visage.

A BOTTLE OF SACRED OIL
LIGHT-WEIGHT • MADE OF OIL & TOXINS

It's not, like, massage oil. It's petroleum oil. But it's still sacred.

PERSONAL RELIGIONS

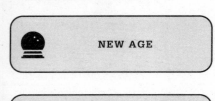

NEW AGE

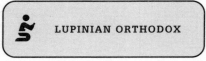

LUPINIAN ORTHODOX

THE CHURCH

ATHEISM

CLUES & EVIDENCE

- Whoever believed in the Church was giving off real Pisces vibes, which was technically heretical.

- A holy relic was discovered atop old wood.

- Whoever was on the grand steps was right-handed.

- Irratino saw a message written in what he thought was Latin: NMAI-CRHA ACLKH SWA EESN OATP A LAMRBE BALS.

- Officer Copper was suspicious of the person who brought sacramental wine.

- The suspect who was an atheist had a weapon made at least partially of wine.

- The suspect who considered themselves Lupinian Orthodox was seen indoors.

- The shortest suspect had a string of prayer beads.

- **The body of the tour guide was found in the belltower.**

SUSPECTS   RELIGIONS   LOCATIONS

WEAPONS

LOCATIONS

RELIGIONS

_____

WHO?

_____

WHAT?

_____

WHERE?

_____

AND?

62. THE DOG SPA MURDER SPREE 🔍🔍🔍

Inspector Irratino got a call from a high-end dog spa. They needed him to solve the attempted murder of a dog. Some detectives might have thought this was beneath them: Irratino thought it was a great honor. And—for just a day—he put the hunt for Logico on hold.

SUSPECTS

GRAYSCALE, CPA

The world's most boring human being.

5'6" • RIGHT-HANDED • BLUE EYES • BLOND HAIR • VIRGO

VICE PRESIDENT MAUVE

A vice president of TekCo Futures. She has been tasked with developing the latest TekCo product: TekTopia. It's like a metaverse in real life.

5'8" • RIGHT-HANDED • BROWN EYES • BLACK HAIR • TAURUS

EDITOR IVORY

The greatest romance editor of all time. She invented the enemies-to-lovers genre, and she was the first person to put a naked man on the cover of a book.

5'6" • LEFT-HANDED • BROWN EYES • GRAY HAIR • SCORPIO

DIRECTOR DUSTY

A true filmmaker. He wants to make a masterpiece. To do that, he might have to make a murder.

5'10" • LEFT-HANDED • HAZEL EYES • BALD • PISCES

LOCATIONS

THE KENNEL ROOM
INDOORS

"Kennel" is a bit of a misnomer, as each of the dogs sleeps in a king-sized bed.

THE BACKYARD
OUTDOORS

Here the dogs can run around and enjoy the imported French dirt and organic grass.

THE RECEPTION AREA
INDOORS

A beautiful lobby with a reception desk where you can check your pooch in.

THE BEDROOM
INDOORS

There's a twin-sized bed for the night watchman to sleep on.

WEAPONS

AN ANGRY CAT
MEDIUM-WEIGHT • MADE OF FUR, CLAWS, & MENACE

Its claws are dipped in poison, which has made it very angry.

AN EMERALD DISH
MEDIUM-WEIGHT • MADE OF EMERALD

One of the dogs can only eat out of an emerald dish (according to his very rich owner).

A GIANT BONE
HEAVY-WEIGHT • MADE OF BONE

What size animal could such a bone come from? And what size dog would eat it?!

A LEASH
LIGHT-WEIGHT • MADE OF COTTON

An expensive designer leash that costs as much as a diamond necklace.

BREEDS OF THEIR DOGS

 THE GREAT DANE

 THE POODLE

 THE MUTT

 THE WIENER DOG

CLUES & EVIDENCE

- Whoever had a weapon made with menace was left-handed.

- The person with an emerald dish had the wiener dog.

- Logico scryed into a fluorescent bulb until he saw these letters: OWHVERE SWA NI ETH CEEONIRPT AAER ADH NROWB YSEE.

- A Pisces was relaxing on the twin-sized bed.

- The suspect who had the Great Dane was seen standing on French dirt.

- Grayscale, CPA, had the poodle: his greatest friend and companion.

- Editor Ivory carried a giant bone with her. Dangerous at a dog spa.

- **The dogicide would have happened on a king-sized bed.**

SUSPECTS   BREEDS   LOCATIONS

WEAPONS

LOCATIONS

BREEDS

_____ **WHO?**

_____ **WHAT?**

_____ **WHERE?**

_____ **AND?**

63. THE DISPROPORTIONATELY BLOODY BLOOD BANK 🔍🔍🔍

Inspector Irratino followed Grayscale's map into the heart of an industrial district, where he found an underground blood bank where people sold their blood for cash. A newspaper columnist had sold too much, it seemed. Or, perhaps, she had been killed when she discovered where Logico was.

SUSPECTS

AGENT ARGYLE

Unlike Agent Ink, Argyle does not have a heart of gold, or a heart at all.

6'4" • RIGHT-HANDED • BROWN EYES • BROWN HAIR • VIRGO

ASTROLOGER AZURE

A stargazer, full of wonder and questions about the exact time and place of your birth.

5'6" • RIGHT-HANDED • HAZEL EYES • BROWN HAIR • CANCER

SISTER LAPIS

A nun who travels the world, doing God's work on His dime. Her habit is cashmere, and her habit is spending.

5'2" • RIGHT-HANDED • BROWN EYES • BROWN HAIR • CANCER

CAPTAIN SLATE

A real-life astronaut. The first woman to travel around the dark side of the moon, and also the first to be suspected of murdering her copilot.

5'5" • LEFT-HANDED • BROWN EYES • BROWN HAIR • AQUARIUS

LOCATIONS

THE DONATION ROOM
INDOORS

They'll pay you a lot for your blood—no questions asked.

THE SECRET ENTRANCE
OUTDOORS

It's in an alley behind a dumpster. You knock three times, then one time, and they'll let you in.

THE TRANSFUSION CENTER
INDOORS

Here's where they put the blood into the people who need it.

THE BLOOD TANKS
INDOORS

They are overflowing with all the extra blood they've received.

WEAPONS

A BAG OF CASH
HEAVY-WEIGHT • MADE OF CANVAS & METAL

This seems totally legitimate.

200-PROOF ALCOHOL
MEDIUM-WEIGHT • MADE OF GLASS & TOXINS

It will go up in flames if you look at it too hotly.

A JAGGED DAGGER
MEDIUM-WEIGHT • MADE OF METAL

See if you can say "jagged dagger" five times fast. (Then get back to solving the murder!)

A PAPERBACK
MEDIUM-WEIGHT • MADE OF PAPER

Too light to hit someone over the head, but the ink is so cheap it's toxic.

BLOOD TYPES

O	TYPE O

AB	TYPE AB

B	TYPE B

A	TYPE A

CLUES & EVIDENCE

- The person with a bag of cash had type A blood.

- They say Virgos are more likely to have type O blood: it was true in this case.

- A Cancer had a weapon that would go up in flames if you looked at it hotly.

- The person who had type AB blood was in the transfusion center.

- The first woman to travel to the dark side of the moon was seen snooping around an overflowing blood tank.

- The person who had type O blood was not at the secret entrance.

- Whoever had a paperback was holding it in their left hand, so clearly they were left-handed.

- The second-tallest suspect was sneaking out the secret entrance.

- **A jagged dagger was used to drain the blood of the donor.**

WEAPONS

LOCATIONS

BLOOD TYPES

WHO?

WHAT?

WHERE?

AND?

64. THE SLAUGHTERHOUSE SLAUGHTER 🔍🔍🔍

Animal-lover Irratino had never seen a more horrifying sight than this slaughterhouse. It would haunt his nightmares for the rest of his life. So it was hard to even notice the dead (human) body, much less focus on solving the mystery.

SUSPECTS

GENERAL COFFEE

An espresso connoisseur, he always drinks his morning brew before sending his men across the battlefield to die. Is it for honor? Is it for glory? Is it for riches? Or is it for the love of the bean?

6'0" • RIGHT-HANDED • BROWN EYES • BALD • SAGITTARIUS

ARISTOCRAT SABLE

Telling the story of the time she was marooned on an island (and suspected of murder!) has been an amazing cocktail party anecdote.

5'5" • LEFT-HANDED • HAZEL EYES • BLACK HAIR • LIBRA

OFFICER COPPER

The best part of being a policewoman criminal is that you can cut out the middleman and fail to investigate your own crimes.

5'5" • RIGHT-HANDED • BLUE EYES • BLOND HAIR • ARIES

COMRADE CHAMPAGNE

A communist and a rich one. Comrade Champagne likes nothing more than to travel the world, sharing the message of communism with his fellow vacationers.

5'11" • LEFT-HANDED • HAZEL EYES • BLOND HAIR • CAPRICORN

LOCATIONS

THE CAGES
INDOORS

Their little animal eyes are so sad, looking through the bars.

THE KILLING FLOOR
INDOORS

Honestly, the location that has been the site of the most murders.

THE PACKING PLANT
INDOORS

What happens here is too horrifying to be printed in a family-friendly book.

THE GIFT SHOP
INDOORS

Here you can buy happy cow plush toys that make you think the animals were treated well.

WEAPONS

A BUCKET OF ▓▓▓▓▓▓▓
MEDIUM-WEIGHT • MADE OF METAL & ▓▓▓▓▓

You don't want to know what's in this bucket. If you learned, it might kill you.

A RUSTY SAW
MEDIUM-WEIGHT • MADE OF METAL

The teeth are rusty, and it's already covered in blood.

A CHICKEN BONE
LIGHT-WEIGHT • MADE OF BONE

Historically, what people have choked on the most.

A SHOVEL
MEDIUM-WEIGHT • MADE OF METAL & WOOD

A multipurpose tool: kill someone and bury them with the same shovel!

DIETS

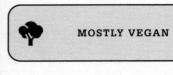 MOSTLY VEGAN

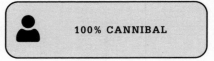 100% CANNIBAL

 CAVEMAN DIET

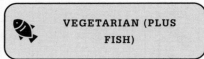 VEGETARIAN (PLUS FISH)

CLUES & EVIDENCE

- A shovel was found next to a happy cow plush toy.

- A Sagittarius had the rusty saw: it was blunt and dangerous, just like them.

- The person who ate mostly vegan was on the killing floor.

- A human blood sample found inside one of the cages contained the following DNA sequence: GGTAT. (See Exhibit C.)

- The suspect with the same height as Aristocrat Sable was not in the packing plant.

- Whoever ate a vegetarian diet (plus fish) was right-handed.

- The suspect with the same height as Aristocrat Sable brought a bucket of ███████████.

- Whoever ate a caveman diet had a medium-weight weapon.

- **A chicken bone was used to commit the murder.**

SUSPECTS DIETS LOCATIONS

WEAPONS

LOCATIONS

DIETS

WHO?

WHAT?

WHERE?

AND?

65. THE MINESHAFT MURDER 🔍🔍🔍

By following ley lines, Inspector Irratino was led to an old abandoned mineshaft. And he knew (in his gut) that a valuable clue might be found at the bottom. But when he traveled into the darkness, he found a dead body instead, surrounded by four suspects of varying degrees of wealth.

SUSPECTS

COACH RASPBERRY

One of the best coaches this side of the Mississippi, regardless of which side you happen to be on. Some people say he has a gambling problem, but he just says he loves danger.

6'0" • LEFT-HANDED • BLUE EYES • BLOND HAIR • ARIES

CARDINAL CINEREOUS

An incredibly respected leader in the Church, second only to the Pope himself . . . for now.

5'10" • LEFT-HANDED • BROWN EYES • BALD • SCORPIO

JUDGE PINE

Master of the courtroom and possessed of a firm belief in justice, as decided by her and her alone.

5'6" • RIGHT-HANDED • BROWN EYES • BLACK HAIR • TAURUS

SIGNOR EMERALD

An Italian jeweler of great renown, Signor Emerald has traveled the world in search of rare, precious stones, which are always falling out of his pockets.

5'8" • LEFT-HANDED • BROWN EYES • BLACK HAIR • SAGITTARIUS

LOCATIONS

THE RUSTED TRACKS
INDOORS

It just needs a little WD-40 and major reconstruction.

THE COLLAPSED OFFICE
INDOORS

Sitting next to the mine shaft, it was long ago abandoned and has since collapsed.

THE LOCKED GATES
OUTDOORS

The rusted iron gates which used to keep out trespassers are now broken.

AN ABANDONED MINE SHAFT
INDOORS

A dark hole that goes down into blackness.

WEAPONS

TAINTED MOONSHINE
MEDIUM-WEIGHT • MADE OF XXX

This'll kill you, that's fer sure. Even the smell is dangerous.

A GEAR
HEAVY-WEIGHT • MADE OF METAL

A cog in a much larger machine. A metaphor for man in society.

A GEODE
MEDIUM-WEIGHT • MADE OF MINERALS

It probably has beautiful crystals inside but you won't know unless you hit someone with it.

A GOLD BAR
HEAVY-WEIGHT • MADE OF METAL

A single bar of gold.

CLASSES

 DIRT POOR

 SORTA BROKE

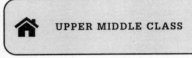 UPPER MIDDLE CLASS

 FILTHY RICH

CLUES & EVIDENCE

- Top numerologists predicted a gear would be found outdoors.

- A splash of "XXX" was found on the clothing of Signor Emerald.

- The person who was dirt poor was in an abandoned mine shaft.

- The person who was sorta broke was not on the rusted tracks.

- Cardinal Cinereous was filthy rich: all of the Church's cardinals were!

- According to the marot, an Aries had the gold bar.

- Someone who was sorta broke smelled a dangerous odor.

- The shortest suspect was seen beside a broken security measure.

- **A cracked-open geode—revealing a crystal inside—was found next to the body.**

	SUSPECTS	CLASSES	LOCATIONS

WEAPONS

LOCATIONS

CLASSES

WHO?

WHAT?

WHERE?

AND?

66. THE VILLAGE BOOK CLUB MURDER 🔍🔍🔍

On the advice of his alchemist, Irratino decided to take a week-long holiday from murder solving. So he traveled to a tiny village with a secret, and there he joined a Dame Obsidian book club. But before their first meeting, one of the members was murdered! Back to work . . .

SUSPECTS

EARL GREY

He comes from a long line of Earl Greys. Yes, those Earl Greys. No, he doesn't sign autographs. But he does always have some bags with him.

5'9" • RIGHT-HANDED • BROWN EYES • WHITE HAIR • CAPRICORN

BISHOP AZURE

A bishop in the Church, Azure has been known to pray for both her friends and her enemies. Of course, she asks for different things . . .

5'4" • RIGHT-HANDED • BROWN EYES • BROWN HAIR • GEMINI

THE DUCHESS OF VERMILLION

A tall, old woman with tall, old secrets. If she is the murderer, then it certainly wouldn't be the first time.

5'9" • LEFT-HANDED • GRAY EYES • WHITE HAIR • PISCES

SIR RULEAN

A sophisticated gentleman who just happens to have been knighted, if you believe the Official Knighting Documents he is always waving around.

5'8" • RIGHT-HANDED • BLUE EYES • RED HAIR • LEO

LOCATIONS

THE VILLAGE PUB
INDOORS

When an outsider walks in, a hush falls over the tobacco-stained pub. Were they talking about the secret?

A SMALL COTTAGE
INDOORS

A weird old man lives here, and he's always muttering. But is he muttering about the secret? Or just about what he wants for lunch?

THE TOWN SQUARE
OUTDOORS

There's a statue of the town founder. Was he secretly a scoundrel? Is that the secret?

THE OLD ABANDONED MILL
INDOORS

It's on the edge of town where they used to mill their grains. Why did it close? Because of the secret?

WEAPONS

A PIANO
HEAVY-WEIGHT • MADE OF WOOD & IVORY

You don't see people get crushed by a piano that often anymore. Until now.

A CROWBAR IN A NEWSPAPER
MEDIUM-WEIGHT • MADE OF PAPER & METAL

The newspaper is the *Drakonian Times,* and it reads, "Major Red to Make Major Announcement!"

A CHESS BOARD
HEAVY-WEIGHT • MADE OF MARBLE

Made of marble and heavier than God.

A SUIT OF DRAKONIAN ARMOR
HEAVY-WEIGHT • MADE OF METAL

Imported from Holy Drakonia before it fell to the Reds. The helmet has a white feather plume.

FAVORITE OBSIDIAN NOVELS

 THE PERPLEXING PROBLEM OF THE PARROT

 MURDER ON THE OCCIDENTAL LOCAL

 A VERY PROPER MURDER

 KNOCK, KNOCK . . . WHO'S THERE? MURDER!

CLUES & EVIDENCE

- Whoever was at the old abandoned mill was left-handed.

- The suspect who was the same height as the Duchess of Vermillion was not in a small cottage.

- Bishop Azure kept rereading *A Very Proper Murder*. Every time, the ending surprised her!

- The person with a piano loved *Knock, Knock . . . Who's There? Murder!*.

- A speck of blood was found on the inside of the suit of Drakonian Armor, and Detective Club bloodwork found it was the only one that contained the following DNA signature: CTAA. (See Exhibit C.)

- The person who was obsessed with *Murder on the Occidental Local* was in the village pub.

- Sir Rulean brought a chess board so he could study how knights move.

- **The murder took place beneath a giant statue of the town founder.**

SUSPECTS NOVELS LOCATIONS

WEAPONS

LOCATIONS

NOVELS

_____

WHO?

_____

WHAT?

_____

WHERE?

_____

AND?

67. ALL ABOARD FOR MURDER 🔍🔍🔍

Inspector Irratino had discovered another lead, and he traveled to this one on a luxury train. But the moment he boarded, he could feel something was off. His suspicions were confirmed when a porter was murdered.

SUSPECTS

LORD LAVENDER

A politically conservative MP in the House of Lords, as well as the musical theater composer behind such hits as *Dogs* and *Mr. Moses Megastar*.

5'9" • RIGHT-HANDED • GREEN EYES • GRAY HAIR • VIRGO

DEAN GLAUCOUS

The dean of some such-and-such department at a massively funded research university. What does he do? Well, he handles the money, for one . . .

5'6" • RIGHT-HANDED • BROWN EYES • BROWN HAIR • VIRGO

CAPTAIN SLATE

A real-life astronaut. The first woman to travel around the dark side of the moon, and also the first to be suspected of murdering her copilot.

5'5" • LEFT-HANDED • BROWN EYES • BROWN HAIR • AQUARIUS

ARCHEOLOGIST ECRU

A great archeologist/grave robber who is famed worldwide for her archeology/grave robbing.

5'8" • LEFT-HANDED • HAZEL EYES • GRAY HAIR • SAGITTARIUS

LOCATIONS

THE SLEEPING CAR
INDOORS

In the nicer beds, they let you turn the lights off at night.

THE DINING CAR
INDOORS

The most expensive food on rails, and some of the worst, too. Maybe someone should murder the chef . . .

THE CABOOSE
INDOORS

The back of the train lets you see where you're leaving, and what you're leaving behind . . .

THE OBSERVATION DECK
OUTDOORS

Here you can gaze up at the stars or shove someone off the side.

WEAPONS

A LUMP OF COAL
HEAVY-WEIGHT • MADE OF ROCK

Leaves a black smudge on anything it touches (like the Earth's atmosphere, for example).

A BOTTLE OF WINE
MEDIUM-WEIGHT • MADE OF · GLASS AND ALCOHOL

Drink and be merry, because somebody else died.

AN ANTIQUE CLOCK
HEAVY-WEIGHT • MADE OF WOOD

Tick-tock, tick-tock. Technically, time is killing us all slowly.

LEATHER LUGGAGE
HEAVY-WEIGHT • MADE OF METAL & LEATHER

This luggage is hideous. The leather looked way better on the cow.

FINAL DESTINATIONS

 ROMANTIC PARIS

 COSMOPOLITAN MADRID

 ETERNAL ROME

 TULIP-FILLED AMSTERDAM

CLUES & EVIDENCE

- Archeologist Ecru had a crush on the person who brought leather luggage.

- A black smudge was discovered in the back of the train.

- The person whose final destination was eternal Rome was on the observation deck.

- The musical theater composer had always wanted to visit romantic Paris, and today they would!

- Irratino gazed into a crystal ball and saw that Dean Glaucous was indoors.

- An Aquarius was in the sleeping car (wide awake).

- The person whose final destination was cosmopolitan Madrid was left-handed.

- Lord Lavender wrote all of his masterpieces using an antique time-keeping device, which he brought on the train with him.

- **An alcoholic red stain was found beside the conductor.**

SUSPECTS   DESTINATIONS   LOCATIONS

WEAPONS

LOCATIONS

DESTINATIONS

_____
WHO?

_____
WHAT?

_____
WHERE?

_____
AND?

68. THE CHESS COMMUNE KILLING 🔍🔍🔍

Since the last time Inspector Irratino had visited this commune, it had been bought by a new cult. This one was led by a mysterious Russian who seemed to treat chess like a religious ritual. Finally, Irratino could get into the game! But then, *nyet!*—the Russian was murdered.

SUSPECTS

THE AMAZING AUREOLIN

A magician who perfected the sawing-your-husband-in-two routine. Then, she made his body disappear.

5'6" • LEFT-HANDED • GREEN EYES • BLOND HAIR • ARIES

TINY TAUPE

He's actually really huge, which is why people call him Tiny.

6'3" • LEFT-HANDED • BLUE EYES • BLOND HAIR • TAURUS

GRANDMASTER ROSE

A chess grandmaster who is always plotting his next move. Like how to bump off his next opponent! (2 . . . Qh4#, and Rose dispatched another challenger.)

5'7" • LEFT-HANDED • BROWN EYES • BROWN HAIR • SCORPIO

BROTHER BROWNSTONE

A monk who has dedicated his life to the Church, specifically to making money for it.

5'4" • LEFT-HANDED • BROWN EYES • BROWN HAIR • CAPRICORN

LOCATIONS

THE BARRACKS
INDOORS

The Russian sleeps in a mansion he has built; everyone else sleeps here.

THE STONE BRIDGE
OUTDOORS

A nice cobblestone bridge across a burbling brook. If you shoved someone off, they'd get wet.

THE STATUE OF A PAWN
OUTDOORS

This pawn is, like, forty feet tall. Imagine how big the king must be!

THE BOARD ROOM
INDOORS

The room with all the chess boards in it.

WEAPONS

LEATHER GLOVES
LIGHT-WEIGHT • MADE OF LEATHER

Beware someone who wears leather gloves. They've already killed a cow: Who's next?!

A CHESS BOOK
MEDIUM-WEIGHT • MADE OF PAPER

It was full of great games, like this one: 1. e4 e5 2. Nf3 Nc6 3. Bc4 d6 4. Nc3 Bg4 5. Nxe5 Bxd1 6. Bxf7+ Ke7 8. Nd5#. Riveting.

PIANO WIRE
LIGHT-WEIGHT • MADE OF METAL

Somewhere out there, there's a piano missing a wire, and it's about to ruin a concert.

A BOTTLE OF WINE
MEDIUM-WEIGHT • MADE OF GLASS & ALCOHOL

Watch out for stains, because the red doesn't come out.

FAVORITE PIECES

 THE STURDY ROOK

 THE SLY BISHOP

 THE TRICKY KNIGHT

 THE POWERFUL QUEEN

CLUES & EVIDENCE

- The tallest suspect carried piano wire in their bag.

- The Amazing Aureolin deeply respected the person who brought a chess book.

- The person with a chess book chose the powerful queen as their favorite piece, mostly because the book said she was the best.

- The Amazing Aureolin was seen between several chess boards.

- The suspect whose favorite piece was the sly bishop was seen outdoors.

- Brother Brownstone was seen praying beside the statue of a pawn.

- A red stain was discovered on a bed where the people slept.

- The suspect whose favorite piece was the tricky knight had blond hair.

- **The Russian was strangled by someone wearing gloves.**

SUSPECTS　　PIECES　　LOCATIONS

WEAPONS

LOCATIONS

PIECES

WHO?

WHAT?

WHERE?

AND?

69. DEDUCT THIS! 🔍🔍🔍

Inspector Irratino traveled to Logico's alma mater, Deduction College, in order to see if he could scrounge up any leads whatsoever. Logico had always regaled him about the greatness of this institution, but when he arrived, all he found were a bunch of nerds and a dead body.

SUSPECTS

STATISTICIAN MARBLE

Now, she has specialized in a specific field of mathematics. Soon, she'll choose a field within statistics.

5'7" • LEFT-HANDED • BLUE EYES • BLOND HAIR • CANCER

COACH RASPBERRY

One of the best coaches this side of the Mississippi, regardless of which side you happen to be on. Some people say he has a gambling problem, but he just says he loves danger.

6'0" • LEFT-HANDED • BLUE EYES • BLOND HAIR • ARIES

PRINCIPAL APPLEGREEN

A strict principal about everything except getting away with murder. His hands are always covered in chalk.

5'11" • RIGHT-HANDED • BLUE EYES • BALD • LIBRA

AGENT INK

An agent with a heart of gold, but a mind for gold, too. She sells more books than Amazon, so don't cross her.

5'5" • RIGHT-HANDED • BROWN EYES • BLACK HAIR • VIRGO

LOCATIONS

THE BOOKSTORE
INDOORS

The biggest moneymaker on campus. A sign offers a 2-for-$500 deal on textbooks.

THE ARBORETUM
OUTDOORS

An arboretum in the middle of campus. It's overgrown with weeds.

THE STADIUM
OUTDOORS

The field features the absolute highest-quality fake grass money can buy.

OLD MAIN
INDOORS

The first building on campus, the most important, and the least maintained. Paint is peeling off the wall!

WEAPONS

A GRADUATION CORD
LIGHT-WEIGHT • MADE OF CLOTH

It would be an honor to be strangled by one of these.

A HEAVY BACKPACK
HEAVY-WEIGHT • MADE OF CLOTH & BOOKS

Finally, a use for all those logic textbooks.

A SHARP PENCIL
LIGHT-WEIGHT • MADE OF WOOD & METAL

Back then, they used actual lead. One stab and you'd die from lead poisoning.

A LAPTOP
MEDIUM-WEIGHT • MADE OF METAL & TECH

The machine you work on. It's connected to every distraction ever made.

FAVORITE SUBJECTS

 RIGOROUS LOGIC

 SOARING RHETORIC

 ESOTERIC MUSIC THEORY

 ADVANCED GRAMMAR

CLUES & EVIDENCE

- Statistician Marble loved to study logic.

- A tiny lead shaving was found beneath a pile of pricey textbooks.

- A weapon made at least partly of cloth was brought by the person who loved grammar.

- Coach Raspberry was betting on sporting events on his laptop.

- The person with a heavy backpack loved to study music theory.

- Agent Ink was very proud of her graduation cord.

- A leaf fell from a tree in the arboretum and landed on a bald head.

- The person who loved rhetoric was not in the stadium.

- **The victim's body was on the steps of Old Main.**

SUSPECTS   SUBJECTS   LOCATIONS

WEAPONS

LOCATIONS

SUBJECTS

WHO?

WHAT?

WHERE?

AND?

70. THE GRAVEST YARD OF ALL 🔍🔍🔍

Inspector Irratino followed the latest lead (a marot card he drew) to a graveyard, where he found an unmarked grave. Terrified it belonged to Logico, he dug up the body and found a fresh corpse! (Not Logico's.) Someone had hidden the body of their victim, but who?!

SUSPECTS

ACTUARY APRICOT

With rough statistical certainty, he can predict the minute you are going to die (especially if he kills you).

5'10" • RIGHT-HANDED • BROWN EYES • BROWN HAIR • VIRGO

BARON MAROON

An incredibly haughty man who famously holds a grudge. Nobody wants to offend the baron. At least, nobody who's still alive . . .

6'2" • RIGHT-HANDED • HAZEL EYES • RED HAIR • SCORPIO

DR. CRIMSON

She believes that everyone—no matter their race or creed—deserves the right to medical care, as long as they can afford it.

5'9" • LEFT-HANDED • GREEN EYES • RED HAIR • AQUARIUS

VICE PRESIDENT MAUVE

A vice president of TekCo Futures. She has been tasked with developing the latest TekCo product: TekTopia. It's like a metaverse in real life.

5'8" • RIGHT-HANDED • BROWN EYES • BLACK HAIR • TAURUS

LOCATIONS

THE WEIRD SHACK
INDOORS

A wooden shack in the corner of the graveyard that you just know contains a secret.

THE COLUMBARIUM
OUTDOORS

A great place to hide a dead body, presuming you've cremated it first.

THE GIFT SHOP
INDOORS

You can buy little knickknack gravestones or a plushie of their mascot, Mr. Skull.

THE ENTRANCE GATE
OUTDOORS

A giant wrought-iron gate with just the right amount of rust for ominous vibes.

WEAPONS

A HUMAN SKULL
MEDIUM-WEIGHT • MADE OF BONE

"Alas, poor Yorick, I knew him. And now I'm swinging his skull at people."

A SKELETON ARM
MEDIUM-WEIGHT • MADE OF BONE

Cause the death of a person with a person who's dead.

A POUCH OF MAGICK POWDERS
LIGHT-WEIGHT • MADE OF VELVET & POWDERS

What is "magick" about these powders is that they are deadly.

A GLOBE
HEAVY-WEIGHT • MADE OF METAL

For plotting world domination or storing drinks.

BURIAL PREFERENCES

 PUT SIX FEET UNDER

 DONATED TO SCIENCE

 BURIED AT SEA

 CREMATED

CLUES & EVIDENCE

- A pouch of magick powders was found outdoors.

- Whoever carried a human skull looked at it with green eyes.

- Based on Irratino's astrological knowledge, he knew a Scorpio had the globe.

- Whoever wanted to be put six feet under when they died was left-handed.

- The person who wanted to be cremated was in the weird shack.

- Actuary Apricot wanted his body to be donated to science.

- The person holding a skeleton arm did not want to be cremated.

- An esoteric ritual with a pendulum convinced Irratino that whoever was at the entrance gate was left-handed.

- Actuary Apricot had never been in the gift shop.

- **The victim's body was found inside a jar of ashes.**

	SUSPECTS				BURIALS				LOCATIONS			

WEAPONS

LOCATIONS

BURIALS

WHO?

WHAT?

WHERE?

AND?

71. THE PUBLISHING HOUSE MURDER 🔍🔍🔍

Inspector Irratino went and visited Deductive Logico's publisher (an imprint of a subsidiary of a subsidiary of TekCo Futures) hoping to find some insight, only to find (instead) the body of a trespasser. (You could say he trespassed away.)

SUSPECTS

DR. SEASHELL, DDS

He's an amateur physicist with a new theory of the universe, and also, a working dentist.

5'7" • RIGHT-HANDED • GREEN EYES • GRAY HAIR • PISCES

EDITOR IVORY

The greatest romance editor of all time. She invented the enemies-to-lovers genre, and she was the first person to put a naked man on the cover of a book.

5'6" • LEFT-HANDED • BROWN EYES • GRAY HAIR • SCORPIO

EXECUTIVE PRODUCER STEEL

The richest, smartest, and meanest producer in Hollywood. She's never seen a check she couldn't cash.

5'6" • RIGHT-HANDED • GRAY EYES • WHITE HAIR • ARIES

AGENT INK

An agent with a heart of gold, but a mind for gold, too. She sells more books than Amazon, so don't cross her.

5'5" • RIGHT-HANDED • BROWN EYES • BLACK HAIR • VIRGO

LOCATIONS

THE OFFICES
INDOORS

Here is where they do the work of making a book: page setting, editing, buying reviews.

THE PRINTING PRESS
INDOORS

The company says they're "vertically integrated," meaning they print their own books in the basement.

THE ROOFTOP
OUTDOORS

Featuring a helipad for the best-selling authors to land their helicopters on.

THE GARDENS
OUTDOORS

Some of their worst-selling writers are buried here, beneath the daisies.

WEAPONS

A GIANT STACK OF BOOKS
HEAVY-WEIGHT • MADE OF PAPER

You can shove this over and crush someone beneath it. But it's hard to carry around.

AN ANTIQUE TYPEWRITER
HEAVY-WEIGHT • MADE OF METAL

You can write with subtlety, or you can hit them over the head with it.

POISONED INKWELL
LIGHT-WEIGHT • MADE OF INK & TOXINS

How was he poisoned? Well.

A PAPERBACK
MEDIUM-WEIGHT • MADE OF PAPER

Too light to hit someone over the head, but the ink is so cheap it's toxic.

FAVORITE AUTHORS

 DAME OBSIDIAN

 DEDUCTIVE LOGICO('S GHOSTWRITER)

 PHILOSOPHER BONE

 BOOKIE-WINNER GAINSBORO

CLUES & EVIDENCE

- A Virgo had the giant stack of books.

- The person whose favorite author was Deductive Logico('s ghost-writer) was on the rooftop.

- The suspect with the same height as Executive Producer Steel had a heavy-weight weapon.

- Dr. Seashell, DDS, was a huge fan of Philosopher Bone (a real red flag, honestly).

- The suspect whose favorite author was Dame Obsidian was left-handed—just like her!

- Whoever was in the gardens was left-handed.

- A smudge of cheap, toxic ink was found outdoors.

- The literary agent was overseeing the "vertical integration" of the company.

- **A few typewriter keys were scattered around the body of the trespasser.**

WEAPONS

LOCATIONS

AUTHORS

WHO?

WHAT?

WHERE?

AND?

72. MURATE AT SEA 🔍🔍🔍

Inspector Irratino's seventh sense told him to take a cruise across the seven seas. And once again, his intuition had guided him straight into a murder: the forty-third mate had been killed. And that wasn't the only issue: everybody had a complaint!

SUSPECTS

BABYFACE BLUE

This is absolutely one fully grown man, and not two kids in a trench coat. They can do adult things like see R-rated movies, buy beer, and stay out way past bedtime.

7'8" • RIGHT-HANDED • BLUE EYES • BLOND HAIR • GEMINI

CHAIRMAN CHALK

He figured out the publishing business years ago and never looked back. He called ebooks a "fad" and still owns a rotary phone. He is worth a billion dollars.

5'9" • RIGHT-HANDED • BLUE EYES • WHITE HAIR • SAGITTARIUS

SECRETARY CELADON

The secretary of defense, and someone who is personally responsible for a number of war crimes, some of which are now named after her.

5'6" • LEFT-HANDED • GREEN EYES • BROWN HAIR • LEO

PATRIARCH PORPOISE

The Holy Drakonian patriarch, the one true leader of all St. Lupinian Orthodox believers, and he won't let you forget it.

5'4" • RIGHT-HANDED • BLACK EYES • BLACK HAIR • CANCER

LOCATIONS

THE DECK
OUTDOORS

Look out over the ocean, but not too far, or someone might push you.

THE ENGINE ROOM
INDOORS

This is a green yacht: it's powered by a nuclear reactor. When the uranium rods are spent, just toss them into the ocean.

OVERBOARD
OUTDOORS

The open ocean. Home of some of history's favorite drowning victims.

THE CROW'S NEST
OUTDOORS

From up here, you can look down on everyone.

WEAPONS

A PAPERBACK
MEDIUM-WEIGHT • MADE OF PAPER

Too light to hit someone over the head, but the ink is so cheap it's toxic.

AN ANTIQUE ANCHOR
HEAVY-WEIGHT • MADE OF METAL

It's covered in moss and the chain is rusty: it looks awesome.

A COMMEMORATIVE PEN
LIGHT-WEIGHT • MADE OF METAL & INK

To commemorate that special event . . . whatever it was. It leaks expensive ink.

POISONED INKWELL
LIGHT-WEIGHT • MADE OF INK & POISON

How was he poisoned? Well.

COMPLAINTS

 AFRAID OF DROWNING

 TERRIBLY SEASICK

 HOME-SWEET-HOMESICK

 BORED TO TEARS

CLUES & EVIDENCE

- The person who was bored to tears was not in the crow's nest.

- The person with a paperback was not afraid of drowning.

- The person who was afraid of drowning was hiding in the engine room.

- A single drop of poisoned ink was lost in a vast, uncaring ocean.

- A commemorative pen was certainly not in the deck.

- Secretary Celadon always carried a paperback with her on long vacations.

- The suspect on the deck had white hair.

- Babyface Blue was home-sweet-homesick.

- **An antique anchor was used to commit the murder.**

SUSPECTS COMPLAINTS LOCATIONS

WEAPONS

LOCATIONS

COMPLAINTS

WHO?

WHAT?

WHERE?

AND?

73. THE CONSPIRACY OF SILENCE (AND MURDER) 🔍🔍🔍

Inspector Irratino received an invitation to a conspiracy theory convention, and he jumped at the chance: if anybody could figure out where Logico had gone, it would be them, he thought. But when he got there, they couldn't even figure out who had murdered the organizer of the conference!

SUSPECTS

PRESIDENT WHITE

The duly elected president of the Royal Resistance, a party of aristocrats who want to retake power. She dreams of yesterday.

5'10" • RIGHT-HANDED • GRAY EYES • WHITE HAIR • LEO

GENERAL COFFEE

An espresso connoisseur, he always drinks his morning brew before sending his men across the battlefield to die. Is it for honor? Is it for glory? Is it for riches? Or is it for the love of the bean?

6'0" • RIGHT-HANDED • BROWN EYES • BALD • SAGITTARIUS

DR. SEASHELL, DDS

He's an amateur physicist with a new theory of the universe, and also, a working dentist.

5'7" • RIGHT-HANDED • GREEN EYES • GRAY HAIR • PISCES

THE CRYSTAL GODDESS

Her followers regard her as a divine being, which is why they give her money.

5'9" • LEFT-HANDED • BLUE EYES • WHITE HAIR • LEO

LOCATIONS

THE BATHROOM
INDOORS

There's no line for the women's room, causing attendees to ask if that's part of the conspiracy.

THE HUGE BOARD
INDOORS

A giant conspiracy board where all the attendees have combined their theories into one mega-theory.

THE CHECK-IN STAND
INDOORS

Where you come up and introduce yourself and get your badge.

THE GREAT HALL
INDOORS

Currently, there's a presentation going on about how the Yeti is actually just a hairy dude.

WEAPONS

RED YARN
LIGHT-WEIGHT • MADE OF COTTON

Used to connect different parts of a conspiracy theory.

A BOOK OF DRAKONIAN CONSPIRACIES
MEDIUM-WEIGHT • MADE OF PAPER

Full of theories about the war between the Reds and Royals, and who is really behind them.

A COMMEMORATIVE COASTER
LIGHT-WEIGHT • MADE OF PAPER

No idea how this could be a weapon . . . and yet!

A BULLETPROOF VEST
MEDIUM-WEIGHT • MADE OF KEVLAR

It would be very ironic to be beaten to death by one of these.

FAVORITE CONSPIRACIES

 EVERYONE IS BEING MURDERED FOR A REASON

 ALIENS CONTROL THE WORLD

 SLEEP IS A SCAM

 TIME BEGAN LAST TUESDAY

CLUES & EVIDENCE

- The Crystal Goddess did not believe everyone was being murdered for a reason.

- Dr. Seashell, DDS, was seen studying the giant conspiracy board.

- The person with red yarn believed sleep is a scam—and they were very tired!

- The head of the Royal Resistance had a medium-weight weapon.

- A blue-eyed Leo brought a book of Drakonian conspiracies.

- The person who believed time began last Tuesday was not in the bathroom.

- The person who believed everyone was being murdered for a reason was in the great hall.

- General Coffee believed that time began last Tuesday, which excused most of his crimes.

- **A bulletproof vest was found beside the victim—ironic!**

SUSPECTS CONSPIRACIES LOCATIONS

WEAPONS

LOCATIONS

CONSPIRACIES

WHO?

WHAT?

WHERE?

AND?

74. BORDERING ON MADNESS & MURDER 🔍🔍🔍

Following President White's lead, Inspector Irratino traveled to the undisclosed location which turned out to be across the disputed Drakonian border. Irratino was terrified when his escort was killed. But still, he had to solve the murder. And you can tell a lot about a suspect from how they carry themselves in battle . . .

SUSPECTS

ADMIRAL NAVY

The firstborn son of an Admiral Navy who himself was the son of an Admiral Navy.

5'9" • RIGHT-HANDED • BLUE EYES • BROWN HAIR
• CANCER

GENERAL COFFEE

An espresso connoisseur, he always drinks his morning brew before sending his men across the battlefield to die. Is it for honor? Is it for glory? Is it for riches? Or is it for the love of the bean?

6'0" • RIGHT-HANDED • BROWN EYES • BALD •
SAGITTARIUS

SERGEANT GUNMETAL

A serious, hard-edged soldier who doesn't take "no" for an answer.

6'0" • RIGHT-HANDED • BROWN EYES • BLACK
HAIR • CAPRICORN

GOVERNOR LEAD

The most feared and least loved of the Free Drakonian governors.

6'2" • RIGHT-HANDED • BROWN EYES • BLACK
HAIR • VIRGO

LOCATIONS

THE FORTIFIED WALL
OUTDOORS

It gets bigger and less effective every year.

THE CANNONS
OUTDOORS

Pointed across the border to be fired in case of invasion (or by accident).

THE SECRET TUNNEL
INDOORS

For smuggling goods—and people—across the border.

THE GUARD POST
INDOORS

A great place to work. You can read all day.

WEAPONS

AN OLD SWORD
HEAVY-WEIGHT • MADE OF METAL

This was used by the bad guys in some old war. It's all rusted.

A BAZOOKA
HEAVY-WEIGHT • MADE OF METAL & EXPLOSIVES

A military classic. Currently manufactured by the Thiwe Corporation.

A SHOVEL
MEDIUM-WEIGHT • MADE OF METAL & WOOD

The great thing about using a shovel for murder is it can also dig a hole to help hide the body.

A CUP OF SCALDING COFFEE
LIGHT-WEIGHT • MADE OF CERAMIC, WATER, & BEANS

The hottest coffee you'll ever taste—and the last!

HOW THEY CARRIED THEMSELVES IN BATTLE

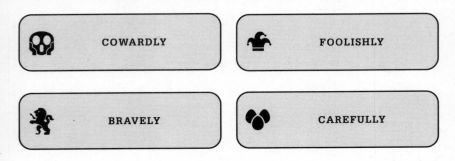

	COWARDLY		FOOLISHLY
	BRAVELY		CAREFULLY

CLUES & EVIDENCE

- A bazooka was found indoors.

- A radio broadcast contained important troop movements, but it was scrambled to avoid decryption: A NRIAPROCC SWA GNSNIATD NI HET RGUDA STOP.

- The person who carried themselves carefully would not climb the fortified wall. In fact, they wouldn't even get near it!

- Admiral Navy brought an old sword from battles long ago.

- The shortest suspect stood next to the fortified wall, but they couldn't see over it.

- The person with a cup of scalding coffee behaved cowardly, hiding behind their cup.

- Whoever carried themselves carefully was giving off real Sagittarius vibes.

- The person who behaved foolishly was hiding in the secret tunnel.

- **The body was found squeezed into a cannon.**

SUSPECTS   BATTLETUDE   LOCATIONS

WEAPONS

LOCATIONS

BATTLETUDE

WHO?

WHAT?

WHERE?

AND?

75. TRIUMPH AT THE WESTERN CITADEL 🔍🔍🔍

The Western Citadel had been the Holy Drakonian western outpost: it protected their great oil fields from advancing armies. Since the civil war, it had changed hands several times. Currently, it was in the hands of the Reds. Negotiations got off to a bad start, and they got worse when one of the ambassadors was murdered.

SUSPECTS

COSMONAUT BLUSKI

An ex-Soviet spaceman whose blood flows red. Sure, that's normal, but for him it's patriotic.

6'2" • LEFT-HANDED • BROWN EYES • BLACK HAIR • ARIES

SECRETARY CELADON

The secretary of defense, and someone who is personally responsible for a number of war crimes, some of which are now named after her.

5'6" • LEFT-HANDED • GREEN EYES • BROWN HAIR • LEO

PRESIDENT WHITE

The duly elected president of the Royal Resistance, a party of aristocrats who want to retake power. She dreams of yesterday.

5'10" • RIGHT-HANDED • GRAY EYES • WHITE HAIR • LEO

SERGEANT GUNMETAL

A serious, hard-edged soldier who doesn't take "no" for an answer.

6'0" • RIGHT-HANDED • BROWN EYES • BLACK HAIR • CAPRICORN

LOCATIONS

THE BARBED-WIRE FENCES
OUTDOORS

Sharp, jagged wires surround
the entire citadel.

THE SECURITY ROOM
INDOORS

Where the guards watch the
CCTV cameras of all the other
rooms.

THE IRON DOOR
OUTDOORS

The great iron door that keeps
the ruffians out of the tower.

THE GRAND HALL
INDOORS

A large conference table for
people to make bloody peace
treaties around.

WEAPONS

A FAKE TOOTH
LIGHT-WEIGHT • MADE OF ENAMEL & TOXINS

Filled with cyanide. The real
trick is getting it into someone
else's mouth.

A SHOVEL
MEDIUM-WEIGHT • MADE OF WOOD & METAL

You can dig holes for all sorts
of reasons if you're not afraid to
get dirty.

A HEAVY BOOT
HEAVY-WEIGHT • MADE OF RUBBER & STEEL

You could swing its steel toes
at someone. (Or, better yet,
kick them with it!)

THE BIG RED BOOK
MEDIUM-WEIGHT • MADE OF PAPER

Written by Major Red, it's filled
with his sayings, like "Some
leaders advocate nonviolence. I
advocate the opposite."

SECRET SOCIETY AFFILIATION

 THE SWORD OF
ST. LUPINE

 THE SECRET POLICE

 THE ORDER OF THE BAT

 THE WHITE GUARDS

CLUES & EVIDENCE

- No White Guards were in the grand hall.

- A blood stain on the copy of the Big Red Book was found to contain this DNA signature: GGCC. (See Exhibit C.)

- Cosmonaut Bluski wore a single heavy boot.

- Whoever was a member of the Secret Police was left-handed.

- Secretary Celadon had dirt all over her clothes.

- The person with a fake tooth belonged to the Sword of St. Lupine.

- A scrambled report came in from the telegram: OSONEME GUD A HEOL ODOROUTS.

- A white hair was found on the barbed-wire fence.

- The person who had joined the Order of the Bat was in the security room.

- **The ambassador's body was slumped against the iron door.**

SUSPECTS   SOCIETIES   LOCATIONS

WEAPONS

LOCATIONS

SOCIETIES

WHO?

WHAT?

WHERE?

AND?

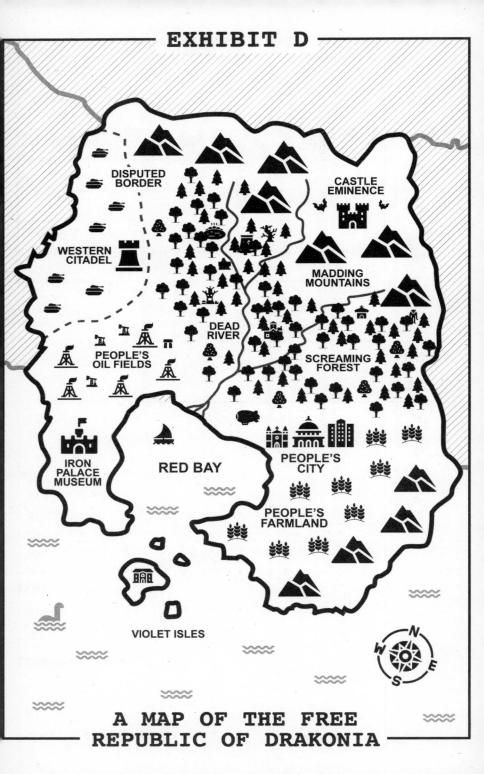

IMPOSSIBLE

Deductive Logico was freed from the Free Drakonians, while Inspector Irratino was handed into their grasp. Free Drakonia was already a spooky nation: it was filled with the terrifying Screaming Forest, the deadly Madding Mountains, and the poisoned Dead River. But what made it truly terrifying was its political situation.

Not so long ago, the Red Revolution had swept across the country, forcing the Iron Tsar from power and establishing a People's Dictatorship, which was really more of a Person's Dictatorship, since Major Red had consolidated every drop of power.

The Iron Tsar had been a terrible menace—brutally repressing any criticism, impoverishing the people, and hanging all heretics to the St. Lupinian faith—but the People's Dictatorship was not much better.

The Reds repressed their critics more than the Tsar had. The civil war impoverished the country even worse than before. And although they had stopped hanging people, they had started chopping off their heads.

All of this made solving murders even more difficult. In these twenty-five mysteries, you have to figure out not only who, what, and where each murder was committed, but why, too. **Everybody has a possible motive, but only one of them is guilty.**

If these mysteries are still too easy for you, then take the Detective Club Challenge: Study the politics of Free Drakonia, and discover the true nature of the latest Drakonian terror: the Gray Walkers. Who are they, and where do they come from?

76. MURDER IN FREE DRAKONIA 🔍🔍🔍🔍

A decade after the brutal civil war, the newly renamed Free Republic of Drakonia was still struggling for peace. Just last month there was a much-publicized murder, which was all over the papers. Can you discover whodunit—and why?

SUSPECTS

PRESIDENT WHITE

The duly elected president of the Royal Resistance, a party of aristocrats who want to retake power. She dreams of yesterday.

5'10" • RIGHT-HANDED • GRAY EYES • WHITE HAIR • LEO

MAJOR RED

The revolutionary leader who freed Drakonia from the grasp of the Tsar and then immediately grasped it himself.

6'2" • LEFT-HANDED • BROWN EYES • BROWN HAIR • ARIES

RADICAL CRIMSON

She thinks the Free Drakonians are too right-wing. She has discovered a new (and even redder) shade of red.

5'7" • LEFT-HANDED • GREEN EYES • RED HAIR • LIBRA

PATRIARCH PORPOISE

The Holy Drakonian patriarch, the one true leader of all St. Lupinian Orthodox believers, and he won't let you forget it.

5'4" • RIGHT-HANDED • BLACK EYES • BLACK HAIR • CANCER

LOCATIONS

CASTLE EMINENCE
INDOORS

Nobody visits the castle of Viscount Eminence if they want to stay alive!

THE IRON PALACE
INDOORS

The iron fortress of the Iron Tsar. It once struck fear in the hearts of all. Now, it's a museum.

THE SCREAMING FOREST
OUTDOORS

The famous wild woods of Drakonia. What horrors lurk inside?

THE PEOPLE'S CITY
OUTDOORS

It used to be called St. Lupine. Now, it's the People's City. But it's still run from the Capitol.

WEAPONS

IVORY NIGHT-EATER FANGS
MEDIUM-WEIGHT • MADE OF SOME POOR ELEPHANT

Ancient Drakonians would wear these to terrify their enemies. Now they're mass-produced.

AN ENORMOUS PAINTING
HEAVY-WEIGHT • MADE OF WOOD & CANVAS

It's a painting of the Iron Tsar, the former ruler of Drakonia. He's wearing his helmet in the painting, too.

AN ANCIENT SWORD
HEAVY-WEIGHT • MADE OF METAL

With this sword (according to legend), Klaus Drakulia subjugated all of Drakonia to his will.

A RED BANANA
LIGHT-WEIGHT • MADE OF EXPLOSIVES

Another name for the sticks of dynamite the Reds used in the Royal Revolution.

MOTIVES

 TO FREE THE PEOPLE

 TO SEIZE THEIR LAND

 TO RULE A COUNTRY

 TO RESTORE THE ARISTOCRACY

CLUES & EVIDENCE

- The person who wanted to free the people was reportedly living in the People's City.

- Major Red was in the southernmost location. (See Exhibit D.)

- The newspaper typesetting on one line was scrambled: A BIRAL RDIAERC THE RDE NAAANB.

- The newspaper article was illustrated with a picture of President White indoors.

- The leader of all St. Lupinian Orthodox believers wanted to seize the land back from the government.

- According to the newspaper's analysts, whoever carried the painting was right-handed.

- An unsettling story described a set of ivory night-eater fangs discovered in the Screaming Forest.

STATEMENTS

(Remember: The murderer is lying. The others are telling the truth.)

President White: I swear under oath I did not bring a Red banana.
Major Red: Radical Crimson did not bring an enormous painting.
Radical Crimson: President White wants to rule the country!
Patriarch Porpoise: I was in the Screaming Forest.

SUSPECTS MOTIVES LOCATIONS

WEAPONS

LOCATIONS

MOTIVES

WHO?

WHAT?

WHERE?

WHY?

77. THE SECRET HIDEOUT MURDER 🔍🔍🔍🔍

Deductive Logico was being held—excuse me, "kept safe"—in a mansion in the woods. This mansion served as the secret headquarters for the Royal Resistance, who wanted to take back their country. Unfortunately for them, one of them had their life taken instead! "Look," another said, "the deductive's already coming in handy."

SUSPECTS

BARON MAROON

An incredibly haughty man who famously holds a grudge. Nobody wants to offend the baron. At least, nobody who's still alive . . .

6'2" • RIGHT-HANDED • HAZEL EYES • RED HAIR • SCORPIO

THE DUCHESS OF VERMILLION

A tall, old woman with tall, old secrets. If she is the murderer, then it certainly wouldn't be the first time.

5'9" • LEFT-HANDED • GRAY EYES • WHITE HAIR • PISCES

LADY VIOLET

The heiress of the Violet Isles, the largest extrajudicial territory in the world.

5'0" • RIGHT-HANDED • BLUE EYES • BLOND HAIR • VIRGO

PRESIDENT WHITE

The duly elected president of the Royal Resistance, a party of aristocrats who want to retake power. She dreams of yesterday.

5'10" • RIGHT-HANDED • GRAY EYES • WHITE HAIR • LEO

LOCATIONS

THE GREAT MANSION
INDOORS

The grandest, oldest, and most dignified mansion you've ever seen, if you haven't seen the Violet Manor.

THE GETAWAY LIMO
INDOORS

They keep it gassed up and ready to go. (Also, fully stocked with alcohol.)

THE DEFENSIVE FORTIFICATIONS
OUTDOORS

Giant stone rocks that look like sharp teeth pointed outward.

THE SCREAMING FOREST
OUTDOORS

In these woods you can hear the screams of everyone you've ever wronged.

WEAPONS

A CHESS BOARD
HEAVY-WEIGHT • MADE OF MARBLE

The only way to play the game of kings. (Unless you can play in your head. Or your phone.)

A CHAMPAGNE FLUTE
LIGHT-WEIGHT • MADE OF GLASS & POISON

Break it and stab someone with it, or just fill it with poisoned champagne.

THE BOOK OF ST. LUPINE
HEAVY-WEIGHT • MADE OF LEATHER & PAPER

It features the wise sayings of St. Lupine, such as "The purpose of life is to die, so good news."

A MAJESTIC CAPE
MEDIUM-WEIGHT • MADE OF SILK

The Iron Tsar used to wear this—when he had a neck he could wear it on.

MOTIVES

 TO PUNISH A TRAITOR

 TO PROMOTE THE OCCULT

 TO FIGHT FOR LOVE

 FOR MONEY

CLUES & EVIDENCE

- The person who wanted to fight for love was in the Screaming Forest.

- Baron Maroon was seen struggling to carry a heavy-weight weapon.

- The person playing the game of kings would kill to punish a traitor.

- The duly elected president of the Royal Resistance was managing the affairs of the Resistance indoors.

- The Duchess of Vermillion did not want money: she had plenty.

- Whoever had the Book of St. Lupine was reading it left-handed.

- A secret message came in, written in the Next Letter Code: SGD ODQRNM VHSG Z LZIDRSHB BZOD CHC MNS VZMS SN OQNLNSD SGD NBBTKS.

STATEMENTS

(Remember: The murderer is lying. The others are telling the truth.)

Baron Maroon: Bah! Here's the truth: the Duchess of Vermillion was in the getaway limo.

The Duchess of Vermillion: President White was not in the getaway limo.

Lady Violet: Whoever had a motive to kill for money was in the getaway limo.

President White: Enough limo talk: the Duchess of Vermillion was in the Screaming Forest.

SUSPECTS   MOTIVES   LOCATIONS

WEAPONS

LOCATIONS

MOTIVES

WHO?

WHAT?

WHERE?

WHY?

78. THE DEATH OF ST. LUPINE 🔍🔍🔍🔍

Everyone knows St. Lupine—the great healer who recruited those three sick orphans, and with their help, built the foundations of the St. Lupinian Cathedral. But just as important as the story of his life is the story of his murder by bandits.

SUSPECTS

BANDIT BLUE

One of the bandits. Definitely the strong and silent type.

5'0" • RIGHT-HANDED • HAZEL EYES • BROWN HAIR • ARIES

BANDIT BLACK

The smart one of the bandits.

4'10" • RIGHT-HANDED • BLUE EYES • BROWN HAIR • GEMINI

BANDIT BROWN

The creative bandit: always dreaming up new schemes.

4'11" • LEFT-HANDED • GREEN EYES • BLOND HAIR • PISCES

VILLAGER WHITE

A villager who just happened to be passing by.

5'10" • RIGHT-HANDED • BROWN EYES • BROWN HAIR • SAGITTARIUS

LOCATIONS

A TORTURED TREE
OUTDOORS

A tree twisted into a very peculiar and punishing shape.

THE STONE FOUNDATION
OUTDOORS

Legend has it that these stones were the foundation of the Great St. Lupinian Cathedral.

THE FENCE
OUTDOORS

A wooden fence that surrounded the old chapel.

A SMALL WOODEN HUT
OUTDOORS

Incredibly small and modest lodgings. St. Lupine was a true ascetic.

WEAPONS

A VAMPIRE BAT
MEDIUM-WEIGHT • MADE OF BAT PARTS

Not an actual vampire (or "night-eater," as the Drakonians call them). But it does have rabies.

A SACRED ROCK
HEAVY-WEIGHT • MADE OF A STRANGE SUBSTANCE

This rock was once held by St. Lupine himself. They say when he held it, it glowed.

A WOODEN STAKE
MEDIUM-WEIGHT • MADE OF WOOD

For killing night-eaters, and people, too. But watch out for splinters.

A POISONED GOBLET
HEAVY-WEIGHT • MADE OF METAL & TOXINS

It contains one of the greatest poisons known to mankind: alcohol.

MOTIVES

 TO FREE THE PEOPLE

 TO STOP THE SAINT'S WORK

 BECAUSE OF RADIATION POISONING

 TO KILL A MONSTER

CLUES & EVIDENCE

- The person who wanted to free the people was in a small wooden hut.

- Over time, historical facts were scrambled, including this one: A ESNDIPOO OGEBTL AWS EDCODEVISR YB A FEENC.

- Bandit Blue hated the person who brought a wooden stake.

- The suspect with the sacred rock also had brown hair.

- The person with a vampire bat desperately wanted to stop the saint's work.

- The creative bandit had a heavy-weight weapon.

STATEMENTS

(Remember: The murderer is lying. The others are telling the truth.)

Bandit Blue: A vampire bat was not in the stone foundation.

Bandit Black: By God Himself, whoever wanted to kill a monster was by the tortured tree.

Bandit Brown: On my honor, Bandit Black was by a tortured tree.

Villager White: If I killed, I'd only do it because of radiation poisoning.

SUSPECTS   MOTIVES   LOCATIONS

WEAPONS

LOCATIONS

MOTIVES

WHO?

WHAT?

WHERE?

WHY?

79. LOCKED UP IN THE FREE JAIL 🔍🔍🔍🔍

Meanwhile, Inspector Irratino was being held in the Free Jail in the People's City. The Reds wanted to interrogate him for information about the Royal Resistance, but first, they needed his help to solve a murder: a guard had been killed.

SUSPECTS

COSMONAUT BLUSKI

An ex-Soviet spaceman whose blood flows red. Sure, that's normal, but for him it's patriotic.

6'2" • LEFT-HANDED • BROWN EYES • BLACK HAIR • ARIES

COMRADE CHAMPAGNE

A communist and a rich one. Comrade Champagne likes nothing more than to travel the world, sharing the message of communism with his fellow vacationers.

5'11" • LEFT-HANDED • HAZEL EYES • BLOND HAIR • CAPRICORN

GOVERNOR LEAD

The most feared and least loved of the Free Drakonian governors.

6'2" • RIGHT-HANDED • BROWN EYES • BLACK HAIR • VIRGO

OFFICER COPPER

The best part of being a policewoman criminal is that you can cut out the middleman and fail to investigate your own crimes.

5'5" • RIGHT-HANDED • BLUE EYES • BLOND HAIR • ARIES

LOCATIONS

THE INTERROGATION ROOM
INDOORS

Two uncomfortable chairs and a table are reflected by the wall-sized mirror.

THE HOLDING CELL
INDOORS

Where the political protestors are held (aka imprisoned) until trial (aka execution).

THE "EMERGENCY EXIT"
OUTDOORS

A euphemism for the 25th-floor window. Where they throw people when they need to get rid of them quickly.

THE OBSERVATION ROOM
INDOORS

One the other side of the two-way mirror, you can watch people being interrogated from a plush sofa.

WEAPONS

THE BAYONET
MEDIUM-WEIGHT • MADE OF METAL

The bayonets these days are produced by International Weapons, known as "the IW."

AN ANTIQUE TYPEWRITER
HEAVY-WEIGHT • MADE OF METAL

You can write with subtlety, or you can hit them over the head with it.

THE BIG RED BOOK
MEDIUM-WEIGHT • MADE OF PAPER

Another great line: "The entire world stands against us. Good. I love a fair fight."

A HAMMER AND SICKLE
HEAVY-WEIGHT • MADE OF METAL

When one weapon won't do, you can use these two!

MOTIVES

 TO FEED THEIR FAMILY

 FOR THE GOVERNMENT

TO ROB A GRAVE

DAD TO AVENGE THEIR FATHER

CLUES & EVIDENCE

- The person with the Big Red Book wanted to kill for the government.

- The person who wanted to feed their family was not in the interrogation room.

- A Virgo was sitting on a plush sofa.

- Two-weapons-in-one were wielded by a left-handed suspect.

- The person who wanted to rob a grave was in the holding cell.

- A prisoner passed Logico a scrambled message: HTE CNEOSD RT-SHEOTS TCEUSSP GUHTORB AN NQEATUI YRTPEIWETR.

- Cosmonaut Bluski preferred the outdoors: it reminded him of space.

STATEMENTS

(Remember: The murderer is lying. The others are telling the truth.)

Cosmonaut Bluski: An antique typewriter was not in the interrogation room.

Comrade Champagne: I was not in the interrogation room.

Governor Lead: On the honor of the Free Drakonians, Officer Copper brought the Big Red Book.

Officer Copper: The Big Red Book was not in the holding cell.

SUSPECTS   MOTIVES   LOCATIONS

WEAPONS

LOCATIONS

MOTIVES

_____ WHO?

_____ WHAT?

_____ WHERE?

_____ WHY?

80. THE TRIUMPH OF THE REVOLUTION 🔍🔍🔍🔍

Governor Lead explained that the civil war had raged for so long that people thought it would never end. But gradually, the Reds conquered almost all of Drakonia, until they had cornered the Iron Tsar in his last remaining hideout: the fortress known as the Iron Palace.

SUSPECTS

RADICAL CRIMSON

She thinks the Free Drakonians are too right-wing. She thinks the Tsar is getting off easy.

5'7" • LEFT-HANDED • GREEN EYES • RED HAIR • LIBRA

TINY TAUPE

He's actually really huge, which is why people call him Tiny.

6'3" • LEFT-HANDED • BLUE EYES • BLOND HAIR • TAURUS

MAJOR RED

The revolutionary leader who freed Drakonia from the grasp of the Tsar and then immediately grasped it himself.

6'2" • LEFT-HANDED • BROWN EYES • BROWN HAIR • ARIES

PATRIARCH PORPOISE

The Holy Drakonian patriarch, the one true leader of all St. Lupinian Orthodox believers, and he won't let you forget it.

5'4" • RIGHT-HANDED • BLACK EYES • BLACK HAIR • CANCER

LOCATIONS

THE GREAT THRONE ROOM
INDOORS

The Iron Tsar sits upon a throne of skulls. (And a soft pillow, technically.)

THE GLORIOUS CHAPEL
INDOORS

It is covered in gold, stolen from the peasants. (Why would a peasant need gold?)

THE GRAVEYARD
OUTDOORS

Filled with the bodies of his enemies, buried upside down.

THE GREAT IRON DOOR
OUTDOORS

Imagine the biggest door you can possibly imagine. It's bigger.

WEAPONS

A RED BANANA
LIGHT-WEIGHT • MADE OF EXPLOSIVES

Another name for the sticks of dynamite the Reds used in the Royal Revolution.

A BAZOOKA
HEAVY-WEIGHT • MADE OF METAL, TECH, & EXPLOSIVES

The signature weapon of the Red Revolution: AKA the People's Cannon.

AN IRON HELMET
HEAVY-WEIGHT • MADE OF IRON & JEWELS

The Iron Tsar used to wear this, when he still had a head to wear it on.

AN ANTIQUE FLINTLOCK
MEDIUM-WEIGHT • MADE OF METAL & WOOD

The gun that fired the silver bullet that started the Drakonian Civil War.

MOTIVES

 THEY WERE ORDERED TO

 TO TAKE OVER DRAKONIA

 FOR THE REVOLUTION

 FOR THE GLORY OF ST. LUPINE

CLUES & EVIDENCE

- The history of the Revolution was often scrambled by time: TYIN PETAU DHA BNEE ERDORED TO LLIK.

- An iron helmet was discovered with a body facing away from it.

- The suspect who wanted to take over Drakonia was seen outdoors.

- The person who wanted the glory of St. Lupine was not near a throne of skulls.

- The person with a "People's Cannon" would kill for the revolution.

- A Red banana was discovered in a room of gold.

- The Libra stood before the great iron door, gazing at its immensity.

STATEMENTS

(Remember: The murderer is lying. The others are telling the truth.)

Radical Crimson: I did not bring an antique flintlock.

Tiny Taupe: I know this with every inch of me: Major Red wanted to take over Drakonia.

Major Red: Whoever had the iron helmet wanted glory for St. Lupine.

Patriarch Porpoise: Radical Crimson was not in the glorious chapel.

SUSPECTS   MOTIVES   LOCATIONS

WEAPONS

LOCATIONS

MOTIVES

WHO?

WHAT?

WHERE?

WHY?

81. MURDER IN THE PEOPLE'S CITY 🔍🔍🔍🔍

Logico argued that if the Royal Resistance got positive press for freeing him from the Reds, they'd get even more positive press for freeing him from themselves. Unable to resist such sound logic, the Royal Resistance set him free, and he hurried to the People's City to rescue Irratino. But first, he had to solve the murder of a newsie.

SUSPECTS

GOVERNOR LEAD

The most feared and least loved of the Free Drakonian governors.

6'2" • RIGHT-HANDED • BROWN EYES • BLACK HAIR • VIRGO

PRESIDENT WHITE

The duly elected president of the Royal Resistance, a party of aristocrats who want to retake power. She dreams of yesterday.

5'10" • RIGHT-HANDED • GRAY EYES • WHITE HAIR • LEO

MAJOR RED

The revolutionary leader who freed Drakonia from the grasp of the Tsar and then immediately grasped it himself.

6'2" • LEFT-HANDED • BROWN EYES • BROWN HAIR • ARIES

COMRADE CHAMPAGNE

A communist and a rich one. Comrade Champagne likes nothing more than to travel the world, sharing the message of communism with his fellow vacationers.

5'11" • LEFT-HANDED • HAZEL EYES • BLOND HAIR • CAPRICORN

LOCATIONS

THE RED BAY
OUTDOORS

Formerly the Bay of St. Lupine, this is where most of the Drakonian shipping goes through.

THE BRUTALIST HOUSING
INDOORS

Immediately, the Reds built this brutalist structure. It poorly houses the poor!

THE COMMUNITY CATHEDRAL
INDOORS

Formerly the Grand Cathedral of St. Lupine, this is now a community center and bingo hall.

THE CAPITOL BUILDING
INDOORS

Formerly the seat of the Iron Tsar's bureaucracy, now the People's House.

WEAPONS

A CHESS BOARD
HEAVY-WEIGHT • MADE OF MARBLE

Made of marble and heavier than God.

A BRAIN IN A JAR
HEAVY-WEIGHT • MADE OF METAL, GLASS, & BRAINS

Philosophers argue you might be a brain in a jar. A great rebuttal is to hit them with one.

THE BIG RED BOOK
MEDIUM-WEIGHT • MADE OF PAPER

Another of Major Red's sayings: "You do not need to die for the Revolution—you need to kill for it."

AN ANTIQUE FLINTLOCK
MEDIUM-WEIGHT • MADE OF METAL & WOOD

The gun that fired the silver bullet that started the Drakonian Civil War.

MOTIVES

TO BECOME A LEGEND

BECAUSE OF RADIA-
TION POISONING

TO MANIPULATE A
GOVERNMENT

FOR THE REVOLUTION

CLUES & EVIDENCE

- The suspect who wanted to become a legend was seen indoors.

- The Big Red Book was not found in the Community Cathedral.

- The newspaper typesetting was scrambled, so one line read: AJMRO RDE TDEWAN TO MNTPAAELUI A MRVETONGEN.

- Whoever wanted to kill for the revolution had hazel eyes.

- Governor Lead would kill because of radiation poisoning.

- A brain in a jar was discovered in the former seat of the Iron Tsar's bureaucracy.

- Forensics determined a weapon made at least partially out of metal was in the Red Bay.

STATEMENTS

(Remember: The murderer is lying. The others are telling the truth.)

Governor Lead: By the glory of Free Drakonia, Major Red brought the Big Red Book!

President White: Governor Lead brought a brain in a jar.

Major Red: An antique flintlock was not in the Community Cathedral.

Comrade Champagne: I say that Governor Lead was in the brutalist housing.

SUSPECTS   MOTIVES   LOCATIONS

WEAPONS

LOCATIONS

MOTIVES

_____ **WHO?**

_____ **WHAT?**

_____ **WHERE?**

_____ **WHY?**

82. A BRUTAL MURDER IN BRUTALIST HOUSING 🔍🔍🔍🔍

Deductive Logico slept that night in the brutalist housing. It had been constructed to fight the housing crisis, but now it *was* the housing crisis. The building was falling apart. The place was a fire hazard. And a resident had just been killed.

SUSPECTS

GRAY WALKER

They shamble about lifelessly, with empty, hollow eyes. You feel cold around them.

5'8" • LEFT-HANDED • BLUE EYES • BROWN HAIR • SAGITTARIUS

TINY TAUPE

He's actually really huge, which is why people call him Tiny.

6'3" • LEFT-HANDED • BLUE EYES • BLOND HAIR • TAURUS

RADICAL CRIMSON

She thinks the Free Drakonians are too right-wing. She thinks anarchy is too controlling.

5'7" • LEFT-HANDED • GREEN EYES • RED HAIR • LIBRA

COSMONAUT BLUSKI

An ex-Soviet spaceman whose blood flows red. Sure, that's normal, but for him it's patriotic.

6'2" • LEFT-HANDED • BROWN EYES • BLACK HAIR • ARIES

LOCATIONS

ROOM 207
INDOORS

All of the rooms are the same.

ROOM 103
INDOORS

All of the rooms are the same.

ROOM 239
INDOORS

All of the rooms are the same.

ROOM 324
INDOORS

All of the rooms are the same. But this one has a poster of Silverton the Legend on the wall.

WEAPONS

A BOTTLE OF CHAMPAGNE
MEDIUM-WEIGHT • MADE OF GLASS & TOXINS

To drink to the success of the revolution. Or just to drink.

A CIGARETTE
LIGHT-WEIGHT • MADE OF TOBACCO

Each one marginally increases your chances of dying early.

BROCCOLI
LIGHT-WEIGHT • MADE OF VEGETABLE

This is green and good for you, like money. It's also the perfect size for choking.

THE BIG RED BOOK
MEDIUM-WEIGHT • MADE OF PAPER

It's filled with the sayings of Major Red, such as "You don't get a museum if you lose."

MOTIVES

 IN A JEALOUS RAGE

 FOR THE REVOLUTION

 TO WIN A SEAT IN PARLIAMENT

 TO AVOID BEING SENT TO THE FRONT

CLUES & EVIDENCE

- A maid wrote a report of the contents of one of the rooms, and her penmanship was horrible: A TLTOEB FO CGPEAMNHA SWA NDOFU NI OMOR 720.

- The Gray Walker did not carry any vegetables. What do these things even eat?

- The second tallest suspect had not been in Room 324.

- When people smoke cigarettes, they want to kill in a jealous rage. That's a fact.

- Everyone with a room number smaller than 220 had a medium-weight weapon.

- Whoever wanted to win a seat in Parliament had a significant figure associated with leadership. (See Exhibit B.)

- The person who wanted to avoid being sent to the front was in a room whose digits add up to 14.

- The person with the Big Red Book wanted to kill for the revolution: it had that effect on a lot of people.

STATEMENTS

(Remember: The murderer is lying. The others are telling the truth.)

Gray Walker: Arrrr—Tiny Taupe not in 103.

Tiny Taupe: Whoever wanted to avoid being sent to the front was in Room 239.

Radical Crimson: Tiny Taupe did not bring the Big Red Book.

Cosmonaut Bluski: The Gray Walker had a cigarette.

SUSPECTS   MOTIVES   LOCATIONS

WEAPONS

LOCATIONS

MOTIVES

_____
WHO?

_____
WHAT?

_____
WHERE?

_____
WHY?

83. MURDER AT THE GUILLOTINE 🔍🔍🔍🔍

Logico raced to the public guillotines in the middle of the People's City. But when he got there, he found people lamenting that there had been a murder. "Oh no!" he wailed. "I'm too late!" But it turns out they didn't mean Inspector Irratino: the executioner had been, ironically, executed.

SUSPECTS

SUPERFAN SMOKY

He knows the shooting locations of every Midnight mystery, but not how to make friends.

5'10" • LEFT-HANDED • BLACK EYES • BROWN HAIR • VIRGO

JUDGE PINE

Master of the courtroom and possessed of a firm belief in justice, as decided by her and her alone.

5'6" • RIGHT-HANDED • BROWN EYES • BLACK HAIR • TAURUS

TINY TAUPE

He's actually really huge, which is why people call him Tiny.

6'3" • LEFT-HANDED • BLUE EYES • BLOND HAIR • TAURUS

RADICAL CRIMSON

She thinks the Free Drakonians are too right-wing. You've heard of two left feet? She has two left hands.

5'7" • LEFT-HANDED • GREEN EYES • RED HAIR • LIBRA

LOCATIONS

THE PLATFORM
OUTDOORS

Where the revolution enacts revolutionary justice.

THE VIEWING AREA
OUTDOORS

Where the people come to witness the justice.

THE OVERLOOK
OUTDOORS

Where you can watch the people watch the justice.

THE GUARD TOWER
INDOORS

Where the guards watch the people watching the people watch the justice.

WEAPONS

A GARLAND OF GARLIC
MEDIUM-WEIGHT • MADE OF VEGETABLE

Keeps night-eaters away from your home and, if wrapped around your neck, blood from your brain.

A STUN GUN
LIGHT-WEIGHT • MADE OF METAL

Advertised as "less than lethal," but anything's lethal if you use it right.

A COMMEMORATIVE COASTER
LIGHT-WEIGHT • MADE OF PAPER

No idea how this could be a weapon . . . and yet!

A HAMMER AND SICKLE
HEAVY-WEIGHT • MADE OF METAL

When one weapon won't do, you can use these two!

MOTIVES

 TO CAST AN EVIL SPELL

 TO LIVE FOREVER

 TO RULE A COUNTRY

 TO STOP THE KILLINGS

CLUES & EVIDENCE

- The person with a garland of garlic did not want to cast an evil spell.

- The person who wanted to live forever was on the platform.

- The person with a paper weapon wanted to stop the killings.

- The second shortest suspect had a hammer and sickle.

- The person who wanted to rule a country was not in the viewing area.

- Black eyes stared out from the guard tower.

- Whoever was in the overlook thought the Free Drakonians were too right-wing.

- Judge Pine was seen nervously clutching a stun gun.

STATEMENTS

(Remember: The murderer is lying. The others are telling the truth.)

Superfan Smoky: Oh, wow! Judge Pine was on the platform.

Judge Pine: A hammer and sickle were not on the platform.

Tiny Taupe: As a big dude, lemme tell you: a commemorative coaster was in the guard tower.

Radical Crimson: As a real revolutionary, whoever wanted to stop the killings was in the viewing area.

SUSPECTS   MOTIVES   LOCATIONS

WEAPONS

LOCATIONS

MOTIVES

WHO?

WHAT?

WHERE?

WHY?

84. VIOLENT MURDER ON THE VIOLET FARM 🔍🔍🔍🔍

According to the papers, the Violet Isles had been turned into the Violet Work Farms, where captured aristocrats were expected to work for their freedom. One of them might have killed for it instead: a Free Drakonian guard was dead!

SUSPECTS

SISTER LAPIS

A nun who used to travel the world, doing God's work on His dime. Her habit is cashmere, and her habit is spending.

5'2" • RIGHT-HANDED • BROWN EYES • BROWN HAIR • CANCER

THE DUCHESS OF VERMILLION

A tall, old woman with tall, old secrets. If she is the murderer, then it certainly wouldn't be the first time.

5'9" • LEFT-HANDED • GRAY EYES • WHITE HAIR • PISCES

SIGNOR EMERALD

Once a jeweler of great renown, Signor Emerald has traveled the world in search of rare, precious stones, but now they've all been confiscated.

5'8" • LEFT-HANDED • BROWN EYES • BLACK HAIR • SAGITTARIUS

GRAY WALKER

They seem bloodless. Not only metaphorically, but also in that they have less blood.

5'2" • LEFT-HANDED • HAZEL EYES • BLOND HAIR • LIBRA

LOCATIONS

THE FARM
OUTDOORS

The garden maze has been razed and replaced by this collective farm.

THE DOCKS
OUTDOORS

Heavily guarded and patrolled by the Red Security.

THE MANSION
INDOORS

It now houses the ostensibly free farmers.

THE CLIFFS
OUTDOORS

This keeps the farmers from leaving—alive, at least.

WEAPONS

A CHAINSAW
HEAVY-WEIGHT • MADE OF METAL & PLASTIC

Rarely seen in whodunits (because of the mess).

AN OTTOMAN
MEDIUM-WEIGHT • MADE OF WOOD & FABRIC

Once, they ruled the world. Now, synonymous with footstools.

A BEARSKIN RUG
HEAVY-WEIGHT • MADE OF A BEAR

Almost certainly haunted by the ghost of the bear.

AN ANGRY MOOSE
HEAVY-WEIGHT • MADE OF MOOSE

Not just angry: furious.

MOTIVES

 BECAUSE THEY HAVE A RAGE PROBLEM

 TO ESCAPE

 OUT OF TOTAL FEAR

 TO TERRIFY THE POPULACE

CLUES & EVIDENCE

- Whoever would kill because they have a rage problem had a medium-weight weapon.

- The Duchess of Vermillion was well known for her support of counter-revolutionary terror: she wanted to terrify the populace.

- A scrambled message was intercepted by the Reds: HET OREPNS THWI A RABNSKEI UGR NWTDAE OT SECAEP.

- The suspect in the mansion had blond hair.

- A Libra had the bearskin rug. It's beautiful and great for snuggling.

- An angry moose stalked the cliffs.

- A former jeweler was wandering where the garden maze used to be.

STATEMENTS

(Remember: The murderer is lying. The others are telling the truth.)

Sister Lapis: My dears, the Duchess did not have an ottoman.

The Duchess of Vermillion: If you ask me, whoever had the chainsaw would kill out of total fear.

Signor Emerald: Strangely, Sister Lapis did not want to escape.

Gray Walker: Ugghhh, ottoman not on cliffs.

SUSPECTS   MOTIVES   LOCATIONS

WEAPONS

LOCATIONS

MOTIVES

_____

WHO?

_____

WHAT?

_____

WHERE?

_____

WHY?

85. CAPITOL CRIMES 🔍🔍🔍🔍

Suddenly, Inspector Irratino and Deductive Logico were apprehended by Red Guards and taken to the Capitol. It was the same building that had been used by the powerless Parliament under the Holy Drakonian Government of the Tsar. But things had changed under the Reds. For example, someone was recently murdered in the building.

SUSPECTS

MAJOR RED

The revolutionary leader who freed Drakonia from the grasp of the Tsar and then immediately grasped it himself.

6'2" • LEFT-HANDED • BROWN EYES • BROWN HAIR • ARIES

TINY TAUPE

He managed to escape that mob by taking refuge in the Capitol, where he'll be tried for his crimes against the mob.

6'3" • LEFT-HANDED • BLUE EYES • BLOND HAIR • TAURUS

MANSERVANT BROWNSTONE

Manservant Brownstone's brother is devoted to God, but he is devoted to the Violets.

6'2" • RIGHT-HANDED • BROWN EYES • BROWN HAIR • CANCER

ADMIRAL NAVY

The firstborn son of an Admiral Navy who himself was the son of an Admiral Navy.

5'9" • RIGHT-HANDED • BLUE EYES • BROWN HAIR • CANCER

LOCATIONS

THE WAITING ROOM
INDOORS

The higher your class, the longer you wait. A reverse of the Tsar's system.

MAJOR RED'S PRIVATE OFFICE
INDOORS

Major Red runs the country—and directs the show trials—from the comfort of his air-conditioned office.

THE SECRETARY'S OFFICE
INDOORS

In a way, the true power center of the government. Anything Major Red signs goes through here.

THE SCREENING ROOM
INDOORS

This used to be where Parliament met. Now, it's where Major Red screens Midnight mysteries.

WEAPONS

AN ANTIQUE FLINTLOCK
MEDIUM-WEIGHT • MADE OF METAL & WOOD

The gun that fired the silver bullet that started the Drakonian Civil War.

THE BIG RED BOOK
MEDIUM-WEIGHT • MADE OF PAPER

Another quote: "Either I will kill the Tsar, or the Tsar will kill me, or someone else will, or we'll die from natural causes."

AN IRON HELMET
HEAVY-WEIGHT • MADE OF IRON & JEWELS

The Iron Tsar was never seen without his helmet, so no one ever saw his face.

A CHEAP PEN
LIGHT-WEIGHT • MADE OF PLASTIC

Getting killed by an expensive pen is bad enough . . .

MOTIVES

 TO SILENCE A WITNESS

 TO RESTORE THE ARISTOCRACY

 TO REDISTRIBUTE THEIR WEALTH

 TO ESCAPE BLACKMAIL

CLUES & EVIDENCE

- The tallest suspect had never been in the waiting room.

- They had to stop a screening of a Midnight mystery when someone found an antique flintlock under their seat.

- The person with a cheap pen wanted to silence a witness.

- An iron helmet was discovered in an air-conditioned office.

- Whoever wanted to redistribute their wealth had blue eyes.

- A secret Red report was written in the Next Letter Code: ZCLHQZK MZUX VZMSDC SN DRBZOD AKZBJLZHK.

- Manservant Brownstone carried a medium-weight weapon.

STATEMENTS

(Remember: The murderer is lying. The others are telling the truth.)

Major Red: Admiral Navy did not bring the Big Red Book.

Tiny Taupe: Admiral Navy was not in the waiting room.

Manservant Brownstone: The person with the Big Red Book wanted to escape blackmail.

Admiral Navy: Tiny Taupe brought the Big Red Book.

SUSPECTS   MOTIVES   LOCATIONS

WEAPONS

LOCATIONS

MOTIVES

_____ WHO?

_____ WHAT?

_____ WHERE?

_____ WHY?

86. A PRESIDENTIAL MURDER 🔍🔍🔍🔍

After solving that capital crime in the Capitol, Deductive Logico and Inspector Irratino were summoned to meet with Major Red. It was a dangerous offer to accept, but an even more dangerous offer to refuse. The danger was underscored by the fact that the last person to meet with him in this office had been murdered—apparently just moments before.

SUSPECTS

GENERAL COFFEE

An espresso connoisseur, he always drinks his morning brew before sending his men across the battlefield to die. Is it for honor? Glory? Riches? Or is it for the love of the bean?

6'0" • RIGHT-HANDED • BROWN EYES • BALD • SAGITTARIUS

DR. CRIMSON

She believes that everyone—no matter their race or creed—deserves the right to medical care, as long as they can afford it.

5'9" • LEFT-HANDED • GREEN EYES • RED HAIR • AQUARIUS

HACK BLAXTON

He's one of the best paid writers in Hollywood, and one of the worst.

6'0" • RIGHT-HANDED • BROWN EYES • BALD • SAGITTARIUS

MAJOR RED

The revolutionary leader who freed Drakonia from the grasp of the Tsar and then immediately grasped it himself.

6'2" • LEFT-HANDED • BROWN EYES • BROWN HAIR • ARIES

LOCATIONS

A SECRET PASSAGE
INDOORS

Exactly where this is or how it works won't be printed here because neither of us wants to die.

A PAINTING OF MAJOR RED
INDOORS

He looks way better in the painting than in real life, but don't tell him that (if you like living).

MAJOR RED'S DESK
INDOORS

Made out of oak from the Screaming Forest. Sometimes, you can still hear it scream.

MAJOR RED'S BOOKS
INDOORS

Almost entirely about revolution, but there're also a few Obsidian whodunits.

WEAPONS

A POLITICAL TREATISE
MEDIUM-WEIGHT • MADE OF PAPER

The densest jargon you've ever read justifying violence, so it's fitting to use it to kill.

IVORY NIGHT-EATER FANGS
MEDIUM-WEIGHT • MADE OF SOME POOR ELEPHANT

Ancient Drakonian warriors would wear these to terrify their enemies. Imported by E. H. Wit.

AN IRON BOOT
HEAVY-WEIGHT • MADE OF METAL

These were the Iron Tsar's boots. They contain four-inch lifts.

A POISONED GOBLET
HEAVY-WEIGHT • MADE OF METAL & TOXINS

It contains one of the greatest poisons known to mankind: alcohol.

MOTIVES

 TO MANIPULATE A GOVERNMENT

 BECAUSE OF THE FULL MOON

 TO HIDE A SECRET TEXT

 OUT OF TRADITION

CLUES & EVIDENCE

- Dr. Crimson was seen near a piece of oak from the Screaming Forest.

- Whoever would kill out of tradition was left-handed.

- Major Red had a set of ivory night-eater fangs.

- The person who wanted to manipulate a government was near Major Red's books.

- A page of inscrutable text was found next to a painting of Major Red.

- Traces of toxins were found on the person who would kill because of the full moon.

STATEMENTS

(Remember: The murderer is lying. The others are telling the truth.)

General Coffee: I was by Major Red's books.

Dr. Crimson: Major Red was in a secret passage.

Hack Blaxton: Picture it: whoever had the iron boot wanted to manipulate a government.

Major Red: By the revolution, a poisoned goblet was in a secret passage.

SUSPECTS   MOTIVES   LOCATIONS

WEAPONS

LOCATIONS

MOTIVES

WHO?

WHAT?

WHERE?

WHY?

87. A SCREAM IN THE SCREAMING FOREST 🔍🔍🔍🔍

Major Red allowed Logico and Irratino to leave and to go wherever they wanted, so long as they avoided the Screaming Forest. So, of course, they went immediately to the Screaming Forest, where Irratino discovered "bad vibes" and Logico found the body of a woodsman.

SUSPECTS

SERGEANT GUNMETAL

A serious, hard-edged soldier who doesn't take "no" for an answer.

6'0" • RIGHT-HANDED • BROWN EYES • BLACK HAIR • CAPRICORN

ELDER ASH

The local wisewoman. She's lived so long she can see the future.

5'5" • LEFT-HANDED • BROWN EYES • BROWN HAIR • PISCES

CHEF AUBERGINE

It is said that she once killed her husband, cooked him, and then served him at her restaurant. It's not true, but even the fact that it's said about her tells you something.

5'2" • RIGHT-HANDED • BLUE EYES • BLOND HAIR • LIBRA

ADMIRAL NAVY

The firstborn son of an Admiral Navy who himself was the son of an Admiral Navy.

5'9" • RIGHT-HANDED • BLUE EYES • BROWN HAIR • CANCER

LOCATIONS

THE TORTURED TREE
OUTDOORS

The tree where, legend has it, St. Lupine was killed by bandits.

THE DEVIL'S STONE
OUTDOORS

A giant rock that looks like the Devil making a rude gesture.

THE DEAD RIVER
OUTDOORS

It used to be called the Living River. Nobody knows what happened.

THE BOILING POOLS
OUTDOORS

Imagine a hot spring but way, way, way hotter.

WEAPONS

A WOODEN STAKE
MEDIUM-WEIGHT • MADE OF WOOD

For killing vampires, and people, too. But watch out for splinters.

A BUNCH OF MAGIC MUSHROOMS
LIGHT-WEIGHT • MADE OF FUNGI

Not psychedelic. What's magic about these fungi is that they're deadly.

A YETI HIDE
MEDIUM-WEIGHT • MADE OF POLYESTER

It looks suspiciously like fake fur, but the guy who sold it swore it was from a Yeti.

THE BIG RED BOOK
MEDIUM-WEIGHT • MADE OF PAPER

Contains all the best Major Red quotes, like "One murder is met by an investigation. Ten thousand are greeted by a parade."

MOTIVES

 TO PROTECT THE TREES

 FOR PROPAGANDA PURPOSES

 TO STEAL A PRIZED BOOK

 TO STAY ALIVE

CLUES & EVIDENCE

- The person who wanted to protect the trees was in the westernmost location. (See Exhibit D.)

- The person who would kill to stay alive was not in the Dead River.

- The Big Red Book was not found by the Devil's Stone.

- Some probably fake fur was found beside a religiously significant tree.

- The person with a bunch of magic mushrooms wanted to steal the woodsman's prized book. (Woodsmen can read, too, you know.)

- The suspect with a wooden stake also had brown eyes.

- A secret government cable was intercepted by the Detective Club, but it remained scrambled: LRMAADI YANV ATENDW OT LLIK FRO APAPDRGONA SSPUROEP.

STATEMENTS

(Remember: The murderer is lying. The others are telling the truth.)

Sergeant Gunmetal: As a soldier, I'll swear that Elder Ash was in the Dead River.

Elder Ash: Chef Aubergine was not in the Boiling Pools.

Chef Aubergine: A Yeti hide was not in the Devil's Stone.

Admiral Navy: Elder Ash brought a Yeti hide.

SUSPECTS   MOTIVES   LOCATIONS

WEAPONS

LOCATIONS

MOTIVES

_____ WHO?

_____ WHAT?

_____ WHERE?

_____ WHY?

88. THE ALMOST-ABANDONED NUCLEAR REACTOR 🔍🔍🔍🔍

When Deductive Logico and Inspector Irratino explored the abandoned facility, they discovered that it wasn't totally abandoned: there were four other people there, too—five if you counted the dead body (which they did). And one of them knew who did it, because it was one of them!

SUSPECTS

VICE PRESIDENT MAUVE
A vice president of TekCo Futures. She has been tasked with developing the latest TekCo product: TekTopia. It's like a metaverse in real life.

5'8" • RIGHT-HANDED • BROWN EYES • BLACK HAIR • TAURUS

BOSS CHARCOAL
A mob boss from the good ol' days when being a mob boss from the good ol' days meant something.

5'11" • RIGHT-HANDED • BROWN EYES • BLACK HAIR • TAURUS

ELDER ASH
The local wisewoman. She's lived so long she can see the future.

5'5" • LEFT-HANDED • BROWN EYES • BROWN HAIR • PISCES

GRAY WALKER
Irratino is now 100 percent convinced that they're just straight-up zombies.

6'2" • RIGHT-HANDED • HAZEL EYES • RED HAIR • SCORPIO

LOCATIONS

THE NUCLEAR WASTE ROOM
INDOORS

Overgrown with vines . . . glowing, green, pulsating vines.

THE DYING GROUNDS
OUTDOORS

The grass is dead, and there's a twisted tree that reminds Logico of something.

THE REACTOR CORE
INDOORS

The nuclear reactor was looted a long time ago. Who knows who has it or what terror has befallen them.

THE LOCKED GATE
OUTDOORS

It's locked but it's also broken, so it's effectively unlocked.

WEAPONS

A BAG OF NUTS AND BOLTS
HEAVY-WEIGHT • MADE OF METAL & CANVAS

You could use this to build all kinds of deadly weapons, like a killer robot or a choking hazard.

A PETRIFIED APPLE
MEDIUM-WEIGHT • MADE OF STONE

This was at the bottom of the fruit pile.

THE BIG RED BOOK
MEDIUM-WEIGHT • MADE OF PAPER

Filled with Major Red quotes, like "A revolution is better on an empty stomach."

A FIRE EXTINGUISHER
HEAVY-WEIGHT • MADE OF METAL & CHEMICALS

You can hit someone over the head with it or just start a fire and do nothing with it.

MOTIVES

 BECAUSE OF RADIA-
TION POISONING

 TO KEEP A HIDEOUT
SECRET

13 BECAUSE OF A
SUPERSTITION

 TO FEED THEIR FAMILY

CLUES & EVIDENCE

- The person in charge of TekTopia just wanted to feed her family.

- The one that Irratino was convinced was a zombie might kill because of radiation poisoning.

- Whoever had the Big Red Book read it with brown eyes.

- Boss Charcoal was wandering outdoors.

- The person who wanted to keep a hideout secret was in the nuclear waste room.

- The person with a fire extinguisher would kill because of a superstition.

- Irratino passed Logico a note written in a shaking hand: A GAB FO SUNT ADN STLBO SAW TON IN TEH RTRAOEC RECO.

STATEMENTS

(Remember: The murderer is lying. The others are telling the truth.)

Vice President Mauve: A petrified apple was in the nuclear waste room.

Boss Charcoal: Look here: a bag of nuts and bolts was on the dying grounds.

Elder Ash: As we used to say, Vice President Mauve was at the locked gate.

Gray Walker: Grrr . . . Elder Ash keep hideout secret.

SUSPECTS   MOTIVES   LOCATIONS

WEAPONS

LOCATIONS

MOTIVES

_____ WHO?

_____ WHAT?

_____ WHERE?

_____ WHY?

89. THE TRUTH OF ST. LUPINE 🔍🔍🔍🔍

And so, Elder Ash told Deductive Logico and Inspector Irratino the true story of how St. Lupine's three helpers came to be orphans, before he took them in and raised them. You see, their single father had been murdered. And they knew exactly who had done it.

SUSPECTS

HELPER BLACK

One of St. Lupine's three helpers. Black is the smart one.

4'10" • RIGHT-HANDED • BLUE EYES • BROWN HAIR • GEMINI

HELPER BLUE

One of St. Lupine's three helpers. Blue is the strong one.

5'0" • RIGHT-HANDED • HAZEL EYES • BROWN HAIR • ARIES

ST. LUPINE

An old Holy Drakonian saint. Perhaps the most important person in Drakonian history: his life is an inspiration to all Drakonians.

5'9" • RIGHT-HANDED • GREEN EYES • BLOND HAIR • LEO

HELPER BROWN

One of St. Lupine's three helpers. Brown is the creative one.

4'11" • LEFT-HANDED • GREEN EYES • BLOND HAIR • PISCES

LOCATIONS

THE NEARBY VILLAGE
OUTDOORS

A quaint little village trying to make it in the Screaming Forest.

THE SCREAMING FOREST
OUTDOORS

Haunted by the ghosts of a million dead soldiers.

A BEAUTIFUL MEADOW
OUTDOORS

A beautiful meadow on the eastern side of the village.

A PILE OF ROCKS
OUTDOORS

A great pile of rocks on the western side of the village.

WEAPONS

A SHOVEL
MEDIUM-WEIGHT • MADE OF METAL & WOOD

The great thing about using a shovel for murder is it can also dig a hole to help hide the body.

A PITCHFORK
MEDIUM-WEIGHT • MADE OF METAL & WOOD

The townspeople use these to bail hay and become a mob, and they're all out of hay.

A SACRED ROCK
HEAVY-WEIGHT • MADE OF A STRANGE SUBSTANCE

This rock was once held by St. Lupine himself. They say when he held it, it glowed.

A HEAVY BOOT
HEAVY-WEIGHT • MADE OF RUBBER & STEEL

You could swing its steel toes at someone. (Or, better yet, kick them with it!)

MOTIVES

 AS AN ACCIDENT

 FOR THE CHILDREN

 OUT OF TOTAL FEAR

 TO KILL A MONSTER

CLUES & EVIDENCE

- Whoever might kill out of total fear was left-handed.

- Part of the story was scrambled by time: TEH PORENS HWO DNTWAE TO AEVS ETH HNCIDREL ASW IN HET RABENY LGLAEVI.

- The strong helper was seen marching east of the village.

- You could tell by the laces that whoever had a heavy boot was right-handed.

- The creative helper did not bring a pitchfork.

- The person who wanted to kill a monster was in the Screaming Forest.

- The smart helper was hauling a sacred rock: it was hard work.

STATEMENTS

(Remember: The murderer is lying. The others are telling the truth.)

Helper Black: A heavy boot was not in the nearby village.
Helper Blue: By St. Lupine, if I killed it would be an accident.
St. Lupine: In God's name, Helper Black was in the nearby village.
Helper Brown: Helper Blue was not by a pile of rocks.

SUSPECTS   MOTIVES   LOCATIONS

WEAPONS

LOCATIONS

MOTIVES

WHO?

WHAT?

WHERE?

WHY?

90. ACROSS THE RIVER DEAD 🔍🔍🔍🔍

Elder Ash pointed a bony finger toward the Madding Mountains, and she said, "You must go to the night-eater in the castle: the worst murderer of all." Logico said that he didn't believe in night-eaters, but he would always look into a murder. But the path ran across the Dead River, and when they tried to cross over the river, the ferry captain crossed over completely.

SUSPECTS

SOCIOLOGIST UMBER

As a representative from the hard sciences, Sociologist Umber is always asking people to question their priors and if they've read Weber.

5'4" • LEFT-HANDED • BLUE EYES • BLOND HAIR • LEO

GRAY WALKER

The only way you can kill a Gray Walker is with any of the normal ways of killing a person.

5'8" • LEFT-HANDED • BLUE EYES • BROWN HAIR • SAGITTARIUS

ADMIRAL NAVY

The firstborn son of an Admiral Navy who himself was the son of an Admiral Navy.

5'9" • RIGHT-HANDED • BLUE EYES • BROWN HAIR • CANCER

TINY TAUPE

He's on the run from the Free Drakonians. (Due to his size, he can't hide.)

6'3" • LEFT-HANDED • BLUE EYES • BLOND HAIR • TAURUS

LOCATIONS

THE DEAD RIVER WATERS
OUTDOORS

Filled with mutant piranhas—nothing else can survive!

THE DIRTY DECK
OUTDOORS

Covered in dirt and blood and junk.

THE BROKEN BRIDGE
OUTDOORS

Before he died, the captain steered the ship like he lived—poorly!

THE ROTTING HOLD
INDOORS

Water leaks through a dozen different holes.

WEAPONS

A HUMAN FEMUR
HEAVY-WEIGHT • MADE OF MINERAL

Spooky to think it belonged to a skeleton.

A PIECE OF WOOD
HEAVY-WEIGHT • MADE OF VEGETABLE

Taken from a lifeboat. So, it's probably already killed those poor people.

A GARLAND OF GARLIC
MEDIUM-WEIGHT • MADE OF VEGETABLE

This can keep vampires from your home and, if wrapped tightly around your neck, blood from your brain.

AN ATTACK CRAB
MEDIUM-WEIGHT • MADE OF ANIMAL

You might not be afraid of this until you hear its claws are dipped in poison!

MOTIVES

 TO FEAST

13 BECAUSE OF A SUPERSTITION

 TO KEEP A HIDEOUT SECRET

 TO FINISH THE REVOLUTION

CLUES & EVIDENCE

- The representative from the hard sciences had not been in the rotting hold.

- Whoever wanted to feast had a heavy-weight weapon.

- The second tallest suspect was seen hanging around beside a mutant piranha.

- Tiny Taupe was seen where the captain steers the ship.

- The person who would kill because of a superstition was on the dirty deck.

- The suspect with the garland of garlic also had brown hair.

- The person carrying poison-dipped claws wanted to keep a hideout secret.

STATEMENTS

(Remember: The murderer is lying. The others are telling the truth.)

Sociologist Umber: Until I've done more reading, all I can say is a human femur was in the rotting hold.

Gray Walker: Uggghhh, no crab in hold.

Admiral Navy: On my honor as a seaman: I brought a human femur.

Tiny Taupe: A garland of garlic was not in the rotting hold.

SUSPECTS MOTIVES LOCATIONS

WEAPONS

LOCATIONS

MOTIVES

WHO?

WHAT?

WHERE?

WHY?

91. THE MONSTER OF THE MOUNTAINS 🔍🔍🔍🔍

Once they had crossed the Dead River, they had to climb the Madding Mountains. They made good progress, and soon they caught up to another group of mountaineers who had run into some trouble: one of them was dead, and another was a murderer.

SUSPECTS

GRAY WALKER

This was once a person, probably. Either that or they've been grown in a lab.

5'6" • LEFT-HANDED • GREEN EYES • BROWN HAIR • LEO

THE ABOMINA-BLE SNOWMAN

Upon closer inspection: an old man who lives in the mountains and has a lot of body hair.

6'3" • RIGHT-HANDED • GRAY EYES • WHITE HAIR • TAURUS

ARCHEOLOGIST ECRU

A great archeologist/grave robber who is famed worldwide for her archeology/grave robbing.

5'8" • LEFT-HANDED • HAZEL EYES • GRAY HAIR • SAGITTARIUS

PATRIARCH PORPOISE

The Holy Drakonian patriarch, the one true leader of all St. Lupinian Orthodox believers, and he won't let you forget it.

5'4" • RIGHT-HANDED • BLACK EYES • BLACK HAIR • CANCER

LOCATIONS

THE MYSTERIOUS CAVE
INDOORS

A great place for a bear to lie in wait to murder you.

THE HIGH CLIFF
OUTDOORS

A great place for gravity to lie in wait to murder you.

THE TWISTING PASS
OUTDOORS

A great place for bandits to lie in wait to murder you.

THE HIDDEN GROVE
OUTDOORS

A nice little grove of trees to relax in.

WEAPONS

A CROWBAR IN A NEWSPAPER
MEDIUM-WEIGHT • MADE OF PAPER & METAL

The newspaper is the *Drakonian Times,* and it reads, "There Are No Gray Walkers, Say Reds."

LEATHER GLOVES
LIGHT-WEIGHT • MADE OF LEATHER

Beware someone who wears leather gloves. They've already killed a cow: Who's next?!

AN ICE AXE
MEDIUM-WEIGHT • MADE OF METAL

For climbing and killing. It leaves a small hole in the rock, and would in your head as well.

A KILLER SNAKE
MEDIUM-WEIGHT • MADE OF SNAKESKIN ET AL.

Sort of self-working. Just shake, throw, and enjoy the show.

MOTIVES

 TO HIDE A SECRET TEXT

 TO FEED THEIR FAMILY

 TO GET REVENGE

 BECAUSE OF THE FULL MOON

CLUES & EVIDENCE

- The Abominable Snowman wanted to feed his family.

- Echoing on the winds, Logico heard a scrambled message he was sure was a clue: TEH NROPES OWH LDWOU IKLL EEUBACS OF HET LUFL OONM AWS OTN NI THE SEOISYRUTM EVCA.

- The Gray Walker was wearing leather gloves.

- Archeologist Ecru was seen hanging around between some nice trees.

- The leader of all St. Lupinian Orthodox believers was afraid of the person who brought a killer snake.

- The newspaper had the fingerprints of a left-handed person on it.

- Whoever was in the twisting pass was right-handed.

- The person who wanted to get revenge was on the high cliff.

STATEMENTS

(Remember: The murderer is lying. The others are telling the truth.)

Gray Walker: Uhhhh—Patriarch in twisting pass!

The Abominable Snowman: Grrr . . . I brought a killer snake.

Archeologist Ecru: Hmm . . . the Abominable Snowman wanted to feed their family.

Patriarch Porpoise: Well, Archeologist Ecru wanted to hide a secret text.

SUSPECTS   MOTIVES   LOCATIONS

WEAPONS

LOCATIONS

MOTIVES

WHO?

WHAT?

WHERE?

WHY?

92. A GOOD OLD-FASHIONED VILLAGE MURDER 🔍🔍🔍🔍

Once Deductive Logico and Inspector Irratino had climbed the Madding Mountains, they arrived at the village at the foot of Castle Eminence. Everyone had locked their doors and was in hiding, on account of the murder of a shepherd.

"It was the night-eater!" said a villager. But Logico wasn't sure.

SUSPECTS

SERGEANT GUNMETAL

A serious, hard-edged soldier who doesn't take "no" for an answer.

6'0" • RIGHT-HANDED • BROWN EYES • BLACK HAIR • CAPRICORN

CRYPTOZOOLO-GIST CLOUD

They know every sighting of Bigfoot, Yeti, Sasquatch, and what the difference is.

5'7" • RIGHT-HANDED • GRAY EYES • WHITE HAIR • SCORPIO

EARL GREY

He comes from a long line of Earl Greys. Yes, those Earl Greys. No, he doesn't sign autographs. But he does always have some bags with him.

5'9" • RIGHT-HANDED • BROWN EYES • WHITE HAIR • CAPRICORN

RADICAL CRIMSON

She thinks the Free Drakonians are too right-wing. She believes in a better tomorrow.

5'7" • LEFT-HANDED • GREEN EYES • RED HAIR • LIBRA

LOCATIONS

THE DYING FIELDS
OUTDOORS

The soil has dried up and the crops have died.

THE EMPTY SHACK
OUTDOORS

This used to belong to farmers, but now it belongs to whoever wants to live here.

THE DRY WELL
OUTDOORS

Only dust and bones at the bottom of this well.

THE ABANDONED MANOR HOUSE
INDOORS

Ancient and rotten, like the aristocrats who used to live here.

WEAPONS

A MUTANT PIRANHA
MEDIUM-WEIGHT • MADE OF FISH PARTS

Like a normal piranha, but twice the size and with twice the teeth, and also, it's always hungry.

A SILVER BULLET
LIGHT-WEIGHT • MADE OF METAL

You could kill a werewolf with this. Or anybody, if you didn't mind the cost.

A ROYAL SIGNET RING
LIGHT-WEIGHT • MADE OF METAL

It's the insignia of the Iron Tsar's family: this used to mean something. Now it's just a ring.

AN UNHEALTHY DIET
HEAVY-WEIGHT • MADE OF BAD FOOD

Over time, nothing is more deadly. (Also, you could choke someone.)

MOTIVES

 TO ADVANCE SCIENCE

 TO HARVEST THEIR BLOOD

 BECAUSE OF RADIATION POISONING

 TO PROMOTE A MANIFESTO

CLUES & EVIDENCE

- Irratino could tell that the silver bullet had once reflected green eyes.
- Whoever wanted to harvest the victim's blood had black hair.
- The suspect who would kill because of radiation poisoning was found outdoors.
- The person who wanted to promote a manifesto was not in the dying fields.
- A scrambled message, written by a starving peasant, was found in the village: RLEA RGEY WAS SENE BIDEES UDTS AND SNBOE.
- A mutant piranha was found in the empty shack.
- A deadly diet was found in an ancient and rotten building.

STATEMENTS

(Remember: The murderer is lying. The others are telling the truth.)

Sergeant Gunmetal: As a soldier, I declare that Radical Crimson wanted to advance science.

Cryptozoologist Cloud: Whoever had the royal signet ring would kill because of radiation poisoning.

Earl Grey: An unhealthy diet was not in the dry well.

Radical Crimson: I was not in the abandoned manor house.

SUSPECTS MOTIVES LOCATIONS

WEAPONS

LOCATIONS

MOTIVES

WHO?

WHAT?

WHERE?

WHY?

93. THE KILLING AT CASTLE EMINENCE 🔍🔍🔍🔍

Lightning flashed and thunder rolled as Deductive Logico and Inspector Irratino arrived at Castle Eminence. Ruined battlements and rusted chains nicely complemented the aesthetic of the cobwebs—and the dead body! It was clear their first task was to solve the murder of this poor soul.

SUSPECTS

RADICAL CRIMSON

She thinks the Free Drakonians are too right-wing. She says the revolution was too traditional.

5'7" • LEFT-HANDED • GREEN EYES • RED HAIR • LIBRA

ARCHEOLOGIST ECRU

A great archeologist/grave robber who is famed worldwide for her archeology/grave robbing.

5'8" • LEFT-HANDED • HAZEL EYES • GRAY HAIR • SAGITTARIUS

SERGEANT GUNMETAL

A serious, hard-edged soldier who doesn't take "no" for an answer.

6'0" • RIGHT-HANDED • BROWN EYES • BLACK HAIR • CAPRICORN

SIR RULEAN

A sophisticated gentleman who just happens to have been knighted, if you believe the Official Knighting Documents he is always waving around.

5'8" • RIGHT-HANDED • BLUE EYES • RED HAIR • LEO

LOCATIONS

THE BAILEY
OUTDOORS

The inner courtyard of the castle: there's a Norton well and some stables.

THE MOAT
OUTDOORS

The moat is dry and filled with bones.

THE GUARDHOUSE
INDOORS

A giant portcullis guards the guardhouse.

THE KEEP
INDOORS

The great tower in the middle of the castle. The light at the top is on.

WEAPONS

A KILLER SNAKE
MEDIUM-WEIGHT • MADE OF SNAKESKIN, ET AL.

Sort of self-working. Just shake, throw, and enjoy the show.

A WOODEN STAKE
MEDIUM-WEIGHT • MADE OF WOOD

For killing vampires, and people, too. But watch out for splinters.

A PETRIFIED HEART
MEDIUM-WEIGHT • MADE OF STONE

Whoever has this truly has a heart of stone.

A GARLAND OF GARLIC
MEDIUM-WEIGHT • MADE OF VEGETABLE

Garlic production is one of the fields where Drakonia really thrives.

MOTIVES

 BECAUSE OF THE FULL MOON

 FOR PROPAGANDA PURPOSES

 TO AVENGE THEIR FATHER

 TO FREE THE PEOPLE

CLUES & EVIDENCE

- A weapon made of snakeskin was brought by the person who would kill because of the full moon.

- The suspect with the same height as Sir Rulean was seen in a great tower.

- Sergeant Gunmetal was seen hanging around next to some bones.

- The person who wanted to free the people was not in the guard-house: it would be a contradiction in terms.

- Radical Crimson brought a petrified heart. She said it was symbolic of the Red Government.

STATEMENTS

(Remember: The murderer is lying. The others are telling the truth.)

Radical Crimson: Whoever had the wooden stake wanted to avenge their father.

Archeologist Ecru: Whoever wanted to avenge their father was in the bailey.

Sergeant Gunmetal: As a soldier, I swear Archeologist Ecru would kill because of the full moon.

Sir Rulean: Archeologist Ecru brought a wooden stake.

SUSPECTS   MOTIVES   LOCATIONS

WEAPONS

LOCATIONS

MOTIVES

WHO?

WHAT?

WHERE?

WHY?

94. CASTLE KEEP YOUR SECRETS 🔍🔍🔍🔍

Deductive Logico and Inspector Irratino looked up at the great castle keep before them. All of the windows were dark, except for a single red light at the top of the tower. That was spooky enough, but then there was a blood-curdling scream! A fair maiden had been murdered.

SUSPECTS

VISCOUNT EMINENCE

The oldest man you have ever seen. The only man nearly as old was the Iron Tsar, and he died ten years ago.

5'2" • LEFT-HANDED • GRAY EYES • BROWN HAIR • PISCES

DR. CRIMSON

She believes that everyone—no matter their race or creed—deserves the right to medical care, as long as they can afford it.

5'9" • LEFT-HANDED • GREEN EYES • RED HAIR • AQUARIUS

GRAY WALKER

This spooky shambler seems right at home in this mysterious castle.

5'6" • LEFT-HANDED • GREEN EYES • BROWN HAIR • LEO

LADY VIOLET

The heiress of the Violet Isles, the largest extrajudicial territory in the world.

5'0" • RIGHT-HANDED • BLUE EYES • BLOND HAIR • VIRGO

LOCATIONS

THE DUNGEON
INDOORS

Chains and torture devices are rusty—not from disuse, but because it adds to the ambience.

THE GRAND HALL
INDOORS

A huge rotting table and a rusted chandelier. Everything is connected by spiderwebs.

THE LIVING QUARTERS
INDOORS

A beautiful viscount-size bed and a roaring fire.

THE BATTLEMENTS
OUTDOORS

You can kill someone with an arrow from up here or just by dropping a rock.

WEAPONS

A FIRE POKER
MEDIUM-WEIGHT • MADE OF METAL

You can poke a fire or somebody's heart with this.

A BRAIN IN A JAR
HEAVY-WEIGHT • MADE OF METAL, GLASS, & BRAINS

Philosophers argue you might be a brain in a jar. A great rebuttal is to hit them with one.

A NUCLEAR FUEL ROD
HEAVY-WEIGHT • MADE OF METAL

Legends say that this can reanimate the dead. It can definitely de-animate the living.

SATIN CURTAINS
MEDIUM-WEIGHT • MADE OF SATIN

One of the most comfortable fabrics to be strangled by.

MOTIVES

TO CAST AN EVIL SPELL

TO BRING BACK THE DEAD

TO STAY ALIVE

OUT OF TOTAL FEAR

CLUES & EVIDENCE

- Nobody with blue eyes was in the dungeon.

- Deductive Logico found a torn-up pile of papers with a message on them. He tried to piece them together, but this is as far as he got: NOTCSVIU MENICENE TAEWDN TO SYAT ILEVA.

- The fire poker was next to (and, in fact, the cause of) the roaring fire.

- Whoever wanted to cast an evil spell had a medium-weight weapon.

- Whoever was in the grand hall had green eyes.

- The Gray Walker was trying to eat his brain in a jar.

- A nuclear fuel rod was found sitting where you might expect an archer.

- Dr. Crimson never set foot in the dungeon.

- Lady Violet would kill out of total fear.

STATEMENTS

(Remember: The murderer is lying. The others are telling the truth.)

Viscount Eminence: Yes, well, satin curtains were in the dungeon.

Dr. Crimson: Viscount Eminence was not in the battlements.

Gray Walker: Fire poker! Aggg! Not in grand hall!

Lady Violet: Viscount Eminence did not bring a nuclear fuel rod.

SUSPECTS MOTIVES LOCATIONS

WEAPONS

LOCATIONS

MOTIVES

WHO?

WHAT?

WHERE?

WHY?

95. THE DEATH OF THE GRAY WALKERS 🔍🔍🔍🔍

Deductive Logico and Inspector Irratino followed the viscount into his living quarters and discovered that he was sick or dying, or otherwise in need of medical care. And also, that somebody had just killed a Gray Walker, while another one stalked about.

SUSPECTS

DR. CRIMSON

She believes that everyone—no matter their race or creed—deserves the right to medical care, as long as they can afford it.

5'9" • LEFT-HANDED • GREEN EYES • RED HAIR • AQUARIUS

MANSERVANT BROWNSTONE

Manservant Brownstone's brother is devoted to God, but he is devoted to the Violets.

6'2" • RIGHT-HANDED • BROWN EYES • BROWN HAIR • CANCER

GRAY WALKER

They are confused, slow, and uncoordinated. Like toddlers but taller.

5'2" • LEFT-HANDED • HAZEL EYES • BLOND HAIR • LIBRA

VICE PRESIDENT MAUVE

A vice president of TekCo Futures. She has been tasked with developing the latest TekCo product: TekTopia. It's like a metaverse in real life.

5'8" • RIGHT-HANDED • BROWN EYES • BLACK HAIR • TAURUS

LOCATIONS

THE HOSPITAL BED
INDOORS

Viscount Eminence collapsed into this bed, barely alive.

THE BALCONY
OUTDOORS

It looks out over all of Drakonia, which stretches out to the horizon.

THE BLOOD TANKS
INDOORS

Giant tanks of blood, each labeled with a different name.

THE GREAT MACHINE
INDOORS

A big electronic beeping machine in between the blood tanks and the hospital bed.

WEAPONS

A COAT OF ARMS
HEAVY-WEIGHT • MADE OF WOOD & METAL

The Iron Tsar's coat of arms. A forbidden symbol for the last decade.

A BOOK OF WAR POETRY
MEDIUM-WEIGHT • MADE OF PAPER

Poems about the war between the Reds and the Royals, full of glory, betrayal, and loss.

A SUIT OF DRAKONIAN ARMOR
HEAVY-WEIGHT • MADE OF METAL

Imported from Holy Drakonia before it fell to the Reds. The helmet has a white feather plume.

IVORY NIGHT-EATER FANGS
MEDIUM-WEIGHT • MADE OF SOME POOR ELEPHANT

Ancient Drakonian warriors would wear these to terrify their enemies.

MOTIVES

 TO PROLONG A LIFE

 TO INHERIT THE CASTLE

 TO EXPLOIT A RESOURCE

 TO AVENGE THE VISCOUNT

CLUES & EVIDENCE

- Whoever wanted to avenge the viscount was right-handed.

- Whoever wanted to prolong a life had a medium-weight weapon.

- According to the scattered files on Dr. Crimson's desk: EHEOWVR WDANET TO IXEPOTL A CROUSREE ASW RIHTG NAEDHD.

- Ivory night-eater fangs were certainly not in the balcony.

- Vice President Mauve carried a forbidden symbol.

- The Gray Walker brought a suit of Drakonian armor.

- The person who wanted to inherit the castle was by the great machine.

STATEMENTS

(Remember: The murderer is lying. The others are telling the truth.)

Dr. Crimson: If you want my medical opinion, a book of war poetry was in the hospital bed.

Manservant Brownstone: Sir, Vice President Mauve was in the hospital bed.

Gray Walker: Grr . . . resource exploitation . . . hospital bed.

Vice President Mauve: Dr. Crimson brought a book of war poetry.

	SUSPECTS				MOTIVES				LOCATIONS			
WEAPONS												
LOCATIONS												
MOTIVES												

WHO?

WHAT?

WHERE?

WHY?

96. THE GRAVEDIGGER OF THE REVOLUTION 🔍🔍🔍🔍

"You see," Dr. Crimson explained, "the true story of the end of the revolution is different than the one the Reds have spread for years. True, someone was murdered. But it wasn't the Iron Tsar. It was a poor corporal in his army."

SUSPECTS

THE IRON TSAR

He ruled Drakonia for decades with an iron fist, and an iron boot, and iron guns, too.

5'6" • LEFT-HANDED • GRAY EYES • BROWN HAIR • PISCES

PATRIARCH PORPOISE

The Holy Drakonian patriarch, the one true leader of all St. Lupinian Orthodox believers, and he won't let you forget it.

5'4" • RIGHT-HANDED • BLACK EYES • BLACK HAIR • CANCER

MAJOR RED

The revolutionary leader who freed Drakonia from the grasp of the Tsar and then immediately grasped it himself.

6'2" • LEFT-HANDED • BROWN EYES • BROWN HAIR • ARIES

TINY TAUPE

He's actually really huge, which is why people call him Tiny.

6'3" • LEFT-HANDED • BLUE EYES • BLOND HAIR • TAURUS

LOCATIONS

THE GREAT IRON DOOR
OUTDOORS

Imagine the biggest door you can possibly imagine. It's bigger.

THE GLORIOUS CHAPEL
INDOORS

It is covered in gold, stolen from the peasants. (Why would a peasant need gold?)

THE GRAVEYARD
OUTDOORS

Filled with the bodies of his enemies, buried upside down.

THE GREAT THRONE ROOM
INDOORS

The Iron Tsar sits upon a throne of skulls. (And a soft pillow, technically.)

WEAPONS

AN ANTIQUE FLINTLOCK
MEDIUM-WEIGHT • MADE OF METAL & WOOD

The gun that fired the silver bullet that started the Drakonian Civil War.

AN IRON HELMET
HEAVY-WEIGHT • MADE OF IRON & JEWELS

For all intents and purposes, this helmet was the Iron Tsar's face.

A BAZOOKA
HEAVY-WEIGHT • MADE OF METAL, TECH, & EXPLOSIVES

The signature weapon of the Red Revolution: AKA the People's Cannon.

A RED BANANA
LIGHT-WEIGHT • MADE OF EXPLOSIVES

Another name for the sticks of dynamite the Reds used in the Royal Revolution.

MOTIVES

 TO BE A HERO

 TO RULE A COUNTRY

 BECAUSE OF AN ANCIENT GRUDGE

 FOR POLITICAL PURPOSES

CLUES & EVIDENCE

- An antique flintlock was certainly not in the glorious chapel: no guns in church!

- Patriarch Porpoise carried a bazooka he called the Holy Cannon.

- An iron helmet was discovered with another body facing away from it.

- Tiny Taupe was huddled indoors.

- The Red banana was thrown by the person who wanted to rule a country.

- The Iron Tsar did not want to kill for political purposes.

- The suspect who wanted to be a hero was brooding indoors.

- The official records of the event had been torn to pieces: A CTSIK FO INTMDYAE ASW UFNDO HAEENBT A GEHU ROOD.

STATEMENTS

(Remember: The murderer is lying. The others are telling the truth.)

The Iron Tsar: Patriarch Porpoise was at the great iron door.
Patriarch Porpoise: A bazooka was not in the graveyard.
Major Red: By the revolution, Tiny Taupe would kill because of an ancient grudge.
Tiny Taupe: I was not in the graveyard.

SUSPECTS   MOTIVES   LOCATIONS

WEAPONS

LOCATIONS

MOTIVES

WHO?

WHAT?

WHERE?

WHY?

97. SISTER VS. SISTER: THE FINAL SHOWDOWN 🔍🔍🔍🔍

Dr. Crimson raced to her helicopter which was waiting by the battlements on top of the keep. There, she was stopped by Radical Crimson, her sister. "What you've done is evil," she said.

"No," Dr. Crimson replied, "what I've done is smart."

"It can be both. And I won't let you get away with it."

SUSPECTS

GRAY WALKER

This Gray Walker seems vaguely familiar to Radical Crimson, like she's hated her before.

5'6" • LEFT-HANDED • GREEN EYES • BROWN HAIR • LEO

GRAY WALKER

This Gray Walker seems unusually physically capable. Can you discover who they all are?

6'0" • LEFT-HANDED • BLUE EYES • BLOND HAIR • ARIES

DR. CRIMSON

She believes that everyone—no matter their race or creed—deserves the right to live forever, as long as they can afford it.

5'9" • LEFT-HANDED • GREEN EYES • RED HAIR • AQUARIUS

RADICAL CRIMSON

She cares about the revolution more than even her own sister, who is (after all) pretty evil.

5'7" • LEFT-HANDED • GREEN EYES • RED HAIR • LIBRA

LOCATIONS

THE HELICOPTER
INDOORS

The blades are spinning, so technically, this location could be a weapon itself.

THE BATTLEMENTS
OUTDOORS

Those fortifications on the top that archers shoot between.

OVER THE EDGE
OUTDOORS

Here you can come face to face with an implacable foe: gravity.

THE STAIRWELL
INDOORS

It's 758 big stone steps to the top which is, honestly, just too many.

WEAPONS

A BAG OF MARBLES
LIGHT-WEIGHT • MADE OF GLASS

You can hit someone with this or pour them out at the top of some stairs.

A PITCHFORK
MEDIUM-WEIGHT • MADE OF METAL & WOOD

The townspeople use these to bail hay and kill monsters, and they're all out of hay.

A CRANIAL SAW
MEDIUM-WEIGHT • MADE OF METAL

Just a regular bone saw. It can be used for brain surgery, vivi-section, or murder.

A SCALPEL
LIGHT-WEIGHT • MADE OF METAL & JEWELS

Somehow it being smaller makes it more dangerous.

MOTIVES

TO ESCAPE

TO STOP HER SISTER

FOR BRAINS

OUT OF CONFUSION

CLUES & EVIDENCE

- Both Gray Walkers were indoors.

- Only the shorter Gray Walker could get into the helicopter without their head being chopped off by the blades.

- Obviously, Dr. Crimson wanted to escape, and Radical Crimson wanted to stop her.

- A scalpel was discovered where an archer might stand.

- A scrambled transmission reported details seen from the ground: DR MICSRNO SWA IHGNNGA EROV HET GEDE.

- The person with a pitchfork wanted to eat some brains.

- The cranial saw was indoors.

STATEMENTS

(Remember: The murderer is lying. The others are telling the truth.)

Gray Walker: Arrr . . . other waaaalker . . . not in copterrr.
Gray Walker: Arrrghr . . . maaarrbbles waaaanted escaaaape!
Dr. Crimson: It's quite obvious, isn't it? I brought a cranial saw.
Radical Crimson: The blue-eyed Gray Walker did not bring a cranial saw!

SUSPECTS · MOTIVES · LOCATIONS

WEAPONS

LOCATIONS

MOTIVES

WHO?

WHAT?

WHERE?

WHY?

98. A CITY ABLAZE

Deductive Logico and Inspector Irratino made it back to the People's City in time to see its burnt-out remains. A coalition of troops supporting President White, and her secret plans to reinstate the Iron Tsar, had set the entire city on fire. Logico and Irratino fled through it, heading for the airport, hoping they could escape. But they had to solve a murder on the way.

SUSPECTS

GOVERNOR LEAD

The most feared and least loved of the Free Drakonian governors.

6'2" • RIGHT-HANDED • BROWN EYES • BLACK HAIR • VIRGO

BOSS CHARCOAL

A mob boss from the good ol' days when being a mob boss from the good ol' days meant something.

5'11" • RIGHT-HANDED • BROWN EYES • BLACK HAIR • TAURUS

SERGEANT GUNMETAL

A serious, hard-edged soldier who doesn't take "no" for an answer.

6'0" • RIGHT-HANDED • BROWN EYES • BLACK HAIR • CAPRICORN

ARCHEOLOGIST ECRU

A great archeologist/grave robber who is famed worldwide for her archeology/grave robbing.

5'8" • LEFT-HANDED • HAZEL EYES • GRAY HAIR • SAGITTARIUS

LOCATIONS

THE RED BAY
OUTDOORS

This is basically the only place that's safe in the city: if you can swim!

THE COMMUNITY CATHEDRAL
INDOORS

Now the *former* former St. Lupinian Cathedral. It will never be rebuilt.

THE CAPITOL BUILDING
INDOORS

The great dome is on fire.

THE BRUTALIST HOUSING
INDOORS

It turns out one of the great ways to save on building costs is to scrimp on fire safety.

WEAPONS

A BAYONET
MEDIUM-WEIGHT • MADE OF METAL

The official weapon of the Red Army, mostly because it doesn't require paying for bullets.

THE BIG RED BOOK
MEDIUM-WEIGHT • MADE OF PAPER

Written by Major Red, it argues for a world without rulers (other than him, anyway).

A NUCLEAR FUEL ROD
HEAVY-WEIGHT • MADE OF METAL

These nuclear materials were supposedly secured by World Horizons International Thermonuclear Energy.

A COAT OF ARMS
HEAVY-WEIGHT • MADE OF WOOD & METAL

The Iron Tsar's coat of arms. A forbidden symbol for the last decade.

MOTIVES

 AS AN ACCIDENT

 TO TURN THE TIDE OF WAR

 TO RULE A COUNTRY

 TO STEAL A RUBY

CLUES & EVIDENCE

- A secret code went out scrambled on the radio: RONORGEV ALDE EDNTWA OT ERUL A UTNYROC.

- Boss Charcoal was following the general fire-safety tip of being outdoors.

- Sergeant Gunmetal had a medium-weight weapon.

- Archeologist Ecru was searching the brutalist housing.

- Whoever had a coat of arms was right-handed.

- The person who might kill as an accident was in the Community Cathedral.

- The person who wanted to steal a ruby was not in the Red Bay.

- A nuclear fuel rod was causing the ocean water around it to bubble.

STATEMENTS

(Remember: The murderer is lying. The others are telling the truth.)

Governor Lead: On the honor of the Free Drakonians, the one with the nuclear fuel rod did not want to rule the country.

Boss Charcoal: Look here: Archeologist Ecru was in the brutalist housing.

Sergeant Gunmetal: A bayonet was not in the Capitol Building.

Archeologist Ecru: Hmm . . . the Big Red Book was not in the Community Cathedral.

SUSPECTS MOTIVES LOCATIONS

WEAPONS

LOCATIONS

MOTIVES

WHO?

WHAT?

WHERE?

WHY?

99. ZEPPE-LET'S GET OUT OF HERE 🔍🔍🔍🔍

Deductive Logico and Inspector Irratino rose out of the burning People's City on the same zeppelin that Logico had arrived on. And they watched below as the city burned beneath them, uncertain of what this would mean for the future. For the present, at least, they had to solve the murder of the replacement zeppelin pilot.

SUSPECTS

MISS SAFFRON

Slowly, the blood is coming back into her face, and the life back into her eyes. She is not a Gray Walker anymore.

5'2" • LEFT-HANDED • HAZEL EYES • BLOND HAIR • LIBRA

CAPTAIN SLATE

A real-life astronaut. The first woman to travel around the dark side of the moon, and also the first to be suspected of murdering her copilot.

5'5" • LEFT-HANDED • BROWN EYES • BROWN HAIR • AQUARIUS

COMRADE CHAMPAGNE

A communist and a rich one. Comrade Champagne likes nothing more than to travel the world, sharing the message of communism with his fellow vacationers.

5'11" • LEFT-HANDED • HAZEL EYES • BLOND HAIR • CAPRICORN

SERGEANT GUNMETAL

He's feverishly ripping the Red Drakonian medals off his uniform and trying to blend in.

5'7" • LEFT-HANDED • GREEN EYES • RED HAIR • LIBRA

LOCATIONS

THE COCKPIT
INDOORS

The robot pilot is still here, ro-boting as well as ever.

THE CARGO HOLD
INDOORS

This used to be filled with lux-ury luggage, now it's filled with whatever people could grab.

THE PASSENGER CABIN
INDOORS

No commercial plane has this much legroom, or a parachute for every passenger.

THE BATHROOM
INDOORS

The bathroom in this zeppelin smells nice, but only because the pipes dump everything into the sky.

WEAPONS

AN ANTIQUE VASE
HEAVY-WEIGHT • MADE OF CERAMIC

Worth more than all of your an-cestors and all of your descen-dants put together.

A HUGE PILE OF PAPERWORK
HEAVY-WEIGHT • MADE OF PAPER

One page is too light to use to kill. But a pile is deadly. Which page makes it a deadly weapon?

A BRIEFCASE OF GOLD
HEAVY-WEIGHT • MADE OF METAL & LEATHER

Everything worth anything is being taken out of Drakonia as quickly as possible.

A HOLY RELIC
MEDIUM-WEIGHT • MADE OF BONE

It's a totem of some long for-gotten god with a terrifying visage.

MOTIVES

 TO COVER UP ANOTHER MURDER

 TO ROB THE VICTIM

 BECAUSE IT WAS TOO CROWDED

 IN A JEALOUS RAGE

CLUES & EVIDENCE

- Whoever wanted to cover up another murder had a medium-weight weapon.

- The recovering Gray Walker had a crush on the person who brought an antique vase: Is a romance blossoming?

- Sergeant Gunmetal was seen hanging around beside a robot pilot.

- The person with a briefcase of gold wanted to kill in a jealous rage.

- Comrade Champagne had a heavy-weight weapon.

- The astronaut was not in the cargo hold.

- The person who would kill because it was too crowded was in the passenger cabin.

- A suspect with an antique vase would not need to rob anybody.

STATEMENTS

(Remember: The murderer is lying. The others are telling the truth.)

Miss Saffron: I might kill to rob someone.

Captain Slate: A pile of paperwork was most definitely not in the bathroom.

Comrade Champagne: Miss Saffron was not in the cargo hold.

Sergeant Gunmetal: Miss Saffron brought a huge pile of paperwork.

SUSPECTS   MOTIVES   LOCATIONS

WEAPONS

LOCATIONS

MOTIVES

WHO?

WHAT?

WHERE?

WHY?

100. THE SECOND DRAKONIAN CIVIL WAR 🔍🔍🔍🔍

And so, the nation descended once again into civil war, with each of the factions quickly staking out their own territory in the country. As an academic exercise, you might like to use your deductive abilities to discern the victor of this protracted war.

In war, like in any murder: the innocent losers tell the truth. The victorious winner lies.

SUSPECTS

PATRIARCH PORPOISE

The Holy Drakonian patriarch, the one true leader of all St. Lupinian Orthodox believers, and he won't let you forget it.

5'4" • RIGHT-HANDED • BLACK EYES • BLACK HAIR • CANCER

VISCOUNT EMINENCE

The oldest man you have ever seen. It is said that he outlived all of his sons and was born before his father.

5'2" • LEFT-HANDED • GRAY EYES • BROWN HAIR • PISCES

MAJOR RED

The revolutionary leader who freed Drakonia from the grasp of the Tsar and then immediately grasped it himself.

6'2" • LEFT-HANDED • BROWN EYES • BROWN HAIR • ARIES

PRESIDENT WHITE

The duly elected president of the Royal Resistance, a party of aristocrats who want to retake power. She wears a signet ring.

5'10" • RIGHT-HANDED • GRAY EYES • WHITE HAIR • LEO

LOCATIONS

THE SCREAMING FOREST
OUTDOORS

The famous wild woods of Drakonia. A perfect place to wage guerilla warfare.

THE WESTERN CITADEL
OUTDOORS

The disputed tower on the western edge of Drakonia. An easily fortifiable base.

THE IRON PALACE
OUTDOORS

It was turned back into a fortress from a museum.

THE MADDING MOUNTAINS
OUTDOORS

The great mountains of Drakonia. Impossible to conquer!

ARMIES

THE SOULS OF ST. LUPINE
MADE OF TRUE BELIEVERS

These are the holy troops of the St. Lupinian faith, an ancient order of deadly monks.

THE PEOPLE'S ARMY
MADE OF "VOLUNTEERS"

Everyone in the People's City is free to join the army. No exceptions.

THE CONVOCATION CORPS
MADE OF WELL-PAID SOLDIERS

The army of the Convocation of Countries. Each soldier has a tablet that lets them order drone strikes.

THE HOLY DRAKONIAN ARMY
MADE OF THE PEASANTS

They've got their sharpened ivory teeth in, and they're ferocious on the battlefield.

TRUE MOTIVES

 FOR EVERLASTING LIFE

 FOR SO MUCH ████████ING MONEY

 FOR NEVER-ENDING GLORY

 FOR LIMITLESS POWER

CLUES & EVIDENCE

- Whoever led the souls of St. Lupine was right-handed.

- The person who wanted never-ending glory was hiding directly south of Castle Eminence. (See Exhibit D.)

- The oldest man wanted unlimited power.

- The Convocation Corps was commanded by a person with a significant figure associated with duality. (See Exhibit B.)

- The Holy Drakonian Army was camped out immediately to the north of the People's City. (See Exhibit D.)

- A commander who was not motivated by ████████ing money had DNA matching this sequence: GCTT. (See Exhibit C.)

STATEMENTS

(Remember: The winner is lying. The others are telling the truth.)

Patriarch Porpoise: As St. Lupine often said, President White wanted so much ████████ing money.

Viscount Eminence: The Holy Drakonian Army was not in the Iron Palace.

Major Red: By the revolution, whoever led the souls of St. Lupine wanted everlasting life.

President White: The souls of St. Lupine were in the Western Citadel.

SUSPECTS   MOTIVES   LOCATIONS

WEAPONS

LOCATIONS

MOTIVES

_____

WHO?

_____

WHAT?

_____

WHERE?

_____

WHY?

101. ONE MORE THING

When Inspector Irratino and Deductive Logico got back to the Investigation Institute, where they hoped to relax for a good long time, they instead found the entire place locked up: the windows were covered with boards and the gates were closed by chains.

The only explanation was on a sign, industrially affixed to the gate, which read:

RG VI OP LC MS OP RG RC EV HW IP RC LC RC EV MS OP AS RB OP HC RG AS UG RC AS

AS RC OC RB RC IP HW LC RG RI RG MS RC OC RB RC IP RG AS RC AS RG RG HC EV AS MS

RG IM LB RG HW AS LB RI RC AS LB AS OP AS AS MS OP LC LB RG HW UG EV RB RI LB RG

HW RC OC OP VI IP IP OP RC OC RB RC IP RG AS RC AS RG RG HC EV IP IP OP AS AS LC

MS RB UG RC RC IM RC MS RG LC RG AS RB OP HC RG AS UG RC AS MS OP RC OC OP IP

LB RG HW AS OP RC AS OP AM RG LC HC RB LB RG HW RC UG RB AM IP IP OP AS RB HC

AS AS MS RC LC OP AS MS RG EV RG AS AM OP RC OP LC LC MS RB RC OC OP IP RC IP HC

RG RC HC HW RB IM RC HC AS RC AT OP MS RG OP AS LB IP RG OC RC LC IP IP OP IM RB

OP HC RG AS UG RC AS RC OC LB RB AM AS MS RC LC OP AS RC LC HC RC EV OP OC HW

AM HW RI LC RC AT OP MS RB VI LC RG RC AM MS OP RG LB RG AS LB RG HW AS MS RB

IM OP LC MS RB LC IP LC RG IM RC HC AS RG AS RB OP HC RG AS UG RC AS IP OP RC OC

MS LB RG AS AS LB RG RI RB AM RB OP AS LB RI LC RC MS AM RC LC MS RG EV RC AS

LB AS OP AS AS MS OP MS RG OP AS RB VI OP AS AS RC OC MS OP AS RG MS OP AS RB

LC LC OP VI MS OP OC RB HC LC RG AS RC AT OP VI RG IP RG HC RB OP AS RC OC OP AS

EV RC AS RC LC LC RB RC LC

Even by putting their heads together, they couldn't solve it. So they turned to the Detective Club, and they asked for their help.

Can you decode this message and help save the Investigation Institute?

HINTS

1. It was the great esoteric investigator Inspector Irratino who consulted the daily horoscope for everyone involved before pronouncing his declaration: Miss Saffron was next to a pigeon. (Sometimes, the stars were pretty down to earth.)

2. Inspector Irratino sent a sky-mail about a vision he had experienced of an incredibly hot liquid spilled on a parachute. He hoped the dark secret wouldn't be too dangerous.

3. A message was waiting for Deductive Logico from Inspector Irratino: "By studying the shape of my coffee grounds, I've determined Captain Slate was beside a drawer of Drakonian dollars."

4. Inspector Irratino had a particularly vivid dream a heavy boot was on the foot of a policewoman.

5. Inspector Irratino texted Logico a riddle he had heard whispered on the winds: "You never find a railing without a piece of dead fish." What did it mean?

6. Inspector Irratino tried to call Logico about a dream he had where the admiral went down with the ferry, but he got his voicemail. (There was no service on the Isles.)

7. Inspector Irratino tried to telekinetically send Logico the following clue: The tallest suspect had the toxic blowfish.

8. Inspector Irratino sent a telegram about a clue he had just uncovered by dowsing: A red stain would be found inside the guest house. (He hoped Logico had figured out the secret by now.)

9. When Inspector Irratino couldn't radio the island, he appeared to Logico in a daydream and told him a Royal weapon was in the main house.

10. A homing pigeon arrived with a message from Irratino: "Don't ask how I know, but Silverton the Legend had a bag of cash."

11. After drawing a marot card, Inspector Irratino pronounced his declaration: A biography of Lord Violet was beside a fountain.

12. Logico was reminded of something that Irratino always used to say: Assassins tended to carry swords, rather than heavy purses or leather gloves.

13. Inspector Irratino sent Logico the following telekinetic message (or maybe the thought just occurred to Logico): "The shortest suspect was by the cliffside."

14. Acting on a hunch, Inspector Irratino sent word of another Drakonian Thanksgiving tradition: the priest always has the gravy boat.

15. Inspector Irratino woke up covered in sweat, shocked by the obvious truth that Christmas-Lover Sable had a candy cane. He wished he could tell Logico!

16. Inspector Irratino discovered that an old Yule tradition was for philologists to carry fire pokers. He tried to radio the island, but he couldn't!

HINTS

17. Inspector Irratino replied to a text Logico had sent: "I wish I was there for New Year's, too. But remember: champagne and maps *always* go together." It didn't go through.

18. Inspector Irratino wished he could tell Logico about his marot reading that proved Chef Aubergine had the crowbar.

19. Inspector Irratino used the whisper network to tell Logico that the cranial saw was *not* on the operating table. When he didn't hear back, he worried it was something to do with the dark secret.

20. Suddenly, Inspector Irratino had the feeling somebody was using his decoy-detective trick. He also had a feeling that Lady Violet had been carrying an empty cage.

21. One night, Inspector Irratino had a dream that the second tallest suspect was seen hanging around in the great hall. Logico was in the dream, too, so he assumed he already knew about that clue.

22. Irratino was in a panic! Logico was in trouble, he knew it, but he couldn't reach him! And he needed to tell him that Cosmonaut Bluski brought the bayonet.

23. Inspector Irratino raced to the airport and bought a ticket to Drakonia. He needed to tell Logico that Manservant Brownstone had the geode.

24. Inspector Irratino screamed into his phone as the dang zeppelin he was on crept across the ocean: "THE FAMOUS ACTOR HAS THE BRIEFCASE FULL OF MONEY!"

25. Inspector Irratino got off the zeppelin in St. Lupine, and saw that the Violet Isles were on fire. But he knew in his heart that Logico had escaped. Just like he knew that the Detective Code was written with A = Z, B = Y, C = X, and so on.

26. Using a technique called scrying, Inspector Irratino stared into the flame of the prayer candle and saw that Dr. Seashell, DDS, was seen between twisting hedgerows.

27. Inspector Irratino cast runes to determine that Supreme Master Cobalt had a cute angel.

28. Logico helped Irratino by showing him CCTV footage of someone playing a distracting murder-mystery web game in the vault.

29. According to a dream Inspector Irratino had, a hypercube was found in Room 101.

30. Inspector Irratino couldn't understand how The Amazing Aureolin did that trick with her compass.

31. Inspector Irratino hiked up to the top of the mountain with a pendulum, and he used it to determine that the tallest suspect had brought a stranglin' scarf.

32. The esoteric detective had a vision of Vice President Mauve with a poisoned cocktail.

33. Inspector Irratino consulted the marot: it told him that to crack the code, look at the letter value table in Exhibit B. The first digit tells you the column, and the second tells you the row.

34. Inspector Irratino used a pendulum, and it swung back and forth between Mathematician Marble and a fire extinguisher.

35. Inspector Irratino stared into a crystal ball and saw that it had been held by Dean Glaucous. (There was a sticker on it that read "Property of Dean Glaucous.")

36. Based on a movie he once saw, Inspector Irratino was confident that the boom mic was on the set of a murder mystery.

37. After "running the numbers," Inspector Irratino came up with an interesting numerological conclusion: the cop had the spoon.

38. Inspector Irratino tried to wake Logico to tell him that Director Dusty had the piano, but Logico was sleeping too soundly.

39. Inspector Irratino had just had a dream about this, but in his dream, it was him in the storm shelter instead of Cosmonaut Bluski.

40. Inspector Irratino reminded Logico that the Next Letter Code was decoded when you replaced every letter of the cipher text with the very next letter in the alphabet.

41. Through careful observation, Inspector Irratino noticed the squirrels really seemed to like broccoli. He did not expect that.

42. Inspector Irratino ran the numbers by Numerologist Night and declared that a poison-dipped claw was found next to five TVs.

43. Inspector Irratino heard a ticking sound in the analysis room.

44. Inspector Irratino called the Institute and had his best psychics do

their best scrying, and then he remarked that Cosmonaut Bluski had been at the side entrance.

45. Inspector Irratino drew two cards: the titanium sphere and the library. Interesting . . .

46. Inspector Irratino drank a special concoction, was sick for an entire day, and then pronounced his revelation: Mx. Tangerine was on brown grass.

47. Inspector Irratino wrote out a list of random numbers and then guessed what number each letter stood for: it spelled out "Sister Lapis beside body of Pythagoras."

48. By reading everyone's palms, Inspector Irratino determined that a block of stone was found next to a lever.

49. Inspector Irratino used a top-secret divination technique called ██████ ████████ to determine that a colored fish was found in a car that Logico wasn't in.

50. Inspector Irratino received a phone call from his alchemist who said that the solutions had turned a certain shade, which signified that Major Red was in the galleries.

51. Deductive Logico called Irratino, but he had to leave a voicemail. "Hey, Irratino. It's me. Apparently I've been detained by the Free Drakonians. They want to negotiate some kind of prisoner exchange. Call me when you get this. Oh! And I just read an article about the Psychic Research Laboratory, and it said that they always put the person in the control group in the actual laboratory."

52. Trying to follow in Deductive Logico's footsteps, Inspector Irratino

used a crime-sniffing dog to locate a chip of brick next to a sign that says "CASH4GOLD."

53. Inspector Irratino examined the medical files of every single suspect, like Logico would have done, and discovered that the DNA sample belonged to Baron Maroon.

54. Deductive Logico left another voicemail. "Hey, Irratino—I'm still stuck in this Free Drakonian jail. If you could give a call back, the number is +█ (█) █-█. Oh, and I was looking over some of the files about the Institute: the person who studied the marot was in the observatory."

55. Trying to do what Logico would've done, Irratino talked to all the witnesses, and he found that a couple of people remarked on seeing the unusual sight of an espresso drunk through a metal straw.

56. By dusting for fingerprints (like Logico might have done), Inspector Irratino was able to determine that the ritual dagger was held by A-List Abalone.

57. "Hey, Tino!" Logico said in another voicemail he left from the Free Drakonian prison. "If you get this, I just want you to know that I'm okay, but you should really reach out to the Reds. Oh, and I saw this wild chessboxing match on the TV in here. Can't believe they played King's Gambit in the middle of a boxing ring!"

58. Inspector Irratino used an occult method to get into the head of Deductive Logico, and he therefore deduced that the person with a fake treasure map loved mystery books.

59. Deductive Logico would have paid careful attention to where every-

one parked, which is how Irratino discovered that the limo was driven by Manservant Brownstone.

60. Inspector Irratino watched the CCTV footage and couldn't help noticing that the person who wanted to fund the Royal Resistance was loudly talking about it at the actual bar.

61. This time, Irratino decided to rely on his own methods, not Logico's, and his gut told him that the atheist was, ironically, at the altar. He just felt it to be true.

62. "Hey, Inspector," Logico said (in yet another voicemail), "I just saw on the news that you were in Drakonia last week? Are you serious?! I mean, I'm not mad. I just really wish you would check your phone. You know, this reminds me of that Great Dane that Editor Ivory always used to bring to meetings. I don't know why it reminds me of that. It just does."

63. Inspector Irratino discovered—through a complicated scientific process too complicated to describe here—that the person with type O blood was in the donation room.

64. Every time Inspector Irratino closed his eyes he had a vision of Aristocrat Sable in the cages.

65. Using forensic financial analysis, Inspector Irratino discovered that the person with a gold bar was dirt poor—at least before they found that gold! But he had missed another call from Logico, and it went: "Hey, I. I., love to hear from you. Just send a diplomatic cable to the Free Drakonian prison and we'll see if we can escape it together."

66. Inspector Irratino used a bizarre technique Deductive Logico called "process of elimination" to determine that the person with a suit of

Drakonian armor probably got the idea from *The Perplexing Problem of the Parrot,* their favorite book.

67. Inspector Irratino carefully studied the timetables and determined that the person with a brick of coal's final destination was Amsterdam.

68. Inspector Irratino studied the journals of all the suspects (which would normally be an invasion of privacy, but when you're investigating a murder you can do whatever you want), and discovered that the Amazing Aureolin's favorite piece was the tricky knight.

69. By carefully examining attendance records, like Logico might have done, Inspector Irratino discovered that Coach Raspberry was seen beside peeling paint.

70. Inspector Irratino felt in his gut that a pouch of magick powders would be found inside a jar of ashes. (Then, he confirmed it with empirical analysis, i.e., by opening the jar of ashes.)

71. By picking up the first *Murdle* book, turning to a random page, and pointing to a random card (a technique called bibliomancy), Inspector Irratino learned that the person with a poisoned inkwell had revered Philosopher Bone.

72. Inspector Irratino drank sixteen cups of coffee and analyzed the leftover grounds. Then, he rushed around telling absolutely everyone that a rusty chain was found in the deck, over and over until the caffeine wore off.

73. Inspector Irratino found a book of Drakonian conspiracies in the bathroom, and honestly, it made for some pretty interesting reading while he was ███████████.

74. Inspector Irratino burned seventy-four occult candles and concluded that the person with a shovel carried themselves carefully.

75. Inspector Irratino had a vision that the person who was a member of the Sword of St. Lupine was by the barbed-wire fences.

76. On page 48, the newspaper article added a crucial detail: Patriarch Porpoise had ivory night-eater fangs!

77. Inspector Irratino used astral projection to tell Logico that the person who wanted to fight for love was in the Screaming Forest, but Logico didn't reply. See, Irratino thought, I'm not the only one who doesn't check their messages.

78. President White made sure to emphasize that the person with a poisoned goblet wanted to kill a monster.

79. Inspector Irratino studied the dialectic and determined, logically and irrefutably, that Officer Copper had the bayonet.

80. Governor Lead went on a tangent during the story, noting that Major Red held the iron crown, as was later widely reported.

81. According to another, unmurdered newsie, the person who wanted to manipulate the government was living in the brutalist housing.

82. Inspector Irratino woke up alone in the middle of the night with a single thought in his head: Cosmonaut Bluski was in room 239.

83. Inspector Irratino kept wildly signaling to Logico that the person with a stun gun wanted to live forever.

84. Inspector Irratino flipped to the back of the newspaper and found the

story continued with a note about a chainsaw having been discovered by Red Security.

85. Inspector Irratino used a pendulum to determine that Tiny Taupe wanted to redistribute their wealth.

86. Inspector Irratino asked Hack Blaxton why he was there: apparently he was trying to adapt a political treatise into a new film for Midnight Movie Studios. Unfortunately, no matter how much he studied, he couldn't figure out a way to visualize the commodification of labor.

87. By studying the rings on the trees and consulting the *Tree Ring Esoteric Dictionary,* Irratino was able to determine that the person with the Big Red Book would kill for propaganda purposes.

88. Inspector Irratino blacked out and, when he awoke, he knew for certain that Vice President Mauve had brought the Big Red Book.

89. Elder Ash went on a bit of a tangent before she revealed that the person who wanted to kill a monster was in the Screaming Forest.

90. Inspector Irratino put his head under the water until he almost died, and he had a (terrifying) vision that the Gray Walker wanted to feast.

91. By studying the weather patterns, and applying the esoteric maxim that everything is connected, Irratino was able to determine that the person with an ice axe wanted to hide a secret text.

92. Inspector Irratino remembered a riddle he had once read: Who wanted to harvest blood? The person in the abandoned manor house. A weird riddle, to say the least.

93. Inspector Irratino spoke with the horses, and by interpreting their

neighs and whinnies, he learned that Radical Crimson would kill for propaganda.

94. Inspector Irratino discovered that two important ley lines intersected beneath the castle: the second tallest suspect was seen beneath chains.

95. Inspector Irratino researched the numerological significance of the serial number on the great machine, and it told him that the person who wanted to exploit a resource was in the hospital bed.

96. Irratino asked about Patriarch Porpoise's strange choice of weapon, and Dr. Crimson scoffed: Patriarch Porpoise wanted to be a hero.

97. Inspector Irratino—riding away on a horse he "freed" from the stables—had a vague premonition that Dr. Crimson had a bag of marbles.

98. Irratino's coat caught on fire, so he stopped, dropped, and rolled, and while he was rolling, he managed to see the person who might kill as an accident in the Community Cathedral.

99. Inspector Irratino flipped through the pages of a book at random and discovered that Sergeant Gunmetal brought a holy relic.

100. Inspector Irratino consulted a sign he had seen in the stars and then pronounced his declaration: The person leading the Convocation Corps wanted so much ██████████ing money.

SOLUTIONS

1. "It was Grandmaster Rose with a red herring in the conspiracy corkboard room!"

Grandmaster Rose was irate. "No! This is all wrong."

Logico asked, "What's wrong about my deductions?"

"Well, for one, I was supposed to get away with it!"

> Miss Saffron | a magnifying glass | the rooftop lookout
> General Coffee | the first *Murdle* book | the detective kit storage
>   room
> **Grandmaster Rose | a red herring | the conspiracy board room**

2. "It was Dr. Crimson with a stun gun in the cargo hold!"

Dr. Crimson was outraged at the accusation, not because she didn't do it, but because she did. "I had a very good reason, and it was for a very good cause, and if you give me a moment, I'll explain."

When they gave her a moment, she grabbed a parachute and jumped out of the zeppelin.

> Captain Slate | a cup of scalding coffee | the passenger cabin
> President White | a fire extinguisher | the cockpit
> **Dr. Crimson | a stun gun | the cargo hold**

3. "It was Boss Charcoal with an exposed wire at the baggage claim!"

He scoffed. "Oh, so it's illegal to electrocute someone to death now?!"

Logico was unsure when that had ever been legal.

Captain Slate | a water bottle | the currency exchange
Chauffeur Bronze | an '80s cell phone | the runway
Boss Charcoal | an exposed wire | the baggage claim

4. "It was Officer Copper with a heavy boot in the interrogation room!"

Officer Copper was flabbergasted. "How can it be illegal if a cop does it?!"

The other Free Drakonians consoled her with reassurances that she would not face consequences.

Officer Copper | a heavy boot | the interrogation room
Comrade Champagne | the Big Red Book | the observation room
Cosmonaut Bluski | a cheap pen | the "emergency exit"

5. "It was the Duchess of Vermillion with a diamond necklace in the captain's quarters!"

The duchess explained that the victim had threatened to reveal their affair. "Now, thanks to you, Deductive Logico, it will be revealed anyway! Therefore, I go!" And she leapt overboard. To her death or her freedom, only her swimming will tell . . .

Admiral Navy | a life preserver | overboard
The Duchess of Vermillion | a diamond necklace | the captain's
 quarters
Uncle Midnight | a fish bone | the deck

6. "It was Uncle Midnight with an attack crab by a single headstone!"

He was adamant that the only reason he did it was to keep the party going. When a boat arrived to pick them up, they left him behind on the tiny island, which is how he became Castaway Midnight. But who would Castaway Sable become?

Castaway Sable | spoiled soup | the lone palm tree
Uncle Midnight | an attack crab | a single headstone
Admiral Navy | a human skull | the shipwrecked ferry

7. "It was Admiral Navy with a toxic blowfish on the wooden dock!"

"That's right!" he said. "I didn't like the look of that rival seaman, so I killed him. And, having killed him, I have no reason to stay. And so, I depart!"

As they watched him swim into the sea, Logico turned to Lady Violet. "Excuse me. My invitation doesn't, by any chance, concern a dark secret on the island, does it?"

Lady Violet laughed and glanced at the tackle shack, but then she answered, "No, of course not. I just wanted you to enjoy the holiday party with us."

> **Admiral Navy | a toxic blowfish | the wooden dock**
> Lady Violet | a broken sword | the tackle shack
> Castaway Sable | a vial of poison | the stone stairs

8. "It was Baron Maroon with a bag of acorns at the statue of Lord Violet!"

Lady Violet declared this was a capital offense. As she explained to Logico, "When the civil war ended, the so-called Free Drakonia never made a claim to this island, and so it became an extrajudicial territory. Unlike those barbarous Reds, we do not execute our prisoners: we simply ask them to leave."

> **Baron Maroon | a bag of acorns | the statue of Lord Violet**
> Lady Violet | a deck of marot cards | the cliffs
> Signor Emerald | a bottle of wine | the guest house

9. "It was Signor Emerald with a flag in the main house!"

Signor Emerald explained that the radio operator was a Red Drakonian spy—and that he had done everyone a favor by killing her. They took a vote, and President White declared him pardoned.

Logico explained to Lady Violet that this was, statistically speaking, too many murders for one holiday party. But Lady Violet just laughed. "You worry too much, dear Logico!"

Signor Emerald | a flag | the main house
President White | a shovel | the greenhouse
Lady Violet | a book of war poetry | the garden maze

10. "It was Viscount Eminence with a piece of wood on the enormous stairs!"

"Yes, I did it. He was an agent of the Revolution, and therefore, he had to go, just as the Red Revolution must go. But Old Drakonia shall remain. The aristocracy shall remain. And we shall have our rights restored. Keep your faith, and hold out, and remember, as St. Lupine said, God Fights For Us!"

And with that, he took it upon himself to leave, and he returned to Castle Eminence, far up in the Madding Mountains, where he continued to do as he had done since the Revolution: wait.

Agent Applegreen | a satin choker | the giant doorway
Viscount Eminence | a piece of wood | the enormous stairs
Silverton the Legend | a bag of cash | the driveway

11. "It was Chauffeur Bronze with a biography of Lord Violet on the balcony!"

When the guests heard about this heroic act, they arranged a party with Chauffeur Bronze as the guest of honor. To these royals, defending property from burglars was akin to saving an orphan from an alligator pit, and everyone whispered about how much it reminded them of the famous story of the death of Lord Violet's Beloved Butler Beryl.

Maid Marble | a marble bust | the guest bathroom
Manservant Brownstone | a poisoned tincture | the guest bedroom
Chauffeur Bronze | a biography of Lord Violet | the balcony

12. "It was the Bloody Assassin with a standard sword on the twin bed!"

When Lord Violet saw his Beloved Butler Beryl dead, he wrested the sword from the Bloody Assassin and fiercely attacked him. But he missed his target, and the sword broke in two, and the Bloody Assassin got away.

Lord Violet took the body of his dear friend and servant, and he buried him on a small island near his home. He and Lady Violet had a private ceremony, and they shared their grief.

Soon, however, this grief turned to rage, fury at the Bloody Assassin, and the Reds who had sent him, and he vowed to spend the rest of his life as an officer for the Holy Drakonian Army.

> Lord Violet | a heavy purse | the tiny window
> Lady Violet | leather gloves | the single chair
> **The Bloody Assassin | a standard sword | the twin bed**

13. "It was Searching Sable with a commercial-grade firework by the statue of Lord Violet!"

Maybe now, one of the aristocrats commented, she would be known as Murderer Sable. But Logico knew the truth: these people had too much money to ever pay for their crimes. (Sable was, however, asked to leave as soon as she finished her drink.)

> Patriarch Porpoise | the Book of St. Lupine | the cliffside
> The Duchess of Vermillion | a carrot | the seating area
> **Searching Sable | a commercial-grade firework | the statue of Lord Violet**

14. "It was Executive Producer Steel with a turkey leg in the kitchen!"

Executive Producer Steel was outraged.

"Oh, you think you can cancel me?! I can never be canceled!" she announced.

> Executive Producer Steel | a turkey leg | the kitchen
> Father Mango | a gravy boat | the pantry
> Lady Violet | a fork | the dining room

15. "It was Bishop Azure with a lump of coal in the fountain!"

Bishop Azure had recognized Santa as another Red spy—that's why his suit was red! And so, she had done what any self-respecting woman of God would do: kill him.

The aristocrats were fine with that, so the bishop was allowed to stay.

> Maid Marble | a gift-wrapped bomb | the secret garden
> Christmas-Lover Sable | a candy cane | the lookout tower
> **Bishop Azure | a lump of coal | the fountain**

16. "It was Chairman Chalk with a log in the stairwell!"

"I hated the cold, but the heater-repair technician tried to slip a manuscript he had written into my bag! *The Joys of Heater Repair*. I hated that a lot more than the cold, so I did what I had to do!"

The aristocrats debated and—in a stirring example of bourgeois democracy—agreed to let him stay by one vote.

> **Chairman Chalk | a log | the stairwell**
> Philologist Flint | a fire poker | the dance floor
> Secretary Celadon | a regular snowball | the bar

17. "It was Judge Pine with ghost pepper flakes in the secret passageway!"

"This is not justice!" she declared. "Only I decide what is justice!"

Nevertheless, she was asked to leave. (Everyone had liked the DJ.)

> A-List Abalone | a really high heel | the stacks
> Lady Violet | a champagne flute | the map room
> **Judge Pine | ghost pepper flakes | the secret passageway**

18. "It was Patriarch Porpoise with a heavy codebook in an empty room!"

Patriarch Porpoise refused to reveal why he was carrying a codebook, or why he committed the murder. But Logico wasn't really that interested in the patriarch's motives; he was interested in what was behind the heavy iron door.

He pushed it open and found . . .

Patriarch Porpoise | a heavy codebook | an empty room
Chef Aubergine | a crowbar | a big locked door
Vice President Mauve | a heavy candle | the main passageway

19. "It was Secretary Celadon with a cranial saw by a giant medical machine!"

But Secretary Celadon was furious. "I was promised a special life-lengthening treatment, and instead it was being done on some random patient! I couldn't have it!"

As Dr. Crimson took Secretary Celadon aside, Deductive Logico looked through an old medical file on Lord Violet. In it, he discovered something that either made no sense at all, or explained everything . . .

It was that time again: he needed to call all the suspects together.

Secretary Celadon | a cranial saw | a giant medical machine
Dr. Crimson | a cheap pen | an operating table
Miss Saffron | a brain in a jar | a medicine cabinet

20. "It was Lady Violet with an empty cage on the leather couch!"

These were the words the real Logico said as he leapt in from the dining hall, revealing he was still alive, a trick he had learned from Inspector Irratino.

Lady Violet was outraged, but then she was relieved. "Killing a decoy is not a crime!"

Logico admitted that was true, and he began his presentation . . .

Lady Violet | an empty cage | the leather couch
Chef Aubergine | a painting of Lord Violet | the fireplace
Maid Marble | a candelabra | the balcony

21. "It was the Iron Tsar with ivory night-eater fangs in the great hall!"

Logico continued, "And yet, solving this mystery only leads us to another! In fact, there are two great mysteries in Lord Violet's life:

1. Why did the Reds send an assassin to kill him, when he was already on their side?

2. Why did the Iron Tsar kill him, once he was fighting for the Royal Resistance?

There was a general murmuring from the guests. "The answer to these two questions is the same: it is the dark secret of the Violet Isles!"

But before he could reveal it, there was a cannon blast!

Governor Lead | the Big Red Book | the throne room
The Iron Tsar | ivory night-eater fangs | the great hall
Major Red | a bazooka | the grand balcony

22. "It was Sergeant Gunmetal with a hammer and sickle on the cliffs!"

But since Logico didn't think that Lady Violet could ask the Reds to leave, he followed her and the other guests into the secret passage in the garden maze!

Sergeant Gunmetal | a hammer and sickle | the cliffs
Comrade Champagne | an exploding cigar | the garden maze
Cosmonaut Bluski | the bayonet | the main house

23. "It was Miss Saffron with a puffy tail comb in the crystal fields!"

But when she protested, and they all heard the boots of the Red Army pursuing them into the caves, they had to make a hard decision: leave her behind, or let a murderer on the submarine with them.

"Goodbye!" Lady Violet told her.

24. "It was the Duke of Vermillion with a flying squirrel in the quarters!"

"Well," he replied, "I had to do it! We were running out of air, or we would have, if my figures are correct." He looked at his figures and realized he had forgotten to carry a two. "Oops."

The submarine began to surface with half its air remaining.

25. "It was Beloved Butler Beryl with a broken sword on the single chair!"

"But what does that mean?" they asked. "He killed himself?"

"No, he did not kill himself," Logico replied. "The two questions I posed were these: Why did the Reds want to kill Lord Violet when he was already on their side? And why, when he had switched sides and was fighting for the Iron Tsar, did the Iron Tsar finally kill him?

"The answer to both questions is the same: they didn't. The Reds didn't try to kill Lord Violet, and the Iron Tsar didn't kill him.

"More specifically, the Reds had no motive to kill Lord Violet. He was supporting their revolution. And, as you have seen from the crystals below his mansion (See Case 23: The Flight Underground), his support would mean a whole lot of money. And not even communists turn away money! No, the Reds did not want to kill Lord Violet. But someone else did.

"Lady Violet!"

He turned to her. "You stood to inherit all of this. But, if your father gave his support to the Reds, then you would lose it either way. Either the Reds would win, and the riches would be given to the people. Or the Reds would lose, and the Tsar would confiscate them for treason. You had to stop him, but how? You needed a partner. Someone who resented your father. Someone who deserved better than he was given. Someone like the so-called Beloved Butler Beryl!

"Beryl hated Lord Violet for two reasons. First, because of his hypocrisy. After all, he was willing to support a worker's revolution, but he treated Beryl so poorly, keeping him in a tiny room, giving him a chair with only three legs. (See Case 12: The Murder of the Butler.) And secondly, because—much like Manservant Brownstone—he was devoted not to the person, but to his class, to his standing, and to his family. It was unseemly for a butler to serve a communist. Undignified! And so, they collaborated. They killed Lord Violet, switched clothes with his butler, and buried him in a private ceremony on the tiny island. (See Case 6: The Tiny Island Murder Mystery.) Then, Beloved Butler Beryl—the new Lord Violet—took up arms in the struggle against the revolution, fighting on the side of the Iron Tsar.

"Because he wore a mask, and because the war took him far from home, he thought that he could pull off the impersonation. However, the Iron Tsar was not fooled: when he saw the brown eyes of Beloved Butler Beryl peering through Lord Violet's mask, he cut him down as an imposter, because he knew Lord Violet's eyes were blue. That is why his portrait shows him with blue eyes (see Case 20: Gathering the Suspects), while his biography says he has brown eyes (see Case 12: The Murder of the Butler). This discrepancy is what I noticed when I saw his autopsy. (See Case 19: The Private Hospital Public Murder)."

Everyone was shocked. And slowly, they all turned to Lady Violet, waiting for a denial and a denunciation. But instead, she simply sighed.

"Fine!" Lady Violet replied. "You got me. I did it. He was going to throw away everything we had for this stupid cause, a pointless revolution. We would have lost our mansion. Our fortune. Our isle!"

But, as Logico pointed out, that had happened anyway. And now, she didn't have her father, either. And that was the dark secret of the Violet Isles.

Beloved Butler Beryl | a broken sword | the single chair
Lord Violet | a heavy purse | the twin bed
Lady Violet | leather gloves | the tiny window

26. "It was Herbalist Onyx with a crystal ball in the observatory!"

Inspector Irratino was outraged! It was going to be hard to keep up the grounds without his top herbalist, but it was even harder to justify continuing to employ a murderer.

"Why didn't I just stick to my plants?" she lamented.

Dr. Seashell, DDS | a prayer candle | an impossible hedge maze
Herbalist Onyx | a crystal ball | the observatory
Numerologist Night | a poisoned tincture | the great tower

27. "It was Supreme Master Cobalt with a cute angel in the apple orchard!"

"This is outrageous!" he replied. "Nobody should be able to invent new numbers except me. And I shouldn't be held accountable for stopping the count! Fortunately, my great mystic faculties will make me impossible to catch!" Then, he ran away really quickly.

Astrologer Azure | a prime steak | the counting room
Supreme Master Cobalt | a cute angel | the apple orchard
Numerologist Night | a hypercube | the calculator room

28. "It was Father Mango with leather gloves in the back room!"

Logico demonstrated how, logically, there was no other way. And Irratino explained that he knew it in his gut: either way, Mango was peeled.

"For the glory of God, murder is permissible!" Mango roared. But by the law of the land, it wasn't.

Chairman Chalk | a laptop | the vault
Father Mango | leather gloves | the back room
Signor Emerald | a bag of gold | the clock room

THE FIRST RIDDLE OF PYTHAGORAS

A: 7. Half 10 is 5. Twice 4 is 8. Only 6 and 7 are between them, and only 7 is odd.

29. "It was Signor Emerald with a hypercube in room 101!"

The concierge had caught Signor Emerald shoving hotel robes and towels into his luggage, and so she had to be eliminated. Now, he reached for the hypercube again, but found it was no longer accessible in our three-dimensional world (i.e. Irratino had hidden it).

"Vai al diavolo!" he exclaimed.

Signor Emerald | a hypercube | room 101
Sociologist Umber | a poisoned muffin | room 202
Mathematician Marble | a laundry bag filled with knives | room 303

30. "It was Principal Applegreen with a 3D printer in the great hall!"

Quickly, Principal Applegreen tried to print a knife, but the convention attendees stepped in. "This whole convention gets an F-plus from me!"

Brother Brownstone | a protractor | the check-in stand
The Amazing Aureolin | a compass | the bathroom
Principal Applegreen | a 3D printer | the great hall

THE SECOND RIDDLE OF PYTHAGORAS

A: 1. The two shortest sides of a triangle must be longer than the third side, or else they won't be able to connect to each other. So 1 cannot be a part of this triangle, because $1 + 3 > 5$ and $1 + 5 < 7$.

31. "It was Deacon Verdigris with poisoned hot chocolate in the woods!"

"Curse you!" Deacon Verdigris replied. "The Church wanted this mountain to build a Cathedral that would rival even the one in Holy Drakonia! And you have ruined it! God will curse you, Logico! He'll curse you for this!"

Irratino reassured Logico that, though God might curse him, Irratino still liked him.

32. "It was Judge Pine with a sack full of golf balls in the dining hall!"

Judge Pine raged, "He cheated at golf! He had to be dealt with!"

While Logico suggested that golf was not worth killing over, the other guests at the country club could not agree less.

Mx. Tangerine | a first-place trophy | the caddy shack
Judge Pine | a sack full of golf balls | the dining hall
Vice President Mauve | a poisoned cocktail | on the eighteenth
    hole

33. "It was Babyface Blue with a shoe knife at the poker table!"

Not only was he guilty of murder, but Logico also suggested that Babyface Blue was possibly too young to be allowed to gamble.

"I want my mom!" Babyface Blue cried out.

Boss Charcoal | a sleeve pipe | the front door
Silverton the Legend | a bag of gold | the cashier
Babyface Blue | a shoe knife | the poker table

THE THIRD RIDDLE OF PYTHAGORAS

A: 5. 5 divided by 2 times 2 is 5.

34. "It was Sociologist Umber with a calculator in the coin-flipping room!"

Sociologist Umber explained how actually, she was not guilty, bolstering her argument with citations from Adorno and Weber until finally, she felt like she had made her point.

"If you disagree," she said, "then I think you need to do more of the readings."

Mathematician Marble | a fire extinguisher | the computer
    room
The Duchess of Vermillion | a sharp pencil | the typewriter
    room
Sociologist Umber | a calculator | the coin-flipping room

35. "It was Dean Glaucous with a crystal ball in the isolation chamber!"

Dean Glaucous replied, "It was so isolating in there! I couldn't handle it. So I killed the first person I saw. And I'll do it again!"

But when he reached for his crystal ball, he saw that Irratino was holding it. Unarmed and exposed, he surrendered.

Astrologer Azure | a dowsing rod | the grounds
Vice President Mauve | a quasi-perpetual motion machine | the
    kitchen
Dean Glaucous | a crystal ball | the isolation chamber

36. "It was President Midnight with a boom mic on Soundstage A!"

President Midnight huffed and puffed. "He was the wrong director for the film! He would have ruined it! So, I had to kill him to get someone better. We need someone with a name—like Director Dusty—not someone who is going to make an art film about poor aristocrats!"

Patriarch Porpoise | a pencil | the statue of Midnight I
Earl Grey | a stage light | the security building
President Midnight | a boom mic | Soundstage A

37. "It was High Alchemist Raven with a fork in the produce section!"

She stammered a reply, "I couldn't believe the prices! I had to do something! Now, every grocery store will know if they charge too much, they might get murdered!"

"Their employees might get murdered," Logico corrected.

"Still, the cost of retraining them should provide a disincentive."

High Alchemist Raven | a fork | the produce section
Chef Aubergine | a corkscrew | the bakery
Officer Copper | a spoon | the deli counter

38. "It was Director Dusty with a piano in my childhood home!"

Just as Director Dusty was about to break down and say something both hilarious and self-incriminating, Logico woke up to a worried Inspector Irratino telling him, "There's a thunderstorm outside! I think there's a tornado! Also, there's been a murder!"

Inspector Irratino | ghost pepper flakes | a local coffee shop
Director Dusty | a piano | Logico's childhood home
Bookie-Winner Gainsboro | the Big Red Book | the clouds

39. "It was Sir Rulean with a satellite dish in a storm-chasing van!"

Sir Rulean protested his innocence, but he did it in a really cagey and unbelievable way. When it was clear nobody believed him, he exclaimed, "Curse you all for what you've done to me!"

Captain Slate | a motorcycle helmet | a tornado
Cosmonaut Bluski | a lightning rod | a storm shelter
Sir Rulean | a satellite dish | a storm-chasing van

40. "It was Comrade Champagne with a laptop in the nature room!"

But instead of getting angry or defensive, he started laughing. "When Major Red unleashes the global revolution, he will free me from jail! But before that happens, I'll just hire an expensive lawyer and post whatever bail they give me."

Comrade Champagne | a laptop | the nature room
Vice President Mauve | a briefcase full of money | the conference
    room
President White | the golden cube | the holostage

41. "It was Cryptozoologist Cloud with a head of cabbage in the llama bed!"

"How can it be murder if I did it to save a life?!" Cryptozoologist Cloud said. "Why is the life of a person I killed worth any more than the thousands of animals they've killed in their lifetime? I did nothing wrong!"

Logico countered that it would more effectively promote a vegetarian lifestyle to not associate it with the murder.

"Well, I didn't expect to get caught!"

> Babyface Blue | a broccoli | the squirrel preserve
> **Cryptozoologist Cloud | a head of cabbage | the llama bed**
> Mx. Tangerine | a carrot | the pig pen

42. "It was Mathematician Marble with a bunch of magic mushrooms in the server room!"

"Yeah, I poisoned him, because he was using math for evil!" she screamed, as she was led away by the Detective Club.

After the drama had died down, Irratino checked the price of his crypto, and then he grew despondent. The CEO being murdered for being evil had done a number on his portfolio.

"Don't worry," Logico said. "I hacked into your phone and sold all your crypto months ago."

> **Mathematician Marble | a bunch of magic mushrooms | the**
> **server room**
> Executive Producer Steel | a hoodie | the computer room
> Sir Rulean | an attack crab | the penthouse

43. "It was General Coffee with a chess book on the top board!"

General Coffee downed his espresso and admitted, "I knew I could never win unless I killed."

"But now you're disqualified," Logico said. "You can't win even though you did kill."

THE FOURTH RIDDLE OF PYTHAGORAS

A: 4. You only need to draw 3 pieces to know you have a pair of one color. If you have 2, you either have a pair or one of each. If you draw a third, you have to have a pair. One more than that is 4.

44. "It was Cosmonaut Bluski with a chess board at the side entrance!"

"Now the Convocation of Countries will be forced to recognize Free Drakonia! All glory to the Reds! Freedom to all oppressed people everywhere!"

Irratino remarked that some of the most oppressed people in the world are the murdered, but Bluski retorted that he did not care about the St. Lupinian babble about the sanctity of human life.

Patriarch Porpoise | an antique flintlock | the back entrance
Cosmonaut Bluski | a chess board | the side entrance
President White | an '80s cell phone | the front entrance

45. "It was Numerologist Night with a prime steak on the back porch!"

But then, the mathematics professor sat up, un-poisoned. "I calculated the odds of that happening years ago, and took precautions against it."

Then, he turned to Logico and said, "I called you here because I have a specific task I need you to undertake for me. It is of incredible global significance."

And he passed Logico a folded note. When Logico unfolded the note, he saw a map.

THE FIFTH RIDDLE OF PYTHAGORAS

A: 6. If 2 students solve 8 problems in 4 days, then each student solves 1 problem per day. Over 2 days, 3 students will solve 6 problems total. Perhaps they could do them faster if they worked together.

46. "It was Mx. Tangerine with a giant metal zero on the grounds!"
"Oh!" they replied. "You think I did this because I wanted to?! I had to do it to save the world!"

Mx. Tangerine fled, and Logico searched the clothes on the dead body. He found, in a hidden pocket, another map . . .

The Duchess of Vermillion | an attack goose | the stairwell
Baron Maroon | a rusted hour hand | the clockworks
Mx. Tangerine | a giant metal zero | the grounds

THE SIXTH RIDDLE OF PYTHAGORAS

A: 9. Since it takes 12 hours for the hour hand to move 360° around the clock, it moves 360°/12 each hour, or 30°. In each minute, it moves 30°/60, or 0.5°. So, in 18 minutes it will move 9 degrees.

47. "It was Sister Lapis with ancient papyrus in the crypt itself!"
"He worshipped numbers instead of the one true faith!" she declared.

"Everybody thinks they have the one true faith," Irratino said, "when in reality—" Logico finished his sentence, "No faiths are true," while Irratino continued, "All faiths are true." In a way, they mean the same.

Suddenly, they heard a creaking sound, and then a crash!

Cosmonaut Bluski | the arm of a statue | the crumbling entrance
Sociologist Umber | a mathematics textbook | the numerological
    hall
Sister Lapis | ancient papyrus | the crypt itself

48. "It was Dr. Seashell, DDS, with a block of stone by a giant stone dial!"

But the murder wasn't the only thing Logico solved. He turned the dial to seven different digits, and then, he pulled the lever. And then . . .

Another chamber opened up, and Logico saw something that was going to change the world.

"Irratino," he said, "do you think you can get one of your friends to let me address the Convocation of Countries?"

Of course, Irratino knew just the person. And a convoy to the Convocation was arranged.

Did you solve the Seven Riddles of Pythagoras? If you think you did, check your answers, upside down, below.

> Aristocrat Sable | a mathematics textbook | a wall of numbers
> **Dr. Seashell, DDS | a block of stone | a giant stone dial**
> Archeologist Ecru | a chalice | a stone statue

THE SEVENTH & FINAL RIDDLE OF PYTHAGORAS

A: 1. Each of the words connects to a number in Exhibit B: 4, 3, 2, so they are counting down, and the blank represents 1.

That means, the answers to the Seven Riddles of Pythagoras, and the numbers Logico entered into the dial, were as follows: 7 1 5 4 6 9 1.

Using Exhibit B, these numbers can be turned into a word. What is it? The answer will be revealed . . . after the next mystery.

49. "It was Officer Copper with a knife pen in the transport car!"

But it wasn't actually Officer Copper, it was an Officer Copper lookalike that had taken Officer Copper's place. She wasn't the same height, didn't have the same color eyes or hair, and (as Irratino was embarrassed not to have noticed) her astrological sign was different.

"What was in that math that's so important?"

"It's complicated. But the password that opened it was simple, and told me everything I needed to know."

"What was it?"

The message hidden in the password is upside down below.

Each of the numbers corresponds to one of the three letters below it on Irratino's numerological primer. With some effort, Logico was able to decode this message, and to find a single word that chilled him to the bone: PANDORA.

These mathematical equations were a modern Pandora's Box. They had the power to change the world completely, or destroy it forever.

And it was for this that people wanted to kill him.

Radical Crimson | a bulletproof vest | the road
Officer Copper | a knife pen | the transport car
Tiny Taupe | a red herring | the decoy car

50. "It was Major Red with a gavel in the galleries!"

Or rather, Inspector Irratino knew that that was what Deductive Logico was planning to say. But Logico did not actually say it, because—to everyone's shock and surprise—Logico went missing! All that was left behind was a mysterious blood stain.

Irratino hoped it wasn't Logico's blood, and he could usually believe anything he wanted, but he worried that this time (and *only* this time), he was deluding himself. He wanted so badly to believe Logico was safe. And yet . . .

Président Amaranth | an exclusive pin | the floor
President White | a ream of paper | the rostrum
Major Red | a gavel | the galleries

51. "It was the Crystal Goddess with a pseudo-scientific apparatus in the roof! And she was being tested for telekinesis!"

She disagreed with all of that except the part about her having telekinesis, and she tried to prove it by killing Irratino with her mind. He left unharmed yet disappointed: it was clear that she knew nothing about Logico's disappearance (or how to kill people with her mind).

> **The Crystal Goddess | a pseudo-scientific apparatus | the roof | telekinesis**
>
> Dr. Seashell, DDS | a dowsing rod | the grounds | aura reading
>
> Herbalist Onyx | a channeled text | the isolation chamber | fortune telling
>
> Supreme Master Cobalt | a hypnotic pocket watch | the actual laboratory | control group

52. "It was Superfan Smoky with a bottle of wine in a used car lot! And he drove a twelve-passenger van!"

"Oh, wow! This is just like a Midnight mystery!" replied Superfan Smoky.

But it was not like a Midnight mystery, because in a Midnight mystery, he would have given Irratino a valuable clue about Logico's disappearance. Instead, he just asked Irratino to sign his autograph book.

> **Superfan Smoky | a bottle of wine | a used car lot | twelve-passenger van**
>
> Sister Lapis | an ordinary brick | the run-down mall | motorcycle + sidecar
>
> Boss Charcoal | an antique clock | a secondhand shop | gas-guzzling SUV
>
> Mx. Tangerine | an axe | a chain restaurant | midlife-crisis convertible

53. "It was Uncle Midnight with a surgical scalpel on the roof! And he had type AB blood!"

Uncle Midnight was outraged. The hospital director had refused to allow him to leave and attend his birthday party—just because he had a contagious disease! So, he did the only thing he could: murder.

"But now that everyone knows you're guilty of murder and that you have a contagious disease, will they still want to come to your birthday party?"

"Yes."

> Dr. Crimson | a clipboard | the gift shop | type A
> Coach Raspberry | a fire extinguisher | the break room | type B
> Baron Maroon | a heavy microscope | the parking lot | type O
> **Uncle Midnight | a surgical scalpel | on the roof | type AB**

54. "It was Supreme Master Cobalt with a poisoned muffin in the observatory! And he studied the marot!"

Supreme Master Cobalt huffed and puffed. "You all think you know about the metaphysical underpinnings of society, but you don't know anything! Only people who join my Group can see the Truth."

Irratino could hear the capitalization in his voice, and he did not trust it. Nor did he trust that this megalomaniac had any idea what had happened to Logico.

> High Alchemist Raven | a Dame Obsidian novel | the big gate | reading coffee grounds
> **Supreme Master Cobalt | a poisoned muffin | the observatory | the marot**
> Sir Rulean | a ritual dagger | the miniature golf course | astrology
> The Amazing Aureolin | a bottle of wine | the grand chateau | numerology

55. "It was Dame Obsidian with a brick in the bean room! And she ordered tea!"

"Would you believe me if I said I did it because I had an important message for you?"

Inspector Irratino was a master of believing in things, but this seemed too self-serving to be true. Nevertheless, he listened as Dame Obsidian told him, "Logico is safe . . . for now."

Then, when he was overcome by emotion, she made her escape.

Booker-Winner Gainsboro | a boiling pot | the counter | regular joe drip

Mayor Honey | a butter knife | the courtyard | Christmas-flavored latte

Dame Obsidian | a brick | the bean room | tea with milk and honey

General Coffee | a metal straw | the bathroom | quadruple espresso shot

56. "It was Silverton the Legend with poisoned popcorn at the concession stand. And his favorite film is *Murdle: The Movie!*"

Silverton the Legend laughed. "Fine, you got me! I wanted him to screen my favorite film—the last one I starred in—but the projectionist refused. So I did him in! But think of the publicity angle: the star of *Murdle: The Movie* murdered for the movie. This is going to definitely raise the profile of the film, and guarantee a sequel."

Irratino thought what would actually guarantee a sequel was finding Deductive Logico. Otherwise, the sequel was going to be pretty depressing.

A-List Abalone | a ritual dagger | the theater | *The Maltese Penguin*

Silverton the Legend | poisoned popcorn | the concession stand | *Murdle: The Movie*

Assistant Applegreen | a stale candy bar | the box office | *Spoons Out*

Booker-Winner Gainsboro | a bag of cash | the lobby | *Who Framed Bobert Bunny?*

57. "It was Boss Charcoal with boxing gloves in the rooftop lounge. And he played the Ruy Lopez!"

Boss Charcoal laughed and admitted it. "He owed me money and he didn't pay. What was I supposed to do?"

Irratino thought about how Logico had never had money, and he worried something similar had happened to him. But Charcoal reassured him that he hadn't killed Logico, even though he had unmasked his murders before. Irratino believed him.

> The Amazing Aureolin | a giant chess knight | the ring | the King's Gambit
> Admiral Navy | a folding chair | ringside | the Fried Liver
> **Boss Charcoal | boxing gloves | the rooftop lounge | the Ruy Lopez**
> Mx. Tangerine | a chess board | the stands | the Italian Game

58. "It was Chef Aubergine with a briefcase full of money in the secret entrance. And she loved dinner theater!"

The treasurer popped up. She wasn't dead at all! Chef Aubergine and the murdered person then took a bow, and Chef Aubergine served dinner.

"I just wanted to host my own dinner theater," she explained. Irratino asked the other members if they would help solve the mystery of Logico's disappearance, but they were too busy eating the entrée.

> **Chef Aubergine | a briefcase full of money | the secret entrance | dinner theater**
> Comrade Champagne | a fake treasure map | the encyclopedia room | books
> Judge Pine | a booby-trapped fedora | the parking garage | murder parties
> Babyface Blue | a golden bird | the main entrance | online games

59. "It was Manservant Brownstone with the Big Red Book on the top floor! And he drove a limo!"

"Fine! I quit serving the Violets when I realized that Lord Violet was just a butler! So I stole his limo, and I became a follower of Major Red."

"Did Major Red want you to kill my source?" asked Irratino.

But instead of replying, Manservant Brownstone leapt off the top floor. Irratino thought he had killed himself, but when he peaked over the edge, he saw he had landed in another limo! It sped off.

60. "It was Tiny Taupe with a heavy purse in the actual bar! And he wanted to fund the Royal Resistance!"

"Argh!" Tiny Taupe declared. "The guy kept going on and on about the great Reds and the evil Resistance, so I had to let him have it. And I think I proved my point! Or, at least, I don't see him making any counterarguments."

Suddenly, a drunkard pulled Irratino aside, telling him (over and over again) that if he wanted to solve the murder of his friend, he needed to go to the Free Republic of Drakonia, and visit the Community Cathedral. Irratino remembered the Latin proverb *in vino veritas,* so, concluding that all drunks told the truth, he traveled to Drakonia.

61. "It was Miss Saffron with a string of prayer beads in the belltower! And she was Lupinian Orthodox!"

Miss Saffron explained that this whole community center was an affront to her religion. It had been stolen from her and turned into a den of iniquity!

Inspector Irratino didn't know if murdering someone made a place less of a den of iniquity. But it was clear that nobody here knew anything about the disappearance of Deductive Logico.

Officer Copper | a bottle of sacred oil | the grand steps | New Age
Miss Saffron | a string of prayer beads | the belltower | Lupinian Orthodox
Mx. Tangerine | a holy relic | the pews | the Church
Chairman Chalk | sacramental wine | the altar | atheism

62. "It was Grayscale, CPA, with a leash in the kennel room. And he loved his poodle!"

Grayscale, CPA, tried to make a deal with Irratino: if he let him off with a warning, he'd tell Irratino where he could find a lead about Logico's disappearance. Irratino agreed, but after Grayscale gave him a map, he immediately turned him in to the Detective Club.

"But we had a deal!" shouted Grayscale, CPA.

"I don't negotiate with wannabe dog murderers," Irratino replied.

Grayscale, CPA | a leash | the kennel room | the poodle
Vice President Mauve | an emerald dish | the reception area | the wiener dog
Editor Ivory | a giant bone | the backyard | the Great Dane
Director Dusty | an angry cat | the bedroom | the mutt

63. "It was Agent Argyle with a jagged dagger in the donation room! And he had type O blood!"

"Fine! I'm broke! I haven't sold a movie in months! So I came here to sell my own blood, and that's when I saw . . . that bloody gossip columnist. I had to kill her. She would have ruined me. Nobody wants an agent who's so broke he has to sell his own blood!"

But Irratino wasn't listening. He was realizing that he had been holding the map Grayscale had given him upside down. It didn't point to an underground blood bank at all. It pointed to some place much more terrifying . . .

Agent Argyle | **a jagged dagger** | **the donation room** | **type O**
Astrologer Azure | a bag of cash | the secret entrance | type A
Sister Lapis | 200-proof alcohol | the transfusion center | type AB
Captain Slate | a paperback | the blood tanks | type B

64. "It was Aristocrat Sable with a chicken bone in the cages! And she was 100 percent cannibal!"

"I can't help it!" she declared. "I developed a taste for human flesh when I was stranded on that island."

Irratino replied, "You were on that island for six days!"

"It was so boring! And is a commoner any different than an animal?"

Irratino felt she was right about that: we are all animals. So, he freed every single animal in the slaughterhouse, and then he burnt the whole building down. Sure, it was a crime, but there were only two people in the world who could solve it. One was him, and the other was missing.

General Coffee | a rusty saw | the packing plant | vegetarian (plus fish)
Aristocrat Sable | **a chicken bone** | **the cages** | **100 percent cannibal**
Officer Copper | a bucket of ██████████ | the killing floor | mostly vegan
Comrade Champagne | a shovel | the gift shop | caveman diet

65. "It was Cardinal Cinereous with a geode on the rusted tracks! And he was filthy rich!"

"The mine should be mine!" Cardinal Cinereous declared. "I discovered that the mine was not depleted, just abandoned. And I could have made so much money—for the Church, of course. But that poor fool was going to announce it to the world and ruin everything. So I did what I had to do."

"Well, you didn't *have* to do it," Irratino suggested. But Cardinal Cinereous explained to him that the good of the Church so exceeded the bad of his deed that, ultimately, he had a moral obligation. Irratino—for once—saw the downside of limitless faith.

Coach Raspberry | a gold bar | an abandoned mine shaft | dirt poor
Cardinal Cinereous | a geode | the rusted tracks | filthy rich
Judge Pine | a gear | the locked gates | upper middle class
Signor Emerald | tainted moonshine | the collapsed office | sorta broke

66. "It was Earl Grey with a piano in the town square. And he loved *Knock, Knock . . . Who's There? Murder!*"

Earl Grey admitted he did it, and he admitted why, too. "To protect the secret! Which I've done."

But Irratino didn't have time for that now. His vacation was over. Logico needed him! The town's secret would have to wait for another time. Or another detective. (Can you discover it?)

Earl Grey | a piano | the town square | *Knock, Knock . . . Who's There? Murder!*
Bishop Azure | a crowbar in a newspaper | a small cottage | *A Very Proper Murder*
The Duchess of Vermillion | a suit of Drakonian armor | the old abandoned mill | *The Perplexing Problem of the Parrot*
Sir Rulean | a chess board | the village pub | *Murder on the Occidental Local*

67. "It was Archeologist Ecru with a bottle of wine on the observation deck. And her final destination was eternal Rome!"

"Okay, fine! I killed the porter! But when he was helping me with my bags, some ancient artifacts fell out of them. And yeah, sure, maybe I broke a few international laws by taking them from the tomb I found them in, but I was going to sell them to a museum, which is where they belong, right? So, no harm, no foul?"

Irratino felt like there was harm, and violating so many laws probably would result in a foul, at the very least. But still, he had learned nothing about Deductive Logico's disappearance.

> Lord Lavender | an antique clock | the dining car | romantic Paris
>
> Dean Glaucous | a brick of coal | the caboose | tulip-filled Amsterdam
>
> Captain Slate | leather luggage | the sleeping car | cosmopolitan Madrid
>
> **Archeologist Ecru | a bottle of wine | the observation deck | eternal Rome**

68. "It was the Amazing Aureolin with leather gloves in the board room! And her favorite piece was the tricky knight!"

"He was going to kick me out! So I had to kill him."

"Why was he going to kick you out?" Irratino asked.

"Because I was going to kill him."

A paradox, Irratino thought. But still, he was no closer to finding Logico.

> **The Amazing Aureolin | leather gloves | the board room | the tricky knight**
>
> Tiny Taupe | piano wire | the stone bridge | the sly bishop
>
> Grandmaster Rose | a bottle of wine | the barracks | the sturdy rook
>
> Brother Brownstone | a chess book | the statue of a pawn | the powerful queen

69. "It was Coach Raspberry with a laptop in Old Main. And his favorite subject was rhetoric!"

"Well, dang, ya got me!" he spat. "But if you'd allow me to elaborate on a few of my theses, I believe I'll be able to turn you to my side. Now, first, I want you to consider—"

But Irratino had no time for rhetoric: he needed to find Logico! He was starting to lose hope.

> Statistician Marble | a sharp pencil | the bookstore | rigorous logic
> **Coach Raspberry | a laptop | Old Main | soaring rhetoric**
> Principal Applegreen | a heavy backpack | the arboretum | esoteric music theory
> Agent Ink | a graduation cord | the stadium | advanced grammar

70. "It was Actuary Apricot with a pouch of magick powders in the columbarium. And he wanted his body donated to science!"
Irratino knew it was him because he had caught him red-handed: the magick powders had left a stain. Also, all the information pointed toward him. And his horoscope said he was a murderer. And also he confessed.

> **Actuary Apricot | a pouch of magick powders | the columbarium | donated to science**
> Baron Maroon | a globe | the weird shack | cremated
> Dr. Crimson | a human skull | the entrance gate | six feet under
> Vice President Mauve | a skeleton arm | the gift shop | buried at sea

71. "It was Editor Ivory with an antique typewriter in the gardens! And her favorite author was Dame Obsidian!"
"Look! He trespassed. He had a manuscript. I had to kill him. That's just our company policy."

Irratino thought she should reflect on her policy of murdering more than her publishing policies. But also, he thought he was getting distracted from his real mission.

> Dr. Seashell, DDS | poisoned inkwell | the offices | Philosopher Bone

72. "It was Chairman Chalk with an antique anchor on the deck! And he was bored!"

"Yeah, I was bored, that's why I did it. I don't know why I came on this cruise anyway. I've got my own yacht. But my wife said, 'Honey, take a cruise. Relax. Enjoy yourself!' And so I did. But I didn't enjoy myself at all! It was miserable. The only thing I enjoyed was murdering that person!"

Inspector Irratino was beginning to wonder if he would ever find Deductive Logico.

73. "It was President White with a bulletproof vest in the great hall. And she believes everyone is being murdered for a reason!"

"That's right, I do," she said. "I killed the organizer of this conference because he was helping them get away with it. But I need someone I can trust to help me unmask this conspiracy and save the person they fear more than anyone."

"Who do they fear?" Irratino asked.

"Why, your friend, Deductive Logico!"

Irratino believed her. And he agreed to follow President White to an undisclosed location. He knew there was danger involved, but he had to risk it.

> President White | a bulletproof vest | the great hall | everyone
>   is being murdered for a reason
> General Coffee | a commemorative coaster | the check-in stand
> | time began last Tuesday
> Dr. Seashell, DDS | red yarn | the huge board | sleep is a scam
> The Crystal Goddess | a book of Drakonian conspiracies | the
>   bathroom | aliens control the world

74. "It was General Coffee with a shovel by the cannons! And he behaved carefully on the battlefield!"

"We needed to open up a new front in the war, and your man was in the way. We did what we had to do, but we're not going to gloat about it. In fact, you can have some official documentation assuring you it was a mistake of war, though one, of course, which we will not take any kind of responsibility for restituting."

Irratino thought that was good. Maybe he would just keep following President White, who was leading him to a giant tower fortress . . . the famed Western Citadel.

> Admiral Navy | an old sword | the fortified wall | bravely
> **General Coffee | a shovel | the cannons | carefully**
> Sergeant Gunmetal | a cup of scalding coffee | the guard post |
>   cowardly
> Governor Lead | a bazooka | the secret tunnel | foolishly

75. "It was Secretary Celadon with a shovel by the iron door! And she was a member of the White Guards!"

Secretary Celadon took Irratino aside and explained, "Look, I did what I did because I had to, and now that it's done, it's over. When you see the ends to which we have striven, you will understand why it was necessary."

Irratino was confused, but then President White announced, "We have made the deal! Our job is complete! We have traded the Reds' prisoner—the great Deductive Logico—for the esoteric Inspector Irratino."

Immediately, Irratino was apprehended by Red soldiers who hauled him away to their jails. And there, he saw Deductive Logico being released by the guards at the same time.

"What's going on?!" Irratino cried.

"I've left you, like, a million voicemails!" Logico exclaimed. "You've got to check your messages!"

Before the Free Drakonians took Irratino's phone away, he finally checked his messages and found a whole bunch of missed calls from Logico, and also a text from the Detective Club, who informed him that the mysterious blood sample was "flipped," so he checked what happened if he reversed the letters. (See Exhibit C.)

Cosmonaut Bluski | a heavy boot | the grand hall | the Secret Police

Secretary Celadon | a shovel | the iron door | the White Guards

President White | a fake tooth | the barbed-wire fences | the Sword of St. Lupine

Sergeant Gunmetal | the Big Red Book | the security room | the Order of the Bat

76. "It was Radical Crimson with a Red banana in the People's City to free the people!"

"The Red Government doesn't go nearly far enough!" Radical Crimson was quoted as saying. "You have taken the land from the rich, but you still govern from their Capitol! And you still accept their money! To be free at all you must be totally free!"

So, as you can see, even a decade later, the country was still a mess.

President White | an enormous painting | Castle Eminence | to restore the aristocracy

Major Red | an ancient sword | the Iron Palace | to rule a country

Radical Crimson | a Red banana | the People's City | to free the people

Patriarch Porpoise | ivory night-eater fangs | the Screaming Forest | to seize their land

77. "It was Baron Maroon with a chess board by the defensive fortifications to punish a traitor!"

"The noble that I killed was a traitor," Baron Maroon declared. "Now, if you'll excuse me, I am feeling weak, and I need to see my physician."

Logico went to the library, where President White was reading from the Book of St. Lupine, the holy book of the St. Lupinian Orthodox Church. She looked up from the book and immediately asked Logico a question: "What was the secret you were going to unveil at the Convocation of Countries?"

Logico answered, "It was Pandora's Box. An ancient mathematical secret that—if known to the world—would unleash unimaginable suffering."

"Let me tell you a story," President White replied.

> **Maroon** | **a chess board** | **the defensive fortifications** | **to punish a traitor**
>
> The Duchess of Vermillion | the Book of St. Lupine | the Screaming Forest | to fight for love
>
> Lady Violet | a majestic cape | the getaway limo | for money
>
> President White | a champagne flute | the great mansion | to promote the occult

78. "It was Bandit Black with a vampire bat by the tortured tree to stop his work!"

"This is why we fight," said President White. "This Red Government is no different than the bandits who came out of the woods and killed our great saint!"

Even Logico was impressed by the soaring rhetoric. She continued, "And so, we must follow the example of the villagers. When they found St. Lupine dead, they did two things: they worked together to finish his cathedral, and they killed those bandits where they stood."

Logico understood. But still, he would not reveal the mathematical secrets he had uncovered in the Tomb of Pythagoras: he would keep Pandora's Box closed.

Bandit Blue | a sacred rock | a small wooden hut | to free the people

Bandit Black | a vampire bat | a tortured tree | to stop his work

Bandit Brown | a poisoned goblet | the fence | to kill a monster

Villager White | a wooden stake | the stone foundation | because of radiation poisoning

79. "It was Governor Lead with the Big Red Book in the observation room for the government!"

"I was told this order came from the highest levels. And when you get an order from the Red Government: you follow it to the letter."

Irratino didn't understand, so Governor Lead told him the story of the death of the Iron Tsar.

Cosmonaut Bluski | a hammer and sickle | the "emergency exit" | to feed their family

Comrade Champagne | an antique typewriter | the holding cell | to rob a grave

Governor Lead | the Big Red Book | the observation room | for the government

Officer Copper | the bayonet | the interrogation room | to avenge their father

80. "It was Major Red with an iron helmet in the graveyard to take over Drakonia!"

" 'I did it!' he would eventually brag. 'I ripped the Iron Tsar's helmet from his face, hoisted it high above my head, and then I brought it down upon his skull, crushing it for the glory of the revolution!' "

Logico was horrified. "Why are you telling me this?"

"To show you," Governor Lead replied, "that if Major Red tells you to do something, you do it."

Radical Crimson | a bazooka | the great iron door | for the revolution

Tiny Taupe | an antique flintlock | the great throne room | they were ordered to

Major Red | an iron helmet | the graveyard | to take over Drakonia

Patriarch Porpoise | a Red banana | the glorious chapel | for the glory of St. Lupine

81. "It was Comrade Champagne with an antique flintlock in the Red Bay for the revolution!"

"These traitorous rebels will never let us govern!" Comrade Champagne declared. "Look at this newsie: he was shouting about all the mistakes the Reds have made. What else were we supposed to do?"

"Fix the mistakes?" Logico asked. But the glare he received showed him that, in fact, the best thing he could do was be quiet.

Governor Lead | a brain in a jar | the Capitol Building | because of radiation poisoning

President White | a chess board | the Community Cathedral | to become a legend

Major Red | the Big Red Book | the brutalist housing | to manipulate the government

Comrade Champagne | an antique flintlock | the Red Bay | for the revolution

82. "It was Cosmonaut Bluski with a broccoli in room 239 to avoid being sent to the front!"

"They were going to force me to go fight on the front lines! But I think my talents are much better spent doing publicity appearances!"

Logico understood that, but more than that, he understood the coded message he had just received, written in Next Letter Code:

"KNFHBN, HS'R HQQZSHMN! SGDX ZQD FNHMF SN BTS NEE LX ANCX! GTQQX! GDKO!"

Gray Walker | the Big Red Book | room 103 | for the revolution

Tiny Taupe | a cigarette | room 324 | in a jealous rage
Radical Crimson | a bottle of champagne | room 207 | to win a
 seat in Parliament
**Cosmonaut Bluski | a broccoli | room 239 | to avoid being sent
 to the front**

83. "It was Tiny Taupe with a commemorative coaster in the viewing area to stop the killings!"

"I had to stop the killings!" he said. "Too many people have died already!"

But the masses knew that this was just more Royal Resistance propaganda, and they attacked Tiny Taupe.

Logico took advantage of the ensuing chaos to free Irratino, and he led him away from the guillotines. "Where are we going to go?" Irratino asked. "Could you take us to that island mansion?"

Logico didn't think they could: he had just read a newspaper article about the Violet Isles . . .

Superfan Smoky | a garland of garlic | the guard tower | to rule
 a country
Judge Pine | a stun gun | the platform | to live forever
**Tiny Taupe | a commemorative coaster | the viewing area | to
 stop the killings**
Radical Crimson | a hammer and sickle | the overlook | to cast
 an evil spell

84. "It was the Duchess of Vermillion with a chainsaw on the docks to terrify the populace!"

Reading about this in the papers, Logico did not feel it had the same effect as actually being there. After all, one murder on one island was not really that terrifying, was it?

"I don't know," Irratino said. "Chainsaws are pretty scary."

Sister Lapis | an angry moose | the cliffs | out of total fear

The Duchess of Vermillion | a chainsaw | the docks | to terrify
the populace

Signor Emerald | an ottoman | the farm | because they have a
rage problem

Gray Walker | a bearskin rug | the mansion | to escape

85. "It was Manservant Brownstone with an antique flintlock in the screening room to restore the aristocracy!"

"You really thought I was a Red? Even after I drove off in a limo?! (See Case 59: The Parking Garage Follow-up.) Like Beloved Butler Beryl before me, I shall live and die to restore the aristocracy to its former glory! And we shall serve them in peace and happiness!"

Multiple Reds tried to convince him that his class interests aligned more with the Revolution than with the Resistance, but he could not be persuaded. So they sent him to the guillotines.

Major Red | a cheap pen | the waiting room | to silence a wit-
ness

Tiny Taupe | the Big Red Book | the secretary's office | to redis-
tribute their wealth

**Manservant Brownstone | an antique flintlock | the screening
room | to restore the aristocracy**

Admiral Navy | an iron helmet | Major Red's private office | to
escape blackmail

86. "It was Major Red with ivory night-eater fangs in a secret passage out of tradition!"

"I didn't want to do it, you see?" Major Red said. "I didn't ever want to kill more than necessary. But even worse than that would be to kill *less* than necessary."

Irratino and Logico struggled to follow that logic.

"You see," Major Red continued, "it is a Drakonian tradition for the leader to eat his vanquished foes—and so I must! Regardless of how I feel about it personally."

Deductive Logico and Inspector Irratino got the ▮▮▮▮ out of there.

General Coffee | an iron boot | his books | to manipulate a government

Dr. Crimson | a poisoned goblet | Major Red's desk | because of the full moon

Hack Blaxton | a political treatise | a painting of Major Red | to hide a secret text

Major Red | ivory night-eater fangs | a secret passage | out of tradition

87. "It was Sergeant Gunmetal with a wooden stake in the boiling pools to protect the trees!"

"These are the people's trees! And I have been tasked with protecting them."

But Logico thought the sergeant had bigger things to worry about: the boiling pools, the tortured tree, and the Dead River were all symptoms of the same cause. The boiling pools had nuclear rods at the bottom of them, which heated the waters. The tortured tree had grown so twisted due to genetic mutations caused by the radiation. And that same radiation had killed all the life in the river.

This forest had been poisoned by an abandoned nuclear reactor, which they soon discovered hidden in the woods.

"See," Irratino said, "I told you there were bad vibes!"

Sergeant Gunmetal | a wooden stake | the boiling pools | to protect the trees

Elder Ash | a Yeti hide | the tortured tree | to stay alive

Chef Aubergine | a bunch of magic mushrooms | the devil's stone | to steal a prized book

Admiral Navy | the Big Red Book | the Dead River | for propaganda purposes

88. "It was Elder Ash with a petrified apple in the nuclear waste room to keep a hideout secret!"

At first, Elder Ash protested, but finally, when Logico explained the case against her, she confessed: "This nuclear site is where we have cultivated our group, the Children of the Helpers."

"Are you with the Red Revolution or the Royal Resistance?" Irratino asked.

"We are with neither," she explained. "Because we know the truth of St. Lupine. Do you want to hear it?" They both agreed that they did.

> Vice President Mauve | the Big Red Book | the reactor core | to feed their family
>
> Boss Charcoal | a fire extinguisher | the locked gate | because of a superstition
>
> **Elder Ash | a petrified apple | the nuclear waste room | to keep a hideout secret**
>
> Gray Walker | a bag of nuts and bolts | the dying grounds | because of radiation poisoning

89. "It was St. Lupine with a pitchfork in the nearby village for the children!"

"You see," Elder Ash explained, "those three helpers were not three sick orphans when they met St. Lupine. He made them orphans when he killed their father. But the so-called St. Lupine needed cheap work, and he saw an opportunity. So he made them orphans. He did it for the children, yes. But not on their behalf. He did it to take them.

"As if that weren't cruel enough, he then made the orphans sick by having them haul the rocks to build his chapel. Those sacred glowing rocks were radioactive, and they poisoned anyone who held them. But he forced them to work all day, and at night, he made them sleep outside in the elements, while he slept in a tiny hut only big enough for one." (See Case 78: The Death of St. Lupine.)

Logico and Irratino were horrified, but Ash continued on. "But the so-called helpers fought back: they put their heads, hands, and hearts together, and they decided to kill him. Those three bandits in the story so revered by the St. Lupinians? They were not bandits, but the three sick orphans themselves, his helpers."

That is why the bandits who killed him were so short, and that is why their motives were fear, and killing a monster, and stopping his work: his work was killing them.

"When the helpers told the villagers who he had really been," Ash continued, "they did not believe them. Instead, the villagers rose up against them, with pitchforks and torches, and killed the three helpers. With them dead, there was no one to question the story of the greatness of St. Lupine. And yet, you cannot hide the truth forever, and the story of the real St. Lupine will survive as long as there are minds to deduce it."

Irratino believed, but Logico questioned, and so, Elder Ash replied, "Ah, I can prove it: the tortured tree by which he was killed does not grow at the site of his cathedral (see Case 61: The Cathedral Killing): it grows beside this nuclear power plant. And the waste from this power plant has poisoned our river, just as the lies of St. Lupine have poisoned our country. That is the true meaning of Holy Drakonia."

> Helper Black | a sacred rock | the Screaming Forest | to kill a monster
> Helper Blue | a heavy boot | a beautiful meadow | as an accident
> **St. Lupine | a pitchfork | the nearby village | for the children**
> Helper Brown | a shovel | a pile of rocks | out of total fear

90. "It was Admiral Navy with a garland of garlic in the Dead River waters to finish the revolution!"

"The only law I live by is the law of the sea!" Admiral Navy announced.

Logico pointed out that this was a river, and the admiral seemed rather perplexed by that for a moment until he figured out the new line he'd take: "I live by the law of all waterways!"

Logico and Irratino moved onward, toward Castle Eminence, debating whether such a thing as night-eaters existed, and whether the Viscount was one. "He's a viscount!" Irratino said. "That feels like a very night-eater title to have."

"But, once again," Logico said, "there is no such thing as night-eaters."

Sociologist Umber | a piece of wood | the dirty deck | because
of a superstition
Gray Walker | a human femur | the rotting hold | to feast
**Admiral Navy | a garland of garlic | the Dead River waters |
to finish the revolution**
Tiny Taupe | an attack crab | the broken bridge | to keep a
hideout secret

91. "It was Patriarch Porpoise with an ice axe in the twisting pass to hide a secret text!"

"Sure, I did it! He was going to spread a document about the true history of St. Lupine. I had to do something, didn't I? I couldn't just let him undo a thousand years of religious tradition, and hand over a powerful weapon to the Reds to use against us. Could I?"

Logico thought that he could. Irratino thought they should continue on.

Gray Walker | leather gloves | the high cliff | to get revenge
The Abominable Snowman | a killer snake | the mysterious cave
| to feed their family
Archeologist Ecru | a crowbar in a newspaper | the hidden grove
| because of the full moon
**Patriarch Porpoise | an ice axe | the twisting pass | to hide a
secret text**

92. "It was Cryptozoologist Cloud with a mutant piranha in the empty shack because of radiation poisoning!"

Cryptozoologist Cloud was stumbling around, screaming at people, declaring that they would all be sorry when a Bigfoot came into their village and ate them.

It was clear that the cryptozoologist had been victimized by radiation poisoning, so it was hard to blame them.

"Maybe the night-eater is who exposed him to radiation, though," Irratino suggested. And when he looked up at Castle Eminence, he was certain he was right.

Sergeant Gunmetal | an unhealthy diet | the abandoned manor house | to harvest their blood
Cryptozoologist Cloud | a mutant piranha | the empty shack | because of radiation poisoning
Earl Grey | a royal signet ring | the dry well | to promote a manifesto
Radical Crimson | a silver bullet | the dying fields | to advance science

93. "It was Sir Rulean with a wooden stake in the bailey to avenge his father!"

"I came here to avenge my father, a peasant who lived in the nearby village. That's right—despite my carefully coifed demeanor, I'm not really a knight! I'm actually a poor peasant's child. And my father was killed, years ago, in this castle! And now, I have repaid that grievous blow by committing another."

"But how can you know it was the same person?"

"It doesn't matter if it's the same person: what matters is that I killed somebody for it."

Radical Crimson | a petrified heart | the guardhouse | for propaganda purposes
Archeologist Ecru | a killer snake | the keep | because of the full moon
Sergeant Gunmetal | a garland of garlic | the moat | to free the people
Sir Rulean | a wooden stake | the bailey | to avenge his father

94. "It was Viscount Eminence with a fire poker in the living quarters to stay alive!"

"Killing a fair maiden?!" Irratino exclaimed. "Clear night-eater behavior!"

Viscount Eminence stood up to his full height, and the moonlight cast a horrifying shadow upon the castle wall. It seemed to be the silhouette of a giant bat! "You dare accuse me?!" the Viscount roared, and yet he turned and fled.

> **Viscount Eminence | a fire poker | the living quarters | to stay alive**
> Dr. Crimson | satin curtains | the grand hall | to cast an evil spell
> Gray Walker | a brain in a jar | the dungeon | to bring back the dead
> Lady Violet | a nuclear fuel rod | the battlements | out of total fear

95. "It was Dr. Crimson with a book of war poetry on the balcony to prolong a life!"

"That's right—I've been draining the blood of various minor aristocrats in order to prolong the life of a major one, the Great Viscount Eminence."

"And these are the Gray Walkers?" Logico asked.

"Yes. My act of mercy," Dr. Crimson replied. "When certain aristocratic individuals visit my hospitals (see Case 19 and Case 53), I simply begin a procedure. It uses their lifeforce to prolong the lifeforce of my chief patient. But I do not kill them. I let them live, even though it would be most effective, and more prudent, to kill them."

"You gave them a fate worse than death," Irratino replied. "And anyway, you did kill this one." He pointed to the dead Gray Walker.

"He was resisting the procedure. I did what I had to do to prolong the life of the viscount."

"Why is this one viscount so important to you?" Logico asked.

"You don't know the true story of the revolution," Dr. Crimson replied. "Let me tell you."

> **Dr. Crimson | a book of war poetry | the balcony | to prolong a life**
> Manservant Brownstone | ivory night-eater fangs | the blood tanks | to avenge the viscount
> Gray Walker | a suit of Drakonian armor | the great machine | to inherit the castle

96. "It was the Iron Tsar with a Red banana by the great iron door to rule a country!"

Once the Iron Tsar had killed the corporal, Major Red and the rest of them stormed in. But the Iron Tsar did what nobody thought he would do: he fled.

He hiked through the Screaming Forest, across the Dead River, and over the Madding Mountains, until he reached the one person he knew he could trust, the old royalist Viscount Eminence. There was just one problem: the viscount, who had been very, very old, was now very, very dead.

But then, the Iron Tsar had an idea, inspired by Beloved Butler Beryl (whom he thought of simply as the Imposter Violet): no one had seen the viscount for years, and no one had seen his face since he became the Iron Tsar. And so, he simply removed his four-inch-high boots (see Case 86: A Presidential Murder), and he took off his helmet (see Case 80, Case 85, and Case 96), and he became the only Viscount Eminence that Deductive Logico had ever known.

(Later, the Detective Club would notify Irratino that he was wrong to think that Major Red's blood was at the crime scene where Logico went missing: it was in fact the blood of Viscount Eminence. When they said that the DNA had been "flipped," they did not mean that it had been reversed, but that they had printed the opposite side of the strand, and that he should replace each nucleobase with its pair, i.e., A = T and G = C.) Dr. Crimson had spilled some of her patient's samples: she carried them with her to match with potential donors.

"And so," Dr. Crimson continued, "the Iron Tsar bided his time, waiting until the Red Government of Free Drakonia finally collapsed, when he could again ascend to the throne. However, for the same reasons that he was able to vanish, Major Red was able to claim victory. He dressed up a corporal as the Iron Tsar, and claimed he killed him, strengthening the foundations of his government. So when the days turned to months and the months turned to years, the Iron Tsar began to worry that he would not live to see the day when the Red Revolution was undone. But that, you see, is where I came in."

Dr. Crimson explained her newly devised method. By draining the blood of the young (and, compared to the viscount, everyone was young), he could prolong his own life and live to see the day when he was reinstated. This she did, not because she supported the Iron Tsar, or cared about the politics of Drakonia, but because she loved money.

"So, wait," Irratino said, "you're saying that he *is* a night-eater?"

"A what?" Dr. Crimson replied.

"No," Logico answered, "she just said that she used a medical, scientific technique—"

"You're telling me he uses the blood of innocents to prolong his own life, and you're arguing that he's *not* a night-eater?"

But Logico had another question: "Why is she telling us this?"

"Because it's done. It's over."

"What do you mean?"

"The day of the Iron Tsar is today. The People's City has been sacked, assisted by the forces of the Convocation of Countries, which has finally unified against the Red Government, due to the sudden disappearance of two of the most famous crime-solvers in the world. Now, President White will reconquer Drakonia for the tsar. It is done!"

Iron Tsar | a Red banana | the great iron door | to rule a country

Patriarch Porpoise | a bazooka | the glorious chapel | to be a hero

Major Red | an iron helmet | the graveyard | for political purposes

Tiny Taupe | an antique flintlock | the great throne room | because of an ancient grudge

97. "It was Dr. Crimson with a bag of marbles over the edge in order to escape!"

Dr. Crimson laid the trap, and her sister fell for it. And then, she literally fell off the tower.

"Like she'd fallen for so many causes before," she would say when she told the story to others. She would talk about her helicopter ride out of the country just as it was collapsing into a second civil war. How she escaped with the secret to immortality.

And, unless you knew Dr. Crimson really well, you wouldn't think anything of it. And you might not even notice that she used to wear flats.

But now she wore two-inch heels.

> Gray Walker | a cranial saw | the helicopter | out of confusion
> Gray Walker | a pitchfork | the stairwell | for brains
> **Dr. Crimson | a bag of marbles | over the edge | to escape**
> Radical Crimson | a scalpel | the battlements | to stop her sister

98. "It was Archeologist Ecru with the bayonet in the brutalist housing to steal a ruby!"

"This is the best chance in a lifetime to recover treasures for a museum, or maybe for my personal collection. What are you going to do? Arrest me?! There's no government!"

Well, there's one thing that they could do, which was not let her on their zeppelin.

> Governor Lead | a coat of arms | the Capitol Building | to rule a country
> Boss Charcoal | a nuclear fuel rod | the Red Bay | to turn the tide of war
> Sergeant Gunmetal | the Big Red Book | the Community Cathedral | as an accident
> **Archeologist Ecru | the bayonet | the brutalist housing | to steal a ruby**

99. "It was Captain Slate with an antique vase in the passenger cabin because they needed air!"

While Captain Slate protested her innocence, she lost confidence as Deductive Logico explained the case against her, which was even further supported by the esoteric proofs of Inspector Irratino. Finally, she confessed.

"I should have stayed in space . . ." she said.

> Miss Saffron | a huge pile of paperwork | the bathroom | to rob the victim
> **Captain Slate | an antique vase | the passenger cabin | because it was too crowded**
> Comrade Champagne | a briefcase of gold | the cargo hold | in a jealous rage
> Sergeant Gunmetal | a holy relic | the cockpit | to cover up another murder

100. "It was President White with the Convocation Corps in the Western Citadel for so much ███████ing money!"

Logico discovered after the fact that President White had heavily invested in the international weapons business. Not only had she sold drones to the Convocation, she had also sold dynamite to the People's Army and ivory to the Holy Drakonian Army. Even greater and more terrible weaponry was devised from the mathematical secrets revealed in the Tomb of Pythagoras, which she cracked in Logico's absence.

All of this she did under other names, but her ego was great enough that she flaunted it at every step. The ivory was imported by E. H. Whit (see Case 86: A Presidential Murder). The bazookas were manufactured by the Thiwe Corporation (see Case 74: Bordering on Madness & Murder). The nuclear materials were controlled by World Horizons International Thermonuclear Energy (see Case 98: A City Ablaze). Even the metal for the bayonets was produced by International Weapons, known as "the IW." Each of them spelled out her name, by anagram or acronym.

And as the four armies fought against each other to the last man, and the country was destroyed in the great conflagration, President White watched the numbers on her portfolio go up, and up, and up.

And that, unfortunately, is the end of *Murdle: More Killer Puzzles*.

Patriarch Porpoise ᛁ the Souls of St. Lupine ᛁ the Iron Palace ᛁ for everlasting life

Viscount Eminence ᛁ the Holy Drakonian Army ᛁ the Screaming Forest ᛁ for limitless power

Major Red ᛁ the People's Army ᛁ the Madding Mountains ᛁ for never-ending glory

President White ᛁ the Convocation Corps ᛁ the Western Citadel ᛁ for so much ████ing money

ACKNOWLEDGMENTS

This is merely an addendum to the acknowledgments in the first *Murdle* book. Everyone who helped then continued to help, and I appreciate them now even more, but space concerns prohibit me from thanking them all again.

Some people, however, have contributed so much that I am compelled to re-thank them, particularly my agent Melissa Edwards, my editor Courtney Littler, and my partner Dani Messerschmidt.

Thank you to Daniel Donohue, Esq., for inspiration and puzzle consultation, and to Bailey Norton, comedic genius, for divining the astrological placements of every suspect.

Thank you to all the puzzle testers in the Detective Club, including newcomers Eiron Page, Miranda Phair, and Ethan N., as well as expert returnees Alexander Maughan, Howie, and Jenny Wilkinson.

Special thanks to Daniel Lisi, all-around book expert, for helping me organize events, and to Amin Osman, for not killing me when I took time off from our movie.

A very special thanks to Tara and everyone at Tara's Himalayan Cuisine, for the garlic tofu that fueled the writing of this book, and for hosting our ongoing murder-mystery dinner theater show.

If you liked the Free Republic of Drakonia, I recommend Bram Stoker's *Dracula* and Isaac Deutscher's three-volume biography of Leon Trotsky. If you liked the Riddles of Pythagoras, I recommend Boris A. Kordemsky's *Moscow Puzzle Collection*, as well as the works of Martin Gardner.

Lastly, this book is dedicated to my mom, who has always believed in me, supported me, defended me, and bragged about me, even when I didn't deserve it. I love you, Mom. Thank you for everything.